Female power and male dominance

On the origins of sexual inequality

Female power and male dominance
On the origins of sexual inequality

PEGGY REEVES SANDAY
University of Pennsylvania

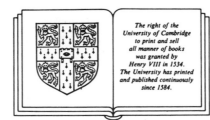

The right of the
University of Cambridge
to print and sell
all manner of books
was granted by
Henry VIII in 1534.
The University has printed
and published continuously
since 1584.

CAMBRIDGE UNIVERSITY PRESS
Cambridge
New York   Port Chester
Melbourne   Sydney

Published by the Press Syndicate of the University of Cambridge
The Pitt Building, Trumpington Street, Cambridge CB2 1RP
40 West 20th Street, New York, NY 10011, USA
10 Stamford Road, Oakleigh, Melbourne 3166, Australia

First published 1981
Reprinted 1982 (twice), 1984, 1985, 1986, 1987,
1988, 1990

Printed in the United States of America

Library of Congress Cataloging in Publication Data
Sanday, Peggy Reeves.
Female power and male dominance.
Bibliography: p.
Includes index.
1. Sex role.   2. Sexism.   3. Power (Social
sciences)   4. Symbolism (Psychology)   5. Sex
(Psychology)   6. Cross-cultural studies.   I. Title.
HQ1075.S26   305.3   80–18461

ISBN 0-521-23618-5 hardback
ISBN 0-521-28075-3 paperback

To Eric and Julie
with love

Contents

vii

Contents

Contents

Contents

Tables and figures

Tables and figures

Tables and figures

Figures

xiii

Preface

When I began this book, I intended to test the explanatory framework for the evolution of female status I had postulated in two published articles. My major question then was: What are the conditions under which the relative status of women changes in the direction of public equality? I assumed that, by and large, men were in a better position to gain both access to and control over strategic resources because of the constraints on the expenditure of female energy posed by their reproductive activities. This assumption corresponded with the then-prevailing view that women were universally subordinated. I hypothesized that women would gain public power by default, in the absence of men. Female power acquired in this fashion, I suggested, would be "legitimized over time through the expressive cultural system"; that is, through the development of female deities.[1]

Supported by grants from the National Institute of Mental Health, I supervised the collection of information on over 150 societies in order to examine this view more closely.[2] It soon became evident that I had to revise my initial hypothesis. This sense of not having seen the forest for the trees was further confirmed upon reading the ethnographies of male and female power published in the 1970s. I was impressed most notably by the work of Albert Bacdayan (Western Bontoc), Jean Briggs (Eskimo), Kamene Okonjo (Igbo), Cara Richards (Onondaga), Susan Carol Rogers (peasants), Alice Schlegel (Hopi), and Nancy Tanner (matrifocal societies).[3]

The realization of the inadequacies in my initial conception was accompanied by the discovery that symbolism played a key role in channeling secular power roles. Preliminary analysis of the data indicated that sacred symbols are not, as I had originally supposed, an epiphenomena of secular power roles. In fact, it became clear that the reverse was more likely: Secular power roles are derived from ancient concepts of sacred power. This realization meant that I had to switch my theoretical stance midstream and become at least semiliterate in symbolic anthropology. Along these lines, I found the work of Clifford Geertz and Mary Douglas the most helpful for seeking meaning below the surface details.

Moving into symbolic territory meant moving away from the positivist framework that normally accompanies the cross-cultural, large-sample approach. Examining various patterns of male dominance and female power in particular historical and cultural settings told me a great deal more than the skeletal information contained in statistical associations. And yet it was precisely these associations that guided my interpretation of specific situations and my overall framework for thinking about female power and male dominance. Only with time was I able to resolve the basic tension between explanation required by the positivist approach and interpretation required by the particular brand of the semiotic approach I adopted.

During this time certain individuals endured my search for intellectual sanity. Julie and Eric Sanday put up with their mother's strange moods after wrestling with "thick description" and the thinness of global comparison. Winthrop D. Jordan's conviction that the book would "make its way" sustained me through numerous drafts. Anyone who has read what he said about migrating men in his book *White over Black* will recognize the imprint of this way of approaching cultural analysis.[4]

Graduate students of the Department of Anthropology at the University of Pennsylvania worked as coders of information and as research assistants. Four students, in particular, contributed in a special way. Very early, Joan Schall convinced me that Mary Douglas's analysis of the meaning of taboos was pertinent. Devon Dederich (then an undergraduate student), Charles Hoffman, and Marilyn Lutz worked closely with me as I made the transition from one framework to another. At various times during the past five years or so, each of them spent hours with me going over questions that led to the point of view I finally developed. Though each contributed in large measure to the final result, each retains skepticism regarding particular details. The final product represents my distillation of the mix between my ideas and theirs.

When it came time to read a completed manuscript, Ruth and Ward Goodenough, Marilyn Lutz, and Charles Hoffman were

particularly helpful. Based on their comments and those of anony-
mous reviewers, I completely rewrote the manuscipt. The final
version benefited considerably from the generous comments of
Rayna Rapp. Finally, I want to thank the two typists who worked
so hard for so long—Marion Pierpont and Renee Ffrench.

Peggy Reeves Sanday

University of Pennsylvania
January 1981

Introduction

This book offers certain answers to some basic questions regarding male and female power. These answers are necessarily tentative, because there are few more difficult questions about human relationships than those about the relationship of the two sexes. Throughout history and among various societies, human beings seem to have handled this relationship in an almost infinite variety of ways. Modern scholarship, particularly as represented by anthropologists, has tended to bifurcate the reasons underlying this reality into two opposites. Starkly put, the dichotomy has been nature versus nurture. In order to get out from under the weight of these polarities, I have tried to frame my questions in the most neutral possible mode. Why, for example, do women play a more prominent role in some societies than in others? Why do men dominate women, either as individuals or as a group? Why do some societies clothe sacred symbols of creative power in the guise of one sex and not of the other?

For several reasons, finding answers to these questions has not been easy. As an anthropologist I have been committed to the task of systematically establishing the full range of variation in male and female power roles before trying to explain this variation. This commitment has meant that I have had to rely on a representative sample of the world's known and well-described societies. I chose more than 150 of these societies for which detailed descriptions are available.[1] Missionaries, colonial officials, and anthropologists provided these descriptions of societies widely divergent in geographical, historical, and social circumstances. These societies are little known and, in many cases, are now extinct. From them, however, we have much to learn about the nature of female power and the reasons for male dominance.

This book is intended for an interdisciplinary audience interested in a global view of female power and male dominance in tribal societies. The following pages present many examples showing the range of variation in the relations between the sexes. In addition, numerous tables display the frequency of male dominance and female power in different environmental, social, and religious settings.

Unfortunately, most of the sources on which I had to rely, which range from the sixth century B.C. to the present, were written by males who paid cursory attention to female attitudes and behavior in the societies they described. As a rule, Western observers of other societies have not thought of women as important contributors to culture. However, despite this paucity of information on the female side of life (in many but not all cases), descriptions of male attitudes and behavior toward women provided important clues to the relationship between the sexes. There are clear differences between societies in which men fear and oppress women and societies in which the sexes intermingle in a friendly way in most activities of everyday life.

The view that emerges in this book is unconventional in that it conforms to no particular theoretical perspective or current style of thinking. Although the legacies of Durkheim, Marx, and Freud haunt the explanatory sections, I did not begin by testing any of the theories associated with these men. Rather, I began by immersing myself in the descriptive material, trying to keep an open mind and a receptive ear to what the actions of men and women in widely different circumstances might suggest regarding the questions I had posed. At the same time I reread the work of Ruth Benedict on cultural selection, Margaret Mead on sex roles, Clifford Geertz on sacred symbols, and Mary Douglas on implicit meanings while trying to keep up with the burgeoning literature written by anthropologists on relative sex status.

The following scenario about male and female power, and the origins of male dominance, does not attempt to summarize all that has been written. Nor do I intend to test one theory and reject others. There is something to be learned from most anthropological treatises on relative sex status. Yet none of them examines the full range of possibilities in a worldwide context. In examining this range, my goal is to focus on why cultures select different styles of interaction between the sexes.

The central argument unfolds by posing questions regarding cultural selection. I assume, as Ruth Benedict said long ago in *Pat-*

terns of Culture, that each culture "selects" or "chooses" from the "great arc" of behavioral possibilities. Human beings, Benedict wrote, build their institutions "upon the hints presented by the environment or by man's physical necessities."[2] How human beings staff these institutions, the freedom and autonomy they grant women relative to men, I argue, is part of a complex interaction between environmental considerations and physical and emotional needs as people construct the "cup of life" Benedict called "culture."

In *Sex and Temperament in Three Primitive Societies,* Margaret Mead argued that cultural selection included the standardization of temperamental types. Within each culture, Mead noted, there is the same range of basic temperamental types established on the basis of heredity. These differences provide "the clues from which culture works, selecting one temperament, or a combination of related and congruent types, as desirable." The choice of the acceptable temperamental type or types was embodied in "every thread of the social fabric – in the care of the young child, the games the children play, the songs the people sing, the structure of political organization, the religious observance, the art and the philosophy."[3]

In addition to selecting approved temperamental types, I suggest, each culture must select a sex-role plan – that is, a template for the organization of sex-role expectations. Because human behavior is so plastic and responsive to many kinds of pressures, as Clifford Geertz says, people must set up "symbolic templates" to set the limits of behavior and to guide it along predictable paths.[4] Sex-role plans form one kind of symbolic template. Such plans help men and women orient themselves as male and female to each other, to the world around them, and to the growing boys and girls whose behavior they must shape to a commonly accepted mold.

In addition to guiding behavior, sex-role plans solve basic human puzzles. Human beings seek answers to such questions as where did we come from; how did we get here; how did others get there; what is our relationship with all the others out there – others being animate, inanimate, and human objects; and what are we to do about the powerful forces within any of these categories not fully understood. Confronted with the obvious, generally accepted, but frequently ignored facts that babies come out of females and female genitals differ from male genitals, people seek to solve the puzzle of sex differences by sorting out how and why the differences came about, what is to be done about the differences, and how the two kinds of people resulting from the differences are to relate to one another and to their environment.

The emphasis in the early part of the book is on describing the symbolic and behavioral components of sex-role plans and showing their diversity. Later sections concern selection. Why do people construct different sex-role plans? Why is there sexual symmetry in some instances and asymmetry in others? Why are women viewed as a necessary part of political, economic, and religious affairs in some societies and not in others? Male dominance is not an inherent quality of human sex-role plans. In fact, the argument suggests that male dominance is a response to pressures that are most likely to have been present relatively late in human history.

The approach of this book represents something of a departure from the mainstream of anthropological analyses of sex roles and status. Much of the current work focuses on the exercise of power and authority in such traditional arenas of anthropological analysis as kinship, marriage, economics, and politics. Increasingly, a positivist framework is employed in which the causes of relative sex status are assigned to either psychological (usually Freudian) or materialist considerations.[5]

There is one notable exception to this general rule. In her analysis of the "universality of female subordination," Sherry Ortner depends "not upon specific cultural data but rather upon an analysis of 'culture' taken generically as a special sort of process in the world." One cannot fully comprehend the actual expression of male or female power, Ortner argues, "without first understanding the overarching ideology and deeper assumptions of the culture that render such powers . . . "[6]

By emphasizing basic cultural premises, Ortner's approach, like mine, begins with the ideational and asks how culture is related to sex status. Although I heartily endorse her approach, I cannot agree with Ortner's conclusion that women are universally assigned to the low ground of nature and men to the high ground of culture. Women are universally devalued, she says, because they are "seen as closer to nature than men, men being seen as more unequivocally occupying the high ground of culture."[7] Because

4

culture's job is to control nature, men are accorded the right to control women – hence, Ortner's conclusion regarding universal female subordination.

Ortner is close to being right about the permeability between the categories of female and nature (in some but not all societies). In societies where the forces of nature are sacralized, as the following pages show, there is a reciprocal flow between the power of nature and the power inherent in women. The control and manipulation of these forces is left to women and to sacred natural symbols; men are largely extraneous to this domain and must be careful lest they antagonize earthly representatives of nature's power (namely, women). Societies that have elaborated this type of relationship between nature and women I refer to as having an *inner orientation*.

Men are not universally aligned so unequivocally with the realm Ortner calls culture, "culture being minimally defined as the transcendence, by means of systems of thought and technology, of the natural givens of existence."[8] On the contrary, in many cases men are inextricably locked into such natural givens as death, destruction, and animality. Just as women are sometimes merged with the powers of the *inner,* men are sometimes meshed with the powers of the *outer.* Men hunt animals, seek to kill other human beings, make weapons for these activities, and pursue power that is *out there.* In other words, when conditions are right, men are unequivocally part of an *outer orientation*.

Looking as an outsider at males and females in the simpler societies of the world – that is, in societies unencumbered by complex literate traditions – one is struck with the degree to which the sexes conform to a rather basic conceptual symmetry, which is grounded in primary sex differences. Women give birth and grow children; men kill and make weapons. Men display their kills (be it an animal, a human head, or a scalp) with the same pride that women hold up the newly born. If birth and death are among the necessities of existence, then men and women contribute equally but in quite different ways to the continuance of life, and hence of culture. The evidence presented in the following pages suggests that, all other things being equal, the power to give life is as highly valued as the power to take it away. The questions at issue are: 1) Why do some societies develop a symmetric as opposed to an asymmetric valuation of these two powers? and 2) How does a symmetric or an asymmetric valuation affect the secular power of men and women?

These questions are addressed in two stages. In the early part of the book, the focus is on symbolic manifestations of a people's sex-role plan, particularly on sacred symbols of creative power. The first three chapters establish a congruence between the gender of a people's creator god(s), their orientation to the creative forces of nature, and the secular expression of male and female power. Scripts for female power are described in Chapter 1. Such scripts accord feminine symbolism and women a prominent role in the sacred and secular domains. Chapter 2 presents metaphors for male dominance and female subordination. Generally speaking, when males dominate, women play an inconsequential role in the sacred and secular domains. Almost always in male-dominated societies, the godhead is defined in exclusively masculine terms. Chapter 3 begins raising questions about selection. How do peoples choose their creator god(s) and weave their orientation to nature? Some sort of orientation to the world, Geertz says, is necessary to formulate general ideas of order. Human beings need to know that "God is not mad" – at least not so mad as to destroy them in a fit of petulance. Because man's innate responses are so general, Geertz points out, symbols and cultural patterns are necessary to make men functionally complete. Without symbols and guidelines, man would be "not merely a talented ape who had, like some underprivileged child, unfortunately been prevented from realizing his full potentialities, but a kind of formless monster with neither sense of direction nor power of self-control, a chaos of spasmodic impulses and vague emotions."[9] As Langer puts it:

[Man] cannot deal with Chaos . . . his greatest fright is to meet what he cannot construe . . . under mental stress even perfectly familiar things may become suddenly disorganized and give us the horrors. Therefore our most important assets are always the symbols of our general *orientation* in nature, on the earth, in society, and in what we are doing . . .[10]

In Chapter 3 I argue that the environment, human subsistence activities, and primary sex differences provide the clues that shape a people's conception of creative power and their orientation to nature. People weave their fantasies about power from their perception of the forces most responsible for what they conceive to be the necessities of life. If these forces revolve around migration and the pursuit of animals, an *outer orientation* becomes prominent. If nature satisfies a people's perception of their primary needs, an *inner orientation* takes precedence. In some cases, both orientations are equally developed.

In addition to orienting peoples to the forces in their universe, sex-role plans determine the sexual division of labor. Whether or not men and women mingle or are largely separated in everyday affairs plays a crucial role in the rise of male dominance. Men and women must be physically as well as conceptually separated in order for men to dominate women. Thus, in determining the conditions that select for male dominance, one must have some prior notion of the conditions favoring sexual segregation.

Chapters 4 and 5 examine the bases for sexual separation or integration. Chapter 4 focuses on the sexual division of labor in technological activities, that is, in activities involving the acquisition and processing of food and making implements, houses, tools, utensils, and so on. Like the gender of a people's major creator(s), plans for the sexual division of labor are formed from a people's adaptation to their environment in pursuing the necessities of life. As such, these plans are part of the same cultural configuration that gives rise to masculine or feminine creator gods and an *inner* or *outer* orientation. Chapter 4 shows that, generally speaking, the sexes mingle in most activities when people perceive the environment as a partner rather than as an opponent. On the other hand, when the environment is defined in hostile terms, the sexes tend to separate from each other.

Chapter 5 extends the analysis of sexual separation to an examination of the belief, found in some societies, that menstrual blood and sexual intercourse are dangerous. The basic argument presented here draws on the work of Mary Douglas, who treats concepts of pollution and danger as a system of meaningful symbols in which the acutal relationship between the sexes plays a negligible role. Following Douglas's suggestion that powers and dangers credited to bodily processes reflect more general fears, I suggest in this chapter that people provide themselves with a stage upon which to control dangerous forces confronting them by projecting their concerns onto the human, usually the female, body.

No matter how it is produced, sexual separation (for whatever reason) creates two worlds – one male and the other female, each consisting of a system of meanings and a program for behavior.

Chapters 6 and 7 concentrate on the "women's world." Chapter 6 discusses the bases for female economic and political power. In societies displaying an *inner orientation,* females control goods and participate in group decision making as a natural extension of the social focus on inner power. In *outer-oriented* societies, female secular power is dependent on practical circumstances giving women access to scarce resources or making them responsible for the conduct of ritual. Where both orientations are evident, the inner and outer conceptions of sacred power support sexually balanced spheres of economic and political power.

When a people combats outside influences, the power of women may disintegrate as new metaphors for sexual identities replace the old and a new sexual division of labor gives men readier access to strategic resources. Examples of the effect of European colonialism on the women's world are presented in Chapter 7. The case studies of the decline in female power presented in this chapter establish a causal relationship between depleting resources, cultural disruption, migration, and the oppression of women.

The rise of secular male dominance is taken up in Chapters 8 and 9. Secular male dominance is defined in terms of: 1) the physical coercion of women, as in wife beating or rape, and 2) the exclusion of women from political and economic activities. Why men dominate women in these ways is a complex question, for which no one answer suffices. In addressing this question it is important to distinguish between "mythical" and real male dominance. "Mythical" male dominance, a term adapted from the work of Susan Carol Rogers, captures the ambiguous and often antagonistic relationship between sexes in societies where females have political and economic power but men act as if males were the dominant sex. Real male dominance, on the other hand, applies to societies in which males dominate women both in theory and in fact. Sexual equality is a third category, in which the balance of power between the sexes is not obscured by the myth that males rule. Such an approach to the definition of male dominance illustrates at the level of secular politics that male supremacism or sexual asymmetry is not as widespread as some anthropologists have argued.

Chapter 8 confirms the relationship between male dominance and cultural disruption suggested in Chapter 7. Basically there are two responses to cultural disruption that have a significant impact on existing sex-role plans. One response is to fight to preserve or reinstate the past; another is to expand the domain of old symbols to control creeping chaos. Regarding the first response, men and not women embrace mass slaughter in defense of a dying tradition. Though a few women have died fighting for the women's world (see Chapter 7), the female role is not conceived in terms that make the acceptance of death in combat a possibility. Because the male role is conceived in these terms, the social body is sometimes entrusted to men as a reward for being the expendable sex. Obviously, if women willingly embraced mass slaughter, there would be no social body to preserve.

In cases of severe social stress or cultural disruption, the fighting takes on a different flavor. Instead of fighting the external oppressor, men band together and turn aggression against women. In these cases male dominance seems extreme because the whole of public life, that is, life that does not revolve around childrearing and family activities, becomes synonymous with the male collective. These primordially based male solidarities exhibit an uneasy strength because they are usually held together by fear of women. In simple societies, I suggest, such primordial attachments develop when culture breaks down, when societies are formed of a mixture of shreds and patches of other cultures, and when ancient power symbols have been drained of their efficacy. When male dominance is based on an exhausted or threatened cultural base, it is, in a sense, a reaction to loss of direction.

The behavioral and symbolic mechanisms for the establishment of male dominance are examined in Chapter 9. Drawing on the work of Mary Douglas and Margaret Mead, I trace the effects of depletion in animal resources, population expansion, and migration in six societies, three of which are male dominated and three of which are not. The purpose of this analysis is to show how a people's orientation to nature and their sacred symbols result in different solutions to stress. Male oppression of women is neither an automatic nor an immediate response to stress. Generally speaking, male dominance is based on a prior foundation formed by an *outer orientation* and sexual segregation.

Another major response to cultural disruption and growing chaos is to generate new symbols or to widen the domain that the gods control. In the Epilogue, I turn to an examination of the symbolic roots of Western sexual asymmetry. I suggest that the patriarchal Judeo-Christian god arose from the lesser figure of Yahweh during a time when pluralism was getting out of hand in Palestine. The Hebrew fathers expanded Yahweh's domain, I argue, in order to preserve the integrity of the social-religious-political identity formed by the exodus from Egypt. Women played an important role in this process because, in all likelihood, Canaanite goddess worship posed the greatest threat to the fledgling identity of the Hebrews in their new land. By raising Yahweh on high to control men, who in turn were charged to control women, the Hebrews reminded themselves that their mission in the new land was one of dominion and not of participation in the surrounding cultural pleasures.

Migrating peoples who take up an abode in a culturally pluralistic land live in a different social universe, as far as maintaining a recognized identity is concerned, than do settled agricultural groups in the same land whose long and deep-rooted ties to one place provide an easier security. Like so many of today's new states, migrating peoples are abnormally susceptible to the overpowering coerciveness of primordial attachments – that is, as Geertz says in discussing the new states, attachments based on the "givens" of social existence. Such givens supply the bonds people seize upon to define themselves in union against others – bonds provided by "congruities of blood, speech, custom, and so on," which have an ineffable coerciveness in and of themselves.[11]

In the case of the Hebrews, the bonds came from religion and membership in one of the semi-nomadic tribes that settled in Palestine. The subsequent religious and ethnic struggles produced, among other things, the guiding symbols for Western male domination – the patriarchal god and the sexual, hence evil, female. In addition to discussing these symbols in Biblical popular culture, I consider in the Epilogue the fate of Gnostic beliefs in early Christianity. These episodes in the Judeo-Christian tradition were marked by warfare between advocates of the participation of women in the inner sacred sanctum and adherents of an all-masculine religious system. The forces resolving this conflict, I suggest in an admittedly speculative analysis, are not unlike those that have accompanied the selection for male dominance in other cultures. Today, after some 2,000 years of relative obscurity, goddess symbols like those present early in the Judeo-Christian tradition are being resurrected by contemporary feminists. The resurrection of these symbols shows that we, like other people, seek to align the sacred with the secular in our sex-role plan.

To summarize, male dominance and female power are consequences of the way in which peoples come to terms with their historical and natural environments and develop their separate identities. Male and female power roles are cast when peoples forge their sense of peoplehood. A sense of peoplehood implies a shared code that guides behavior, including the behavior of the sexes, not only in relation to each other but also in relation to valued resources and to the supernatural. Power is accorded to whichever sex is thought to embody or to be in touch with the forces upon which people depend for their perceived needs. Conceiving power in this way, one can say that in some societies women have more power, or men have more, or both sexes have an approximately equal amount.

When a people's identity is formed in adverse circumstances or when this identity is endangered by new circumstances, they may become heavily dependent on the aggressive acts of men. Male dominance results if adversity is blamed on matters having to do with women. Males may claim that the supposed tyranny or incompetence of females actually forces men to dominate women. Or, the association of women with sin and evil gives men the right to dominate. The spectacle of the female temptress in the Garden of Eden is by no means unique. The reasons peoples give for their afflictions provide a starting point for investigating dominance–subordinance relations between the sexes.

Because the plan that guides the behavior of the sexes in everyday life is part of the foundation of a people's culture, it does not change easily. As people transmit their culture from one generation to the next, they transmit sex-role principles. Human beings do not invent new paths for males and females to follow from one generation to the next. Rather, young people are inexorably bound by the sexual life-styles of their parents. No matter how hard they try to be different, young males and females eventually experience the tidal pull of their culture and history. Things change when tensions are such that without change things would come apart.

How does all this affect us? It does so by suggesting possible answers to some of the questions our current sex-role revolution poses. For example, male dominance is not universal, as some people have suggested. Then, too, there is a connection between religious thought and male and female power, which feminists have been arguing since the nineteenth century. Changing sex-role relationships will involve more than changing a few laws, though the latter is clearly part of the process of change. The relative power between the sexes will change as our culture changes. Change the cultural plot and sex roles are conceived differently. Change sex roles and the plot will change. For example, give women access to sacred roles and much else will change – our concept of the sacred, the standard interpretation of the Bible, our concept of "human rights," and so on. Which is to say that the traditional fabric of our culture will be involved if the current move toward sexual equality succeeds.

PART I

Plans for sex-role behavior

Women shall be considered the progenitors of the Nation. They shall own the land and the soil.

> The Constitution of the Five Nations
> 60-LX, TLL, in Parker (1916)

To the women he [God] said, "I will greatly multiply your pain in childbearing; in pain you shall bring forth children, yet your desire shall be for your husband, and he shall rule over you."

> Genesis 3:16

1 · Scripts for female power

In Western society, as individual males and females, we understand the meaning of the divine command in the Garden of Eden – "yet your desire shall be for your husband, and he shall rule over you" – and we are affected by the attitude toward women expressed in the events that led to the fall of Adam and Eve. We also understand that when our founding fathers declared "that all men are created equal; that they are endowed by their creator with certain unalienable rights," they had men and not women in mind. It comes as no surprise to any of us that women are excluded from many of the behavioral domains in which the right to rule is exercised.

Religious and secular codes, such as those found in the Garden of Eden story and in the Declaration of Independence, present basic propositions regarding expected behavior. Often these propositions explicate the relationship between the sexes and the meaning of being male and female. From the propositions by which a people codify their social and religious identity we can infer the historically approved plan structuring the relationship between the sexes.

As a rule, the logic of sex-role plans is transmitted from one generation to the next almost intact. These plans are subject to change only when a people's traditional culture has been shattered by environmental or social exigencies. When this happens, either a new code for social identity is formulated or a people become extinct as a unique social unit. It is not unusual to find in reformulated social codes new forms of sexual identities and a revised sex-role plan.

The plans that structure the relationship between the sexes can be categorized as follows: The sexes are either merged or they are segregated; the power to make decisions is either vested in both sexes or is dominated by one sex. Sex-role plans are cultural and

15

not biological. This means that they do not derive from human genetics but from the historical and political circumstances in which people find themselves when they are forced to come to terms with their environment and themselves as a social unit. If sex-role plans were derived from the human biological structure, we would not find the variety of plans that do exist.

In this chapter and the next, differences in sex-role plans are demonstrated by displaying the scripts that direct the sexes in nine widely scattered and very different kinds of societies. These scripts are revealed by the mythical representation of the sexes in creation stories and the behavior of the sexes in everyday life. Sex-role scripts are as unique to a culture as the turn of phrase or splash of brush is unique to poet or artist. Consequently, each culture can be shown to have different ideas about what it means to be male, what it means to be female, and how the two sexes should interact. Although the scripts are rich and various, the underlying plans are not. The task in these first two chapters, then, is to uncover the plans by analyzing the scripts.

Creation stories tell us something about how people conceive the nature and origin of creative power. The main actors in these stories can be interpreted as metaphors for ancient but still salient sexual identities. Whether the creator is conceived in masculine or feminine terms has important consequences for the evolution of the authority relationship between the sexes. In order to understand female power and male dominance, it is important to clarify from the outset the interconnection between supernatural power and sex-role plans. Once this is accomplished we will want to examine the question of how and why people choose their creative agents – Why is the creative mother found in some societies and not in others? After this, the task will be to examine first the forces that divide the sexes and, second, the bases for female power and male dominance.

From "the complete perfect unity": the Balinese

The Balinese of insular Southeast Asia exemplify in theory, if not altogether in fact, the unisexual society. In religion, politics, economics, kinship, and dress, Clifford Geertz says, "Bali is a rather 'unisex' society, a fact both its customs and its symbolism clearly express." Even in those contexts where women do not play much

16

of a role – music, painting, certain agricultural activities – their absence "is more a mere matter of fact than socially enforced."[1]

In other realms of life also the Balinese merge what we in the West ordinarily keep distinct. The arts, religion, ritual, and collective life are elaborately developed and interrelated. Fantasy and reality are so closely connected that one cannot be understood without reference to the other. When a single religious concept, myth figure, or fairy tale is accepted by the Balinese, the whole culture becomes to some extent modified. This is because children are brought up on these tales and parents' attitudes are consistently modified in concordance with current belief.[2]

Social groups are also internally undifferentiated. The generic term for any organized group is *seka,* which means "to be as one." In any *seka* all members have equal rights and duties, and decisions are reached unanimously in meetings of the whole. Leadership is nominal and nonauthoritative. The *seka* principle demands that groups be viewed as having one, and only one, basis of organization. This protects the integrity of a social group against its parts. It ensures its autonomy as a functioning unit in its own terms rather than as a mere derivative of its components.[3]

The egalitarian structural principle so important in Balinese life is reflected in the mythical representation of the sexes. It is difficult to be very specific about Balinese creation stories because there are so many of them and because the Balinese themselves are, by Western standards, disarmingly imprecise about "origins." They have a myth about the origin of just about everything. As one plows through these tales, a sense of total confusion rings in the Western ear. Yet this confusion is precisely indicative of the Balinese character: The Balinese enmesh themselves in a fantasy world populated by an uncountable number of wondrous beings of uncertain sex.

Consider this legend concerning origin:

The gods concentrated to make human beings and produced two couples; one yellow in color: Ketok Pita and Djenar; another red: Abang and Barak. From the yellow couple was born a boy, Nyoh Gading, "Yellow Coconut," and a girl named Kuning. The second couple had also two children, a boy named Tanah Barak, "Red Earth," and a girl Lewék. Yellow Coconut married Lewék; Red Earth married Kuning; and their descendants did the same until the population of Bali was created.[4]

17

There are endless similar tales about the Balinese legendary "original couple." This couple, and those like it, are usually male and female twins who appear to be a union of the eternal male and female principles, rather than specific persons.

Male and female creative forces are believed to stand in complete and perfect unity within the supreme deity, Siwa. Siwa is "the esoteric combination of all the gods and all the forces of nature."[5] Another god – The Solitary – combines the characteristics of both sexes and seems to have preceded the separation of male and female in Balinese cosmology, coming before all other gods.[6]

The notion of divine unity is repeated in the Balinese perception of the rights and duties of the sexes. An important feature of Balinese culture is the crossing of sex roles: the merging into an undifferentiated male–female type and the redivision of the sexes, which restores the polarity between them. This thinking is reflected in their attitude toward the development of the child. This new being is presumed to be created out of the union of the separated male and female elements. In this respect the child is like a god. The child is a straight-line descendant from the undifferentiated male–female element, which will, as it grows and develops, again divide as either its male or its female potential is realized.[7]

The distinction between the sexes is irrelevant in much of everyday life, and the two sexes are often interchangeable. If a man has no son to carry on his line, a daughter will do. Priestly functions may be carried out by women as well as by men. Child dancers may be boys or girls, or boys dressed as girls or girls dressed as boys. Boys and girls wear almost identical clothing, as do men and women. From a short distance it is not unusual to mistake a man for a woman, or a woman for a man. One can tell males and females apart from the way they sit or from what they are doing. Women sit one way, men another. Women weave, men climb coconut trees. When, as occasionally happens, individuals wish to be of the opposite sex, "it is precisely by doing such things as climbing coconut trees or weaving that they express this wish."[8]

One can see from this example that sex-linked behavior does exist. This is especially so during the years of young courtship, when there is more emphasis on the differences between male and female. While skills are being acquired there is a division of labor by sex that emphasizes sex differences. But once a man and woman marry and form a household, either one may act for the pair. Husbands and wives "are like partners, of whom either one can represent the firm."[9]

The creative grandmother of the primeval sea: the Semang

Undifferentiation, to which the Balinese adhere in theory, is practice among the Semang. When they were described in 1925, the Negrito Semang were nomadic gatherers and hunters inhabiting the tropical forest of the Malay peninsula. The following description represents their way of life in the 1920s.

The Semang have a "plant oriented mentality" in the food they procure and in their ritual thought and practice.[10] They wander through their forest "lightfooted, singing, and wreathed with flowers," with the blowgun over their shoulders, searching the treetops for game or honey. Every expedition is a new experience for them. They place a high value on freedom of movement and disdain the sedentary life of agriculture.[11]

Semang women are the main contributors to the diet, since they gather wild plant food, which is the dietary staple. Men occasionally hunt small game, but they do not hunt large game nor do they engage in any kind of warfare. Men do not band together for either hunting or warfare and, perhaps as a result of this, they are more involved with their families and with childrearing. Semang men will sometimes join the women on gathering expeditions. Everyone joins together in harvesting fruit.[12]

The ceremonials and symbolism connected with the fruit harvest reflect male and female principles in interesting ways. Blood is the major fertility symbol: The more of it that is sacrificed, the more abundant will be the fruit harvest, because the blood cast against a thunderstorm enters the umbels of the fruit, which hang from tendrils to the ground.[13] In no sense does blood have the connotation of taking life; rather, it is given to increase life and to atone for sins committed. The blood sacrifice consists of nothing more than men and women (usually women) cutting their legs with knives, catching drops in a piece of bamboo, and casting it toward the sky. This is done whenever it thunders. It is believed to appease angry or evil spirits and to bring the important deities together in a manner that increases the abundance of fruit.

These deities are male and female. The major female deity, Manoij, lives in the earth, and the most important male deities, Karei and Ta Ped'n, live "above the firmament." They feed on the fruits of the celestial trees, whose juice they suck. The rinds and seeds dropped to earth become fruit trees for human beings. Karei gives humans various commandments or taboos and he punishes transgressors with lightning, falling trees, the tiger (who is his policeman), or sickness. Karei shows his displeasure through thunder and is appeased by the blood sacrifice. However, the blood that is offered is both for Karei living above and for Manoij living in the earth. When Karei roars forth thunder and lightning, Manoij comes out of the earth, bringing with her the blood the Semang have poured on the ground, and begs Karei to allow himself to be placated.[15]

In one performance of the blood sacrifice, the blood is first directed to Manoij, who is considered to be "the grandmother of the inhabitants of heaven who cause thunder." She is asked to go up and ask them to cease thundering and to announce to Ta Ped'n that the expiation for the offense has been offered. He receives the blood, cooks it, and puts it into the umbels of fruit trees, through which many fruits will flourish. There are many other celestial male and earthly female deities, although Manoij and Ta Ped'n are mentioned most frequently. Although all deities are paired in a male–female unit, these two "practically merge into a bisexual being."[16]

In one creation story, Manoij performs the main acts of creation with the aid of her grandsons:

In the beginning there was only water. Manoij and her two grandsons floated on this primeval sea and Manoij commanded one of the grandsons to bring her the branch from a wild rambutan. This she used to pierce the back of the monster that dwelt in the deep, after which the water began to ebb and the water bed became visible. A beetle then lifted the earth out of the ooze, and the earth grew, but there were only hills. A bird hopped about on the earth and by flipping its tail, smoothed down the hills, so that habitable land was formed between the hills and mountains.[17]

Human beings were made out of flowers. Manoij dreamed about a child and asked her grandson (who is identified as Ta Ped'n in the story of the creation of people) for one. The two of them went into the forest where the grandson made a clay figure and wrapped it in a mat. The next day it became a girl. This process was repeated and the new clay figure became a boy, who cohabited with the girl when he grew to manhood. This couple made the first human couple by transforming a flower with a stone in it into a girl who grew into a woman. This woman went into the forest and came across a shrub which she plucked, and it turned into a boy. These two cohabited and were responsible for bringing human children into the world. [18]

Manoij plays a mediatory role both in ritual and in the story of creation. Because she acts as intercessor she inspires confidence. Although the heavenly deity has ultimate control over thunderstorms and is appealed to directly to end the storm quickly, the plea to the earth mother is more intense. [19]

Thus, the male and female principles are both central to Semang thought, ritual, and everyday behavior. Neither one is superior to the other. The earth mother is perhaps closer to human affairs and the sky father more distant. He makes the thunder and she helps the people to appease him. She is the nurturant figure and he the commanding figure. In this sense they are different, but the difference is balanced by their equal capacity to do good.

Sex roles among the Semang are, by and large, integrated and equal; that is, males and females participate jointly in many of the activities of everyday life. Both have rights to property and participate in decision making. To the extent that leadership exists, it is based on the ability to be assertive. This women can do as well as men. For example, a woman named Isan is described by a Western observer as "a very alert and voluble woman who had the ability to assert herself even with men."[20] Other observers refer to a Semang woman, perhaps the same woman, as "the ruler of the Negritos."[21] It is likely, however, that political authority was less formally developed than these remarks would indicate. Isan, and women like her, was simply a respected voice in public decision making.

Father, mother, lover, friend: the Mbuti

Minimal differentiation of sex roles also exists among the Mbuti, who form the largest single group of pygmy hunters and gatherers in Africa. Their habitat and their heaven is the Ituri Forest.

The Mbuti have no creation myth per se. The forest is their godhead, and different individuals address it as "father," "mother," "lover," and/or "friend." The Mbuti say that the forest is everything: the provider of food, shelter, warmth, clothing, and affection. Each person and animal is endowed with some spiritual power that "derives from a single source whose physical manifestation is the forest itself." Disembodied spirits deriving from this same source of power are also believed to inhabit the forest; they are considered to be independent manifestations of the forest.[22] The forest lives for the Mbuti. It is both natural and supernatural, something that is depended upon, respected, trusted, obeyed, and loved.[23]

The forest is a good provider. At all times of the year men and women can gather an abundant supply of mushrooms, roots, berries, nuts, herbs, fruits, and leafy vegetables.[24] The forest also provides animal food. There is little division of labor by sex. The hunt is frequently a joint effort. A man is not ashamed to pick mushrooms and nuts if he finds them or to wash and clean a baby.

In general, leadership is minimal and there is no attempt to control or dominate either the geographical or human environment. Decision making is by common consent: Men and women have equal say because hunting and gathering are both important to the economy.[25] The forest is the ultimate authority. It expresses its feelings through storms, falling trees, poor hunting – all of which are taken as signs of its displeasure. But often the forest remains silent, and this is when the people must sound out its feelings through discussion. Diversity of opinion may be expressed, but prolonged disagreement is considered to be "noise" and offensive to the forest. Certain individuals may be recognized as having the right and the ability to interpret the pleasure of the forest. In this sense there is individual authority, which simply means effective participation in discussions. The three major areas for discussion are economic, ritual, and legal matters having to do with dispute settlement. Participation in discussions is evenly divided between the sexes and among all adult age levels.[26]

The avoidance of differentiation between the sexes is consistent with the principle of egalitarianism that rules Mbuti life in the forest. Some sexual differentiation, however, occurs in the emotional connotations associated with mother and father and is acted out in one of the most important Mbuti ceremonies. Motherhood is associated with food and love, and fatherhood with authority,

22

although fathers physically nurture their children. The mother is regarded as the source of food; all food that is collected or hunted is cooked and distributed by women. Hungry children look to their mothers for food, not to their fathers.[27]

Sexual differentiation is acted out in the *molimo* ceremony, which is held irregularly, when someone dies or when conditions of life are generally poor. Its goal is to awaken and "to rejoice the forest." The festival symbolizes the triumph of life over death. The central ceremonial symbols are the *molimo* fire and the *molimo* trumpets. Both are associated with life, regeneration, and fertility. Both are believed to have been once owned by women and stolen from them by the men. The trumpet is sometimes referred to as an "animal" of the forest: It is symbolically fed, it is passed through the fire, and during a dance it is used by a young man to imitate the male and female parts in the sexual act. The trumpet is the only sign of the presence of a supernatural power during the *molimo* festival. The trumpet is supposed to sing and to pass on the song of the Mbuti into the forest. It is kept out of the sight of women and children, who are supposedly forbidden to see it. The Mbuti do not consider the trumpet to be sacred in itself; it is simply a vehicle for transferring power between the Mbuti and the forest.[28]

The *molimo* festival includes two rituals that separate male from female. Both focus on an old woman who symbolically kills and scatters the *molimo* fire (the symbol of life) and later ties all the men together with a roll of twine. The old woman dances the fire dance led by a chorus of women singing *molimo* songs (supposedly known only by men). The men follow in obedient chorus. The high point of the dance comes when the old woman jumps into the flames, whirls around, and scatters the *molimo* fire in all directions within the circle of men surrounding her. The men, still singing, gather the scattered embers, throw them back onto the coals, and dance while the flames begin to rise again as if they had brought the fire back to life. The old woman repeats her dance, each time seeming to stamp the fire out of existence, after which the dance of the men gives it new life. Finally the old woman and the women leave the scene.

A little later the old woman comes back alone. The men continue singing while she ties them all together, looping a roll of twine around their necks. Once all are tied they stop singing. The men then admit to having been bound and to the necessity of giving the woman something as a token of their defeat, so that she will let them go. After a certain quantity of food has been agreed upon, the old woman unties each man. No one attempts to untie himself, but as each man is untied he begins to sing once more. This signifies that the *molimo* is free. The old woman receives her gifts, and before leaving several weeks later, she goes to every man, giving him her hand to touch as though it were some kind of blessing.

These are indeed fascinating acts. Colin Turnbull, the major ethnographer of the Mbuti, suggests that in the fire dance women assert their prior claim to the fire of life and their ability to destroy and extinguish life. However, he asks, was the old woman really destroying the fire? Perhaps when she kicked the fire in all directions among the men she was giving it to them, to gather, rebuild, and revitalize the fire with the dance of life.[29] In discussing these ceremonies, Turnbull suggested to me the possibility that they symbolized the transferance of power from women to men. As he put it, "Women have the power which they give to men for them to control" (personal communication). If this is indeed the case, and it is difficult to be sure, then whereas in some societies men take power from women (see the description of Mundurucu in the next chapter), Mbuti women give power to men.

The Mbuti attitude toward blood is similar to that of the Semang. Blood symbolizes both life and death. Menstrual blood in particular symbolizes life. Between husband and wife it is not a frightening thing as it is in so many societies. The blood that comes for the first time to the young girl comes as a gift, received with gratitude and rejoicing, because she is now a potential mother and can proudly take a husband. The girl enters seclusion, taking with her all of her friends. Here they celebrate the happy event and are taught the arts and crafts of motherhood by an old and respected relative. They learn to live like adults and to sing the songs of adult women. Pygmies from all around come to pay their respects, because for them this occasion is "one of the happiest, most joyful occasions in their lives."[30]

The mother of the earth beings who fell from the sky: the Iroquois

With the Iroquois we come to a very different patterning of the relationship between the sexes. Sexual differentiation among them

24

was extreme, with the main emphasis placed on the female principle. The ceremonial and political importance of females in Iroquoian culture is well known. In the nineteenth century the Iroquois were described as matriarchal, and in the twentieth century they have frequently been cited as an example of sexual equality. Female symbolism dominated the Iroquoian ceremonial cycle and belief system. The earth was thought to belong to women, which gave them religious title to the land and its fruits. Female agricultural activities and the fertility and bounty of nature were highly respected and revered. The major activities celebrated in the communal ceremonial cycle were those related to female food production.[31]

Iroquois is the name given to the famous North American Indian confederacy that was formed around the middle of the fifteenth century at Onondaga (Syracuse, N.Y.). Consisting at first of five nations – Mohawks, Oneidas, Onondagas, Cayugas, and Senecas – a sixth nation, the Tuscaroras, joined the confederacy in about 1710. Their geographical position in interior New York made the Six Nations vital to the fur trade during the Colonial period. Not only was their own country rich in beaver, but they were located at the gateway to lake routes to the distant interior. As early as 1612, they obtained firearms in trade from the Dutch, which enabled them to defend themselves and expand their hegemony over other Indian groups. Their military strength is said also to have maintained the balance of power between French, English, and Colonial Americans for more than a hundred years.[32]

The importance of women is clearly reflected in the story of the founding of the confederacy and in the Constitution of the Five Nations, which consists of the confederate Iroquois laws. The League was founded by the legendary Deganawidah who, early in his life, set out on a journey "to stop the shedding of blood among human beings." This was a time when the Five Nations existed as independent bodies, with similar dialects and customs but with no political coherence. They fought constantly with one another and, faced with raids from other tribal units, were in a precarious situation. Before Deganawidah's birth, his name and mission were disclosed to his grandmother in a dream in which she was visited by a messenger from the Great Spirit. The messenger instructed the grandmother that when Deganawidah reached manhood she was to "place no obstacle in his way when he desires to leave

25

home to spread the New Mind among the nations."[33]

This dream would appear to be a minor incident in the story, were it not common in Iroquois culture for people to act on these "wishes of the soul." The Iroquois believed that a dream revealed the wishes of the dreamer and of the supernatural who appeared in the dream. Because frustration of wishes of a supernatural was believed to be dangerous, the dreamer through whom the supernatural spoke often assumed the role of prophet, messiah, public censor, and adviser. Such prophets were known to make detailed recommendations about such matters as diplomatic policy toward other tribes.[34] Viewed within the context of the Iroquoian theory of dreams, the grandmother played an important role in the founding of the League by delegating this task to her grandson.

Returning to the Legend of Deganawidah, early in his journey he met a woman "who lived by the warriors' path which passed between the east and the west." To this woman he told his message, "that all peoples shall love one another and live together in peace." She replied by saying, "Thy message is good but a word is nothing until it is given form and set to work in the world. What form," she asked, "shall this message take when it comes to dwell among men?"

This question prompted Deganawidah to set forth the basic structure of the League, one that replicated that of the family. The League, Deganawidah said, was to "take the form of the long-house in which there are many fires, one for each family, yet all live as one household under one chief mother. Hereabouts are five nations, each with its own council fire, yet they shall live together as one household in peace. They shall be the Kanonsionni, the Longhouse." In that longhouse, he declared:

The women shall possess the titles of chiefship. They shall name the chiefs. That is because thou, my Mother, wert the first to accept the Good News of Peace and Power. Henceforth thou shalt be called Ji-gonhsasee, New Face, for thy countenance evinces the New Mind, and thou shalt be known as the Mother of Nations.[35]

The traditional Iroquois dwelling unit was called a *longhouse*. It was a kind of family barracks in which lived a number of family groups who were related through women and headed by an influential matron. Archeological evidence suggests that these structures existed before the formation of the League, as did the influ-

26

ence of women, who were the cardinal food providers. The adoption of familial symbolism in structuring the League indicates again the pivotal role of women.[36]

The Constitution of the Five Nations, transmitted orally for generations and rendered in written form in the late nineteenth century, lists Deganawidah's Words of the Law and codifies the central role of women as follows: "The lineal descent of the people of the Five Nations shall run in the female line. Women shall be considered the progenitors of the Nation. They shall own the land and the soil. Men and women shall follow the status of the mother."[37]

The theme of women as progenitors of the people is not unique to the Legend of Deganawidah or to the Constitution, as this Seneca creation story shows:

A woman, called the Ancient-bodied, is responsible for most of earthly life. The story begins in the sky-world, which is dominated by "man-beings" and chiefs. One chief, because he suspects that his wife has borne him a daughter by another man, angrily uproots a tree near his lodge, causing a hole to appear. The chief pushes his wife and her girl-child through the hole and, as the mother falls, she grabs some earth from the sky-world. She falls onto Turtle's back with her daughter, still gripping the earth from the sky-world (there is no land to fall upon). With this earth she makes land. During her fall she is given utensils, an ear of corn, and a mortar and pestle for grinding grain. The Ancient-bodied causes the earth to increase in size and the plants to grow. She commands that there be a sun and a day in which the sun rises and sets. At night she creates the stars and names the constellations.

The girl-child, the Ancient-bodied's daughter, becomes pregnant by the Wind and two male twins are born. The twins and their grandmother continue to create, the girl-child remaining insignificant in the rest of creation. One twin asks for game animals, which he receives after competing successfully in a race with the Wind's other two sons. He carries the game animals home in a bag and lets them loose in the forest. The Ancient-bodied names all the big game animals that men hunt and tells the man-beings to name the rest. Thereafter the twins become accustomed to hunting in the woods together, where one of them is eventually killed.[38]

The division of male and female spheres is reflected clearly in this myth. The Ancient-bodied is responsible for corn and the

27

male twins for hunting, although the Ancient-bodied names the important game animals. A similar division of labor characterized Iroquoian division between the sexes. Men were warriors and hunters and were active in League affairs; senior women planted and harvested the crops, managed the households, and named the men who were to assume vacated League titles. Both men and women participated in village decision making, the women caucusing behind the scenes in town meetings attended by both sexes. Women were entitled to demand publicly that a murdered kinsman or kinswoman be replaced by a captive from a non-Iroquoian tribe. A woman's male relatives were morally obligated to join a war party to secure captives, whom the bereaved woman might either adopt and let live or adopt and consign to torture or death. Thus, Iroquois women participated in consensual politics in theory and in fact.[39]

In the symbolic, economic, and familial spheres the Iroquois were matriarchal, that is, female dominated. Iroquoian women headed the family longhouse, and much of the economic and ceremonial life centered on the agricultural activities of women. Men were responsible for hunting, war, and intertribal affairs. Although women appointed men to League positions and could veto their decisions, men dominated League deliberations. This tension between male and female spheres, in which females dominated village life and left intertribal life to men, suggests that the sexes were separate but equal, at least during the confederacy. Before the confederacy, when the individual nations stood alone and consisted of a set of loosely organized villages subsisting on the horticultural produce of women, females may have overshadowed the importance of males.[40]

One couple from the sky and one couple from the earth: the Ashanti

The Ashanti, one of the great West African Kingdoms, duplicate the essential outlines of the segregated-but-equal sex-role plan. The Ashanti are divided into a number of chiefdoms composed of dispersed matriclans (descent groups recognizing a remote common ancestress). There are eight of these clans, most of which can be found in each Ashanti chiefdom. To understand the importance of Ashanti women, it is necessary to consider briefly the Ashanti political structure.[41]

At the apex is the king, the Asantehene, with his court in Kumasi, the traditional center of the Ashanti empire. He is a member of the Oyoko clan, the royal clan that supplied heads of chiefdoms and new kings. Clustered around Kumasi are a group of Ashanti chiefdoms. The system of government regulating the relationship of these chiefdoms to Kumasi was first described in 1817 and again in the early twentieth century, when the main features appeared unaltered. The chiefs were of coordinate rank with the king in Kumasi. Each segment within the chiefdoms constituted a largely autonomous unit that, in major outline, reproduced the higher jurisdiction of the king in Kumasi. Each chief had a council of hereditary advisers or elders, and succession to chiefly office (like succession to the title of king) was inherited through the female line. A festival (*odwira*) was held annually, in which subordinate chiefs affirmed or reaffirmed allegiance to the chief. This festival, however, could not be held until after the chief had himself attended the king's *odwira* in Kumasi, thereby confirming his allegiance to him. The ties between the chiefdoms and the capital were maintained through restrictions on the autonomy of the chiefs, which included taxation, maintaining the last court of appeal in the capital, and requiring the use of local forces for the national interest or restricting the use of local forces when inimical to the national interest.

A man named Osei Tutu, of the Oyoko royal clan, was responsible for consolidating the Ashanti chiefdoms in this form of political structure. He built the capital at Kumasi and became the first king of the new state in the late seventeenth century. The unity of the new empire was symbolized in the Golden Stool which, being without past, was regarded as having descended from the sky. Older symbols of political authority were ritually buried near Kumasi "because it was considered improper that any stool in the nation should be regarded as having preceded the Golden Stool."[42]

The Golden Stool contains the *sunsum* (soul or spirit) of the Ashanti nation. The people's power, health, bravery, and welfare reside in it. If the stool were taken or destroyed, the Ashanti nation would sicken and lose its vitality and power.[43] The stool symbolizes the union of a number of previously autonomous but culturally similar groups, each of which is ruled by a paramount chief whose insignia of office, also a stool, was passed on in the female line.[44]

Everyday life is organized around the group of related men and women who live in village or township wards. These groups, called *localized lineages,* trace their descent through females. Each has a male head, who is often one of the chief's councillors. He is chosen by the consensus of the older men and women and with their assistance is responsible for the welfare of the entire group. In lineage affairs there is, according to Meyer Fortes, a "high degree of equality between male and female members." The lineage head is assisted by a senior woman informally chosen by him and his elders. This is extended to the kingdom as a whole and to each chiefdom.[45]

The senior woman of the royal lineage is the Queen Mother. She has her own stool, which is senior to the chief's stool. Traditionally, the Queen Mother has had the most to say in selecting a new chief or king. No one can be put upon the stool who is vetoed by the queen. After the chief or king is "enstooled," he sits down on the right of Queen Mother to receive the homage and oaths of allegiance of the assembled subchiefs or chiefs. As long as he is in power, Queen Mother's place is on his left hand.[46] In the centuries before British hegemony over Asante, Ashanti queens might accompany an army to war. Others assumed responsibility for civil government in the absence of the king on a military campaign. When Asante came under British military occupation in 1896, the powers of Queen Mothers were largely curtailed.

Today, in addition to her power to select a king when the stool is vacant, the senior Queen Mother controls all the Queen Mothers of Asante. It is her responsibility, for example, to hear cases involving individual Queen Mothers.[47] The Ashanti regard for women comes from their idea that the lineage – and the clan that incorporates several lineages – is synonymous with blood, and that only women can transmit blood to descendants. A man cannot transmit blood, and so no Ashanti can have a drop of the male parent's blood in his or her veins. Males transmit *ntoro,* meaning soul or spirit. The Ashanti trace blood through the female line alone, because of the blood observed at menstruation and childbirth. It is agreed that a male has blood in his body, but he does not transmit it to his offspring. People say that "if a male transmitted his blood through his penis he could not beget a child."[48] The word *ntoro* is sometimes used to mean semen.

Ashanti women are definite about their own importance. They say:

I am the mother of the man . . . I alone can transmit the blood to a king . . . If my sex die in the clan then that very clan becomes extinct, for be there one, or one thousand male members left, not one can transmit the blood, and the life of the clan becomes measured on this earth by the span of a man's life.[49]

In 1922 the Queen Mothers and women of Ashanti presented, as a wedding present to Her Royal Highness the Princess Mary, a silver stool that was a replica of one belonging to the Queen Mother of one of the Ashanti chiefdoms. In her speech, which was translated and sent with the stool to England, the Queen Mother designated as spokeswoman made some interesting comparisons between the Silver Stool and the Golden Stool, the power of Ashanti women and the power of English women. She said:

Lady Guggisberg, wife of His Excellency, I place this stool in your hands. It is a gift on her wedding for the King's child, Princess Mary. Ashanti stool-makers have carved it, and Ashanti silversmiths have embossed it. All the Queen Mothers who dwell here in Ashanti have contributed towards it, and as I am the senior Queen Mother in Ashanti, I stand as representative of all the Queen Mothers and place it in your hands to send to the King's child (Princess Mary).

It may be that the King's child has heard of the Golden Stool of Ashanti. That is the stool which contains the soul of the Ashanti nation. All we women of Ashanti thank the Governor exceedingly because he has declared to us that the English will never again ask us to hand over that stool.

This stool we give gladly. It does not contain our soul as our Golden Stool does, but it contains all the love of us Queen Mothers and of our women. The spirit of this love we have bound to the stool with silver fetters just as we are accustomed to bind our own spirits to the base of our stools.

We in Ashanti here have a law which decrees that it is the daughters of a Queen who alone can transmit royal blood, and that the children of a king cannot be heirs to that stool. This law has given us women a power in this land so that we have a saying which runs: "It is the woman who bears the man" (i.e., the king). We hear that her law is not so, nevertheless we have great joy in sending her our congratulations, and we pray the great God Nyankopon, on whom men lean and do not fall, whose day of worship is a Saturday, and whom the Ashanti serve just as she serves Him, that He may give the King's child and her husband long life and happiness, and finally, when she sits upon this silver stool, which the women of Ashanti have made for their white Queen Mother, may she call us to mind.[50]

The importance of women is also seen in Ashanti religion and ritual. Priestesses participate with priests in all major rituals. Sky and Earth are the two great deities. The Ashanti creation story emphasizes the complementarity of male and female and of sky and earth:

It is said that a very long time ago one man and one woman came down from the sky and one man and one woman came up from the earth. From the sky also came a python who made its home in a river. The first men and women did not bear children, they had no desire, and conception and birth were not known at that time. The python, on learning that the couples had no offspring, bade them to stand face to face and plunging into the river he rose up and sprayed water on their bellies and then ordered them to return home and lie together. The women then conceived and brought forth the first children into the world.[51]

Asase Ya, the name of the Earth Goddess, means "the soil, the earth," but not what grows or stands on it. People say: "We got everything from Asase Ya, food, water; we rest upon her when we die . . . every one must pass into the earth's wallet."[52] Just as the sky is believed to be the source of the Golden Stool, the symbol of the Ashanti confederacy, the earth is believed to have been the source of the aristocracy of the Ashanti clans. On Thursdays, the day set aside for the observance of "Old Mother Earth," the Ashanti farmer will not break soil. In the past, infringement of this rule was punishable by death. Today, at the first plowing the farmer takes *eto* (mashed plantain or yam) cooked by his wife or sister together with a fowl to the land where cultivation is to be commenced. He stands on the land and wrings off the neck of the fowl, allowing the blood to drip upon the *eto* and upon the earth. Addressing himself to the earth, he says:

Grandfather So-and-so, you (once) came and hoed here and then you left (it) to me. You also Earth, Ya, on whose soil I am going to hoe, the yearly cycle has come round and I am going to cultivate; when I work let a fruitful year come upon me, do not let the knife cut me, do not let a tree break and fall upon me, do not let a snake bite me.[53]

Female power among the Ashanti, as among the Iroquois, is associated with a ritual orientation to plants, the earth, and fertility. The Ashanti also equate menstruation and childbirth with hunting and warfare, emphasizing the complementarity of female reproductive functions and male activities considered vital to social survival. This kind of orientation, together with the belief that the child is formed from the mother's blood, gives Ashanti women power and authority in everyday affairs. Before the formation of the Ashanti confederacy, which brought the Golden Stool into being and signified the ritual importance of the sky, it is possible that the earth–female–blood emphasis of the Ashanti supplied the primary ritual focus. If this were the case, then we could hypothesize that there was a time in Ashanti history when women were the central focus of everyday life.

The female creative principle

It is evident from these descriptions that creation symbolism and sex-role behavior are joined. When the female creative principle dominates or works in conjunction with the male principle, the sexes are either integrated and equal in everyday life (as they are, at least in theory, among the Balinese and in practice among the Semang and the Mbuti), or they are separate and equal (as they are among the Iroquois and Ashanti). In no sense are women portrayed as being responsible for sin and the fall of man, nor are they relegated only to conception and obedience in everyday life. In some of the stories presented in this chapter it is men who are associated with the beginning of evil and women with the bringing of the first people into the world. Hence what we know in our own culture is reversed in other cultures.

In these stories, men and women participate in the power of the divine. That is, in a sense, they are made "in the image of" their divine rather than out of the dust or from a rib. The first people are associated more with plants or blossoms than they are with animals. Such notions about first creation are reminiscent of the first version of creation in Genesis. In Chapter 1 of Genesis male and female are created "in the image of God," after which they are

33

given only vegetable food to eat (see Genesis 1:29). According to a well-known Biblical commentator, the vegetarian status of humans and animals in Chapter 1 of Genesis signifies that by "God's" design there is to be "no shedding of blood within the animal kingdom, and no murderous action by man!" Rather, he says, harmony and purposefulness are meant to reign in the cosmos.[54] In the next chapter we will see that creation metaphors for male dominance reflect on the evil of women, separate humans from the divine, and introduce bloodshed and war.

2 · Scripts for male dominance

Male dominance in myth and everyday life is associated with fear, conflict, and strife. In the creation stories drawn from the societies described in this chapter, disobedience in the face of Allah results in a mother losing her children; sexuality is equated with animality; warfare and cannibalism cause natural disasters bringing the world to an end. In these societies, males believe that there is an uncontrollable force that may strike at any time and against which men must be prepared to defend their integrity. The nature of the force and its source are not well defined, but often they are associated with female sexuality and reproductive functions. Men believe it is their duty to harness this force, with its power over life and death, to prevent chaos and to maintain equilibrium. They go to extraordinary lengths to acquire some of the power for themselves so that they will not be impotent when it is time to fight. Men attempt to neutralize the power they think is inherent in women by stealing it, nullifying it, or banishing it to invisibility.

Eve's transgression, God's punishment, and female power: the Hausa

Sexual segregation is extreme among the Hausa of northern Nigeria. Women do not contribute much to food production, and men are only distantly involved with their children. The relationship between mother and child is warm, but the father is stern and "gruffly commands small tasks to be performed." [1] According to Islamic law, "Hausa women must not hold political office; they are legal minors and their proper place is in the home . . . when married, they were secluded inside the compound." [2] Before Islamization, which was a result of the Holy Wars of 1804–10, some Hausa women held political positions and others were rulers. They could achieve economic independence by owning farms or self-employment. Just as the spread of Christianity affected the

35

status of women, intensive Islamization was accompanied by rapid change in the status of Hausa women. What happened to Hausa female political power? It was pushed underground, where today it remains in the form of a spiritual guerrilla movement.

The nature of Hausa female power is revealed in the Hausa creation story. In this story all things and events have their ultimate beginnings with Allah:

> *A few hundred years ago Allah made the universe from his own dung, and later made humans and animals from the earth's dirt. The first people were Adam and Eve, who were told by Allah to produce many children to present to him. As their offspring increased, Eve suggested to Adam that Allah might destroy all of their children when they were presented. She decided to hide one-half of the children. When Allah called for their presentation he said, "You have hidden one-half of your children. I did not tell you to do this, but since you have hidden them, they shall remain so forever."*[3]

Eve's children, banished by Allah to invisibility, play an important part in Hausa life. They are called the "Bori spirits" and are central to the operation of the Bori cult, which is controlled mainly by women. Bori spirits have clandestine power, for they

inflict illness on hidden and unknown evil-doers; they are the fountains of fortune and misfortune, wealth and poverty, happiness and sorrow. The characters of the individual spirits, as shown in their dance movements, are attributes of particular human beings – anger, envy, love, passion, sensuality, nobility, humility, restraint, illhealth, health, violence, etc. The spirits control the moral community by controlling the community's economic activities and its natural environment – epidemics, rainfall, storms, etc.[4]

Both Muslim and pagan Hausa believe in the power of the spirits, though the Muslim Hausa are more ambivalent. Those possessed by Bori form a loosely organized group; they have a meeting house where the chief officials of the association live and where other members can rally for the possession rituals and rites. The head of the Spirit Owners is generally a woman who has female and male assistants. The male assistants are less important; the female assistants help to initiate new members into the secrets and techniques of Bori. Through Bori and spirit possession women wield their lost power. Because the spirits are beings of great force and must be treated with submissiveness and subservience, pos-

36

sessed women can defy not only the domestic authority of their husbands but also that of political authorities.

The Bori cult was the mechanism by which indigenous female power was consolidated and maintained during the years of Islamization. The rise of nationalism in Hausaland during 1950–65 provided the social circumstances for its reexpression. A small but significant female political coalition grew through the Bori cult. The organizing women included the female head of the Bori cult and her followers.[5] Without the Bori institution, it is questionable whether women would have had the institutional means for reasserting their authority. This raises the question of whether women in other parts of the world touched by the great religions remain excluded from the public domain because of the absence of prior female public power or because of the absence of an institutionalized mechanism for consolidating and conserving female symbolic power during colonization.

The merging and splitting of animals, mothers, and males: the Mundurucu

Among the Mundurucu of the tropical forest of South America there is a rigid separation of the sexes. Although males and females contribute heavily to food production, they do so separately. Females are completely excluded from all formal positions of leadership and all religious offices.[6] Men associate with men in this society and women with women.[7] Fear of women, however, dominates male-oriented myths and ritual behavior.

The central figure in the tale about Mundurucu origins is a culture hero called Caru-Sacaebe. He is not a divine being, although he performs magical acts. There are two versions of his exploits – one described in 1875 and the other in 1952. In both, Caru-Sacaebe can be viewed as the heroic leader of a group of men migrating into a new territory where they must learn to hunt, garden, and find wives. This is the earlier version, paraphrased:

Caru-Sacaebe appeared on the earth along with the first men. He was responsible for the appearance of the larger game and for teaching men how to hunt. He had neither father nor mother, but he had a son and a companion who acknowledged him as master. Caru-Sacaebe became angry with the hunters who refused several times to grant him a request for fowl, and he retaliated by changing everyone into wild pigs. There is a cave that still exists today from which, the Mundurucu say, can be heard the grunts of wild pigs and cries of agony. Others say that women's ornaments as well as other vestiges of the catastrophe may be found near the cave entrance. The culture hero is reported to have left with his companion, who was the only survivor of the disaster. On arriving at a certain place, he stamped his foot on the ground, and from the large fissure that resulted he drew one pair of Mundurucu, one of white people, one of Indians, and one of Negroes. All but the Mundurucu couple set off to populate other lands. Caru-Sacaebe laid out a field and sowed it, and thus began the practice of agriculture. He taught people to build ovens and to make manioc flour. He made a small wooden statue and gave it life; thus his second son came into being. To provide this son with a mother, he took as consort a maiden of another tribe. When this son was grown he was seduced by some women who had eluded the vigilance of the chosen mother. Caru-Sacaebe changed his son into an ant and his mother and the guilty women into fish. Caru-Sacaebe caused his original companion to be snatched away by the clouds and he himself disappeared. Since then no one has known where he is, but the Mundurucu faithfully preserve the memory of his deeds and paint themselves, their wives, and their children in the same fashion as he was painted.[8]

In the second, later version of the Mundurucu origin tale the hero is called Karusakaibo and is portrayed as a transformer, not as a creator:

Karusakaibo transforms people into animals to punish them for their sexual exploits. He changes his son into an animal with well-endowed genitals for consorting with women who enter his bed and seduce him. In another instance, people become wild pigs, because when Karusakaibo tells them to eat their food they misunderstand him, thinking he was telling them to have sexual intercourse. While proceeding with coitus they make the usual grunting sounds and gradually these noises turn into the grunts of wild pigs.

The theme of drawing the people from the ground is reported with an interesting variation:

After drawing the people from the ground, Karusakaibo decided to make more women, since he was the only man to have a wife. He made many women out of clay, but they lacked vaginas, and these were made by various animals, who formed the vaginas by having intercourse with the clay figures . . . After the vaginas were made,

Daiiru [the armadillo-trickster] dabbed a bit of rotten Brazil nut on the mouth of each one. It is because of the animals who made the vaginas that they are of different shapes and sizes today, and it is because of the armadillo that the female organ smells as it does.[9]

Thus, women are equated with animality and sexuality; and when men engage in sexual intercourse, they are portrayed as animals.

The Mundurucu believe that there was a time when women ruled and the sex roles were reversed, with the exception that women could not hunt. During that time women were the sexual aggressors and men were sexually submissive and did women's work. Women controlled the "sacred trumpets" (the symbols of power) and the men's houses. The trumpets contained the spirits of the ancestors, who demanded ritual offerings of meat. Since women did not hunt and could not make these offerings, men were able to take the trumpets from them, thereby establishing male dominance.

The trumpets are long, hollow tubes in which the ancestral spirits are believed to dwell, "just as the real cavities of women contain the regenerative potential of the people and the clans." A Mundurucu male who sees a woman sitting with her legs apart will call out that *his* mouth is open. The sacred trumpets have a mouth, and on certain ritual occasions a gourd of meat is placed before the mouth of each instrument, a symbolic offering of food to the totemic ancestors who are contained within. In the mouth of the trumpets there are two strips of the wet and pliant root of the paxiuba palm, placed side by side and bound together near each end. Blowing through the mouth causes the halves of the unbound middle section to vibrate, making a deep, rather mournful-sounding note. It is believed that the ancestral spirits are pleased by the playing of the trumpets, as they are by being fed meat after a successful hunt.[10] Feeding the spirits and playing the trumpets is a form of fertilization; it pleases the spirits and the game increases.

The pliant, wet opening of the mouth of the trumpets and the internal cavity containing the ancestral spirits is suggestive of vaginal and uterine symbolism.[11] By taking the trumpets, men symbolically seize ownership and control of female generative capacities. The trumpets are secured in special chambers within the men's houses and no woman can see them, under penalty of gang rape In order to please the trumpet spirits, men bring back heads of non-Mundurucu they have taken in warfare. Men also seek enemy trophy heads to offer to the spirit mothers of animals, who must continually be propitiated to ensure success in hunting. Trophy heads are believed to charm the spirit mothers into improving the supply and availability of game.[12]

Just as men once gained control from women by robbing them of the sacred trumpets, men attempt to gain power over the spirit mothers. This can only be done by shamans, men believed to have special powers to contact the supernatural world. The shaman acquires power over the spirit mothers by killing certain animals when they are pregnant and extracting the fetus. But the spirit mothers also have power over the shaman: If he is not careful to observe certain rituals, they can turn the shaman into an animal.[13]

To conclude, the primary axis of power in this society poses men against women and symbolic animal/females. Uterine power symbolism dominates the realm of the supernatural. Male power is based on symbolic castration, that is, on acquiring the symbols of uterine power. Men extract the fetus from a pregnant animal in order to gain control over the spirit mothers. The myth of former female power also echoes the theme of castration, of taking by force something that naturally belongs to females. Having acquired from women these symbols of power, men go to extraordinary lengths to keep women from gaining them back. One cannot help wondering who is, in fact, the most powerful in Mundurucu society – males or females?

By Western standards, Mundurucu women would be considered subordinate to men, because only men occupy formal positions of leadership in religious and political activities. However, the Mundurucu world of power and influence extends far beyond such activities into the realm of magic and the supernatural, where female symbolism dominates. Mundurucu women do not believe themselves inferior, nor do men think of them as such. Mundurucu women neither like nor accept their subordinated position in everyday life. Men must be on constant guard lest women seize from them the power they once had. The relationship between the Mundurucu sexes cannot be described as one of simple domination and submissiveness. Rather, this relationship is characterized by ideological dissonance and real opposition.[14]

Nullifying female power: the Papagoes

Early in the twentieth century, the Papagoes of Southwest North America lived somewhat like the Mundurucu, with an interesting twist – men dominated political and economic activities but male and female symbolic power were equivalent. Whereas Mundurucu women had their power stolen from them, Papago women were believed to be the vehicle of a "terrific force" that was manifested during menstruation and that had to be nullified. Papago women were excluded from communal ceremonies and council meetings. The sexual division of labor was "so sharp that it kept the two sexes in separate groups during daylight hours." There was also division of labor by age, so that the young labored and the old directed. Like women, the younger generation had no voice in council meetings. Young men could not participate in the planning of a war raid and young women did not manage their households. Both were considered unfit for thinking and planning, and in the household and the village the commanding positions belonged to the old. Older women managed the household and men, the village.[15]

Papago inequality in public decision making, then, was based on sex and age, with elder men ranking in the highest position and young people of both sexes almost always uninvolved. If we concentrated solely on Papago public decision making, we would conclude that women were subordinated because they were excluded. However, public decision making was not the focus of Papago life; the focus was in communal and individual power ceremonies that sought to promote growth and prevent disorder in an arid environment where the threat of warfare was constant.

General disorder and warfare are reflected in the elaborate Papago origin tale. The tale begins when all was darkness and Earthmaker and Yellow Buzzard were floating in a void:

Earthmaker formed a world from the gum produced by the lice on a plant, gum which he made from "something from his heart" or "the dirt from his skin." Earthmaker pounded the world, and as it flattened, he placed mountains on it, and in the mountains he placed shamans (humans with magical powers). As the earth flattened, the mountains and the shamans were spread everywhere. The earth spread until it reached the edge of the sky, then it spun around until the edges were joined. From this union sprang a being who leaped up and down four times, shouting: "I am the child of earth and sky." Earthmaker named this new being "I'itoi." He was a small man with a beard and white, or golden, hair.

Earthmaker made people from his body. Since there was no death and the people murdered one another for relief, Earthmaker and I'itoi produced a flood. They did this by creating a Handsome Man who impregnated all the girls of the land. The morning after Handsome Man's visit each girl bore a child. So did Handsome Man. When he deserted the child he bore from his own body, it wept and its tears made the flood.

When Earthmaker, I'itoi, and a foolish but powerful being called Coyote (who had previously been involved in helping to make the Universe) emerged from the flood, they made a new population for the earth out of clay. Only I'itoi's creatures were normal human beings. Earthmaker's were misshapen and Coyote's were deformed. Earthmaker and I'itoi quarreled over their creations and, after attempting to pull down the sky, Earthmaker gave up and sank through the earth, spreading disease as he went.

As I'itoi's clay people came to life they became the various groups in the area and I'itoi chose the Papago for his own. He taught them arts and ceremonies including the bow and arrow, the house, and the drinking ceremony. His teaching done, he retired to a cave where the people sent delegates when they had difficulties. In his old age I'itoi became hostile to his people and assaulted their maidens at girls' puberty ceremonies. The people killed him three times, but he always came back to life. Finally Yellow Buzzard, after consultation with the sun, shot I'itoi with an iron bow (gun).

After four years I'itoi came back to life. He sought help from people who lived under the ground. These people emerged and moved about, fighting with people who spoke their own language (presumably these were Papago people). The Papago moved around, then returned home and settled in their present country. The western Papago were defied by Yellow Buzzard, I'itoi's assassin in the former incarnation. The story ends with Buzzard being killed and scalped, which explains why his head is bare of feathers to this day. I'itoi is said to have returned underground after the country was settled and the feasts were instituted. Since then he has appeared occasionally when his help was needed.[16]

In this tale, competing and opposing creative forces vie for power. The conflict brings on a flood that temporarily relieves tensions. The flood is instigated by male sexuality and desertion of a child. The movements of peoples suggest the theme of migration; historical evidence indicates that the Papago did indeed migrate to their present location. The environment they came to was arid, causing a constant concern over the need for rain to make the crops grow.

The aridity of the Papago environment and a concern with fertility motivates the Papago quest for power. Male and female power is essentially identical; both have equal, although different, force. Female power is conceived as having an inherent negative charge. At first menstruation, Papago women become the vehicle of a force that is equated with the dangerous magic men can acquire only by ceremonial effort. The mysterious force that comes to women during menstruation is dangerous to men. A man who touches a menstruating woman might die; to see her would cause weakness. Contact takes the strength from his weapons and poisons his food. For the sake of everyone, a menstruating woman is segregated whenever the magic comes upon her. She must undergo ritual purification, which nullifies the power within her.[17]

One is tempted to say that all Papago women are born powerful whereas only some Papago men achieve power. Power comes to men only after performing one of three ritual acts – killing the enemy, killing an eagle, or fetching salt from the ocean. Any one of these acts automatically brings the man into dangerous contact with the supernatural. The fetish he acquires – scalp, sea shells, or eagle feathers – is avoided by everyone. The power conferred is equally potent for good or for evil. The man, too, must undergo ritual purification. However, the purification both nullifies the evil and manipulates the power for good. Purification ceremonies are required for males and females, but they are more rigorous for men. Failure to complete the rituals of purification

meant danger, both to the individual and to the community. If a "ripe man" did not guard and "feed" his fetish properly, "he could make us all sick." If a girl omitted her ceremony her village might be struck by lightning. This constantly expressed fear of the misuse of power is one of the basic elements in Papago religion. Shaman, eagle killer, enemy slayer, salt pilgrim, and woman were objects of constant suspicion, lest their supernatural contact should be improperly treated.[18]

The psychological attitude underlying male and female purification ceremonies equates the warrior with the childbearing woman.[19] The warrior who takes a scalp is instantaneously at the mercy of supernatural power – just like the woman who begins to menstruate. He must retire from battle immediately and begin the purification ritual. He is segregated like the menstruating woman; he undergoes 16 days of isolation and fasting and performs certain rituals to induce the visions that give him power. This power benefits both his family and the village.[20] While he is isolated, the scalp is raised on a pole in the village so that it will call the clouds to bring the rain to make the corn grow.[21] Once the power contained in the scalp has been tamed, it becomes part of the warrior's family. He takes it into his arms and calls it "my child." The scalp is taken home, wrapped in many layers of buckskin or put in a jar, and, because of its potential danger, is kept in a crevice in rocks. He visits it regularly, supplies it with offerings, and, if he is a hunter, gives it food. He must speak to it affectionately and recite ritual over it. Having obtained a scalp, he is generally regarded as a "ripe man," which allows him to sit in the council and have the right to speak.[22]

The nature and function of Papago male and female power is both negative and positive. At first it is a destructive force and is then tamed for bearing and growth. Males can cause fertility through death and dismemberment (taking a scalp); females promote pregnancy through taming the danger brought by menstruation. Papago scalp taking is not unlike Mundurucu headhunting – both result in food increase. The trophy head pleases the "mothers" and the scalp becomes "a child." Both involve taming enemy power for the good of the community. The Papago warrior takes power from the enemy by shedding his blood. Menstrual blood, however, takes power from the warrior and strength from his weapons; for this reason a warrior whose wife is menstruating cannot go to war. Blood binds the warrior and the childbearing woman. The blood that comes to women at first menstruation is dangerous but, if properly tamed, can be transformed into childbearing. The man who takes a scalp emulates female biological functioning: He acquires a dangerous power that is tamed and

44

transformed to bring the rain that makes the corn grow. At the same time he acquires a child for his family. Papago male and female principles are balanced, in that both contribute in different ways to life and growth, death and destruction.

The fierce people: The Yanomamo

The Yanomamo Indians have been referred to as "one of the most aggressive, warlike, and male-oriented societies in the world."[23] They live in southern Venezuela and adjacent portions of northern Brazil in some 125 scattered villages ranging from 40 to 250 inhabitants. In the 1960s they were one of the largest unacculturated tribes left in South America and were still actively conducting warfare. According to one of their myths, it is the nature of man to fight "because the blood of 'Moon' spilled on this layer of the cosmos, causing men to become fierce." Napoleon Chagnon, who studied and lived among them between 1964 and 1968, calls them "the fierce people" because, he says, "that is how they conceive themselves to be, and that is how they would like others to think of them."[24]

The Yanomamo survived contact with Europeans and the spread of the rubber trade because they were "foot" Indians of the backlands whose nomadic way of life protected them.[25] Traditionally they were hunters and gatherers, but today 85% of their diet consists of cultivated plants that are high in calories but low in protein. Hunting and fishing are the only source of protein, and men spend as much time hunting as they do gardening. The Yanomamo are aware of their need for animal protein. They have two words for hunger: One means an empty stomach and the other means a full stomach that craves meat. Game animals are not abundant and an area is rapidly depleted, keeping groups constantly on the move. Chagnon accompanied prolonged hunting parties in areas that had not been hunted for decades and reported that frequently there was insufficient meat to feed the hunters. On other occasions, however, enough game was collected in one day to feed an entire village.[26]

Because of the emphasis on warfare and hunting, male babies are preferred. Men make it known that their wives had better deliver a son or suffer the consequences. Women will kill a female infant or allow it to starve to avoid disappointing their husbands.

45

The shortage of women produced by infanticide is exacerbated by taboos prohibiting sexual intercourse at certain periods and by the tendency for influential men to have more than one wife. In one village, for example, there were 122 males and 90 females. About 25% of the politically important men in that village had two or more wives. Sexual intercourse is prohibited when a woman is pregnant or nursing. This creates considerable concern within the village over the acquisition and possession of sexually active females. Teenage males frequently have homosexual affairs because the females of their own age are usually married. By the time a young man is 20, however, he is anxious to display his masculinity and becomes an active competitor for the favors of sexually active women. This leads to considerable friction between men within the village.[27]

Although boys spend most of their time with their mothers, they quickly learn that there are status differences between males and females. From an early age, boys are treated with considerable indulgence by their fathers. Boys are encouraged to be "fierce" and are rarely punished for beating girls in the villages, as their fathers beat their wives.[28] Many Yanomamo women show the effects of brutal treatment by men: They are covered with scars and bruises from violent encounters with seducers, rapists, and husbands. By displaying their ferocity against women, men show other men that they are capable of violence and had better be treated with respect and caution.[29]

Women respond to their husbands as a slave does to a master: When men return from a hunting trip or a visit, wives stop whatever they are doing to hurry home and quietly but rapidly prepare a meal. Should a wife be too slow in doing this, she may be beaten. Some husbands chop their wives with the sharp edge of a machete or axe, shoot them with a barbed arrow in some nonvital area, or hold the hot end of a glowing stick against them, causing serious burns. If a wife is suspected of infidelity she will be seriously injured, perhaps killed.[30]

The men of a village are constantly fighting among themselves or going off to raid other villages. An enraged husband who has caught another man with his wife will challenge him to what is called a club duel, in which the two will flail at one another's heads with heavy clubs resembling pool cues, 8 to 10 feet long. When the blood starts to flow from one of the blows, almost all of the men in the village will rip a pole out of the house frame and join in the fight in support of one of the contestants. Warfare between villages is commonly for abducting women, due to the imbalanced sex ratio created by female infanticide. The Yanomamo regard fights over women as the primary cause of their wars.[31]

Yanomamo male supremacy is part of a self-perpetuating cycle of violence. Males are reared to be fierce in order to compete for protein resources, garden plots, and women. To display their fierceness, men beat women, fight other men, and go to war. To defend against counterattacks, more fierce males are needed, and male infants are favored over female infants. Infanticide is necessary in order to achieve a balance between population size and protein resources. The shortage of women causes sexual frustration and jealousy. Having several wives is the insignia of power and influence, which only increases the level of sexual frustration and the motivation for going to war.[32]

In their account of the nature of the cosmos and the origin of the present population, the Yanomamo explain why they fight so much and why some villages are more warlike than others. The cosmos is comprised of four parallel layers, analogous to historical stages, lying horizontally, each on top of the other. The uppermost layer is at present considered to be "empty" or "void," but long ago some things originated there and then moved down to the other layers. This layer is called the "tender" plane and is sometimes described as "an old woman," a phrase used to describe an abandoned garden or a female no longer able to produce offspring. This layer or stage does not figure prominently in everyday life. It is something that is thought to be there and to have once had a function. It is associated with women, abandonment of what may have been a former gardening phase or territory, and, perhaps, barrenness in women.

The next layer is called *hedu*, "the sky." Its top surface is made of earth and is the eternal home for the souls of the departed. Its inhabitants are spirits of men who garden, make witchcraft, hunt, and eat. Everything that exists on earth supposedly has its counterpart in *hedu*. Its bottom surface is the visible portion of the sky. Man dwells below the sky on what is called "this layer" or *hei*. It originated when a piece of *hedu* broke off and fell to a lower level. It consists of a vast jungle in which the numerous Yanomamo villages are dispersed. Finally, there is another place underneath

47

this layer, which is almost barren. A single village of spirit men, the Amahiri-teri, live underneath the earth layer. It was formed after the earth layer when another chunk of *hedu* fell down and crashed through the earth. It hit earth where the Amahiri-teri lived and carried their village down to the bottom layer. When this happened, only their garden lands were carried to the lower layer; the Amahiri-teri thus have no place in which to hunt for game and must send their spirits up to earth, to capture the souls of living children and eat them.

The present-day Yanomamo are descended from the "first beings," or "those who are now dead." The "first beings" lived on earth and departed for *hedu* after a major disaster in which most of them were killed. In the beginning, most "first beings" were dirt eaters and hunters. Some among them, however, knew plant and fruit cultivation. Others knew how to make fire and cook. But they did not share their knowledge, and other "first beings" acquired it by wily and devious means. Cooperation and sharing are conspicuously absent from the Yanomamo tale about the "first beings."

The chain of events bringing an end to the "first beings" and resulting finally in the creation of the "fierce people" is set off by meat hunger, cannibalism, and rape:

A mother who keeps her knowledge of fruit cultivation a secret gives a piece of fruit to a child, who then dies. Hungry for meat, another woman, who is the daughter-in-law of the offending mother, asks if she may eat the child, and her request is granted. Also hungry for meat and out of revenge, the father of the eaten child eats the mother of the child eater. This man is killed by the sons of the mother, who then become afflicted with sex hunger, which may be equated with meat hunger since the Yanomamo use the same verb for eating and copulating. To satisfy their sex hunger, the two sons rape the daughter of another "first being." They then change the girl's vagina into a mouth, with teeth that bite off the penis of the next man who seduces her.

One of the brother's sons gets very thirsty, and to quench his thirst, the father digs a deep hole from which water flows, causing a great flood in which many of the "first beings" are drowned. Those who escape do so by climbing mountains, which is why the first beings may be said to have ended up in the sky, or hedu. *The mother of the girl who had been raped and whose vagina had been changed into a mouth plunges into the lake caused by the flood, and eventually she makes it recede. She still remains there, having been changed into a snakelike monster by one of the brothers. To this day, the Yanomamo are afraid to cross large rivers, for fear that she will eat them or create large waves.*

Among the very few original beings left after the flood was the Spirit of the Moon. He comes down to earth from hedu to eat the soul parts of children. Eventually some earth beings (it is not clear whether these are "first beings") manage to pierce his flesh with an arrow, causing him to bleed profusely. Where his blood hit the earth, a large population of men (no women) are born. Most of the Yanomamo alive today are descended from the blood of the Spirit of the Moon. Where his blood fell the thickest, wars were so intense that the people in that area exterminated themselves. Where it was thinner, the people were less fierce and did not become extinct. The most docile Yanomamo are thought to have been created from the right leg of one of the blood men, and women from the left leg.[33]

Thus, there are three types of Yanomamo—fierce men, docile men, and women.

According to the tale, only men appear to have survived the flood, with the exception of the raped girl's mother. Only men are thought to have been created from the blood of the moon spirit. This, in addition to the idea that there are different types of Yanomamo, suggests the theme of a group of migrating males who, long ago, came from another land and, along the way, killed or incorporated men from other groups to obtain sexual access to women and rights to hunting territory. The treatment accorded Yanomamo women certainly appears to perpetuate the relationship between conquerors and the conquered in a harsh environment.

To conclude, the cycle of violence and sexual inequality we observe among the Yanomamo can be viewed as part of an extreme adaptation to extreme circumstances in the struggle for survival. In their origin tale, cannibalism, rape, and murderous revenge are responses to the tensions created by a precarious existence and by the perception that the universe contains powerful and uncontrollable forces that may at any moment destroy all life. These forces are set in motion by the minds of men in their struggle to maintain the upper hand in a losing battle. If the Yanomamo believe that they exterminated themselves once before, they must live with the fear that it will happen again.

The psychological bedrock

Creation metaphors for male dominance resolve tensions between opposing forces and conflicting wills. Described within the context of sex-role behavior, these metaphors express the psychological bedrock of male dominance. Men fear, envy, and oppress women. Eve defies Allah in the Hausa Garden of Eden and one-half of her children are banished to invisibility. These spirit children represent indigenous female power usurped by the Holy Wars and Islamization. Today, Hausa women manipulate these spirits in a revitalization of former female power. The Mundurucu believe that women once had all the power in the days when the sex roles were reversed. Mundurucu men took the symbol of power from women; today they keep it carefully guarded and hidden in an inner chamber of the men's houses. This symbol turns out to represent the generative capacities of women. Papago men also perceive a dangerous power in women, which they seek to nullify in order to divert its flow toward the aim of growth in an arid environment. The Papago are oppressed by their environment and are in perpetual conflict with their neighbors. They seek to concentrate all energy sources – both male and female – to balance destruction with growth. The Yanomamo are perhaps the most oppressed by environmental and human sources. Their lives are motivated by a cycle of self-perpetuating violence in a struggle for limited protein and other food resources. In this society men beat up men as well as women. One is hard pressed to say who is more oppressed – Yanomamo males or females.

The theme of conquest and migration ties together the discussion of these four societies. One wonders how often in human history groups of migrating males have endeavored to find a new place for themselves. The oppression of women may be an outcome of taking wives in the new land and regarding them as part of the force they must continue to control in order to survive. Or, men and women may migrate together into an arid environment that forces people to concentrate their ritual energies on finding and renewing the sources of growth. Once a stance of control and manipulation is adopted, it is not easily abandoned. Success confirms the need to adhere to past practices. Success can also give a people a taste for more of the same.

PART II

Constructing sex-role plans

Mawu, the female principle, is fertility, motherhood, gentleness, forgiveness; while Lisa is power, war-like or otherwise, strength and toughness. Moreover, they assure the rhythm of day and night. Mawu is the night, the moon, freshness, rest, joy; Lisa is the day, the sun, heat, labour, all hard things. By presenting their two natures alternately to men, the divine pair impress on man the rhythm of life and the two series of complementary elements of which its fabric is woven. The notion of twin beings . . . expresses the equilibrium between opposites, which is the very nature of the world.

> From Mercier's (1954:219) description of
> the Dahomean Mawu-Lisa cult

I am all the forces and objects with which I come in contact. I am the wind, the trees, and the birds, and the darkness.

> Patty Harjo, American Indian

3 · The environmental context of metaphors for sexual identities

Once a sex-role script is established, it is easy to see how it is almost perpetually self-reinforcing as both sexes transmit the proper cues to their offspring. It is especially difficult, however, to understand why any particular script becomes established in the first place. Why one and not another? We deal here with origins. How do different cultural patterns get started? This is an old and very difficult question.

In *Sex and Temperament*, Margaret Mead addresses the question of how cultures come to pattern the relationship between sex and approved temperamental types. Noting "the differences between the standardized personalities that different cultures decree for all their members, or which one culture decrees for the members of one sex as contrasted with members of the opposite sex," Mead asks, "why do these striking contrasts occur at all?" To explain the basis upon which the personalities of men and women have been differently "standardized so often in the history of the human race," she offers the following hypothesis, which "is an extension of that advanced by Ruth Benedict in her *Patterns of Culture.*" Assuming that there are temperamental differences between human beings that are hereditary, Mead argues that "these differences are the clues from which culture works, selecting one temperament or a combination of related and congruent types, as desirable." The choice of the favored temperament is embodied "in every thread of the social fabric – in the care of the young child, the games the children play, the songs the people sing, the structure of political organization, the religious observance, the art and the philosophy."[1]

Mead leaves unanswered the question of why the clues "from which culture works" differ from society to society. Why is male aggression selected in one society and not in another? Why does one society choose female passivity and another female aggression? It is not the purpose of this book to answer such questions directly. The goal here is to uncover the bases for the underlying plan that directs the authority relations of males and females in symbolism and behavior. In the pursuit of this goal, however, it will become clear that sex-role plans are embodied in much of social behavior. In the chapters of this section, for example, we shall see that the way the roles of the sexes are cast in creation stories is reflected in childrearing practices and in work activities.

Origins cannot be determined with certitude. All that we can do is show that in many societies certain relationships are evident that are suggestive of origins. In particular, there is evidence of a subtle interconnection between sex-role plans and certain environmental circumstances.

This chapter begins to deal with origins by examining the relationship between symbolic manifestations of sex-role plans and environmental circumstances. The environmental context of gender symbolism in origin stories is the main focus. Gender symbolism in origin stories provides ancient and hence reliable metaphors for sexual identities. Such metaphors provide emotional guidelines in times of stress when institutionalized guides for behavior are absent or do not seem to work. As Clifford Geertz says about symbolic templates, "It is in country unfamiliar emotionally or topographically that one needs poems and road maps."[2] Because they give guidance in times of need, metaphors for sexual identities persist long after the circumstances giving rise to them have changed.

The proposition argued in this chapter is that gender symbolism in origin stories is a projection of a people's perception of the phenomenon of human birth and of their experience with their environment. This proposition, as will be seen, is not new. In subjecting this proposition to rigorous scrutiny, the approach will change from the descriptive mode adopted in the first two chapters to a more analytic mode, in which a large sample of societies will form the information base. This sample, frequently employed in cross-cultural research, is called the Standard Cross-Cultural Sample (see Appendix A for technical details). The Standard Cross-Cultural Sample consists of 186 societies and is said to be representative of the world's known and well-described societies. The main reason for employing such a large sample consisting of disparate societies (ranging in historical time from 1750 B.C. to the present) is to distinguish what is generically human from what is caused by circumstances of time, place, and history in the patterning of sex-role behavior.

Gender symbolism in creation stories: inward females and outward males

Most peoples of the world are concerned with how things came into being. Creation stories contain within them a conception of the natural or initial order of things. By articulating how things were in the beginning, people supply more than a logic for sexual life-styles – they make a basic statement about their relationship with nature and about their perception of the source of power in the universe. This relationship, and its projection into the sacred and secular realms, holds the key for understanding sexual identities and corresponding roles.

Creation stories tell us whether a people have what will be defined as an *inner* orientation in their perception of the sources of power or an *outer* orientation. Though widely diverse in content, creation stories display an underlying regularity in structure. These stories reveal three consistent themes: 1) Some sort of creative agent is described; 2) There is reference, either implicit or explicit, to the place from which the creative agent originates; and 3) The method by which the creative agent brings people into the world is described. There is a clear-cut pattern associating these three themes. Female creators originate from within something – such as earth or water – and create from their bodies. Male, animal, and supreme being creators originate from without – such as the sky or another land – and produce people magically. Couple creators, on the other hand, originate from within and without but they tend to produce by natural reproductive processes. These patterns lead to the conclusion that an "inner" orientation is joined with feminine gender symbolism in creation stories, whereas an "outer" orientation is joined with masculine gender symbolism. (See Appendix C for a detailed demonstration of these patterns in a sample of 39 stories.)

Most creation stories begin by resolving the puzzle of who is the main agent in creation. How the creator is conceived tells us something about where people locate the major source of power in the universe. Since power figures so prominently in the way the

57

sexes interact, it is intriguing to see how power is projected in fantasy. In the stories presented in Chapters 1 and 2 the following six types of creative agents are depicted:

1. An androgynous or sexless figure is the main agent (Balinese story).
2. A female is the creator or first mover (Semang and Iroquois stories).
3. A couple creates jointly (Ashanti story).
4. A male culture hero or ancestor is the first mover (Mundurucu story).
5. An animal is the creator or ancestor (Papago story).
6. A supreme being or force (such as the Spirit of the Moon) is the creator (Hausa and Yanomamo stories).

Creative agents depicted as feminine are usually associated with the water or the earth. Masculine and animal agents, on the other hand, live higher, such as in the sky, in "god's hill," in "the flat land above the sky," or they are depicted as omnipresent. In those cases where male and female agents create jointly, often the male is described as coming from the sky and the female from the earth. Culture-hero and ancestor creative agents are portrayed in more human terms. Usually the latter are described as having migrated from another place.

There are two primary modes for creating people – from the creator's body, as in sexual union, birth, and self-propagation; or from other than the body, as in making people magically out of clay, transforming people from plants or animals, or chiseling people from wood. With a few exceptions, female and couple agents create from the body. Male, animal, and supreme being creators create from other than the body.

Thus, the female in creation stories is associated with nature and natural processes, the male with the sky and magical processes. This finding is consistent with Erich Neumann's analysis of the feminine archetype in myth and art, which is symbolically manifested in what he calls the "Great Container."[3] Any symbolic projection in myth or art that implies containment (such as earth, body, vessel, belly, egg, water) and anything that is naturally derived from such symbols (such as plants from the earth, babies from the body, ships on the water), he proclaims, is associated with the feminine.[4]

Table 3.1. *Geographical distribution of types of gender origin symbolism in creation stories (A05) in 112 societies*

Geographical area	Feminine		Couple		Masculine		Row totals	
	N	%	N	%	N	%	N	%
Africa	1	5	7	35	12	60	20	100
Circum-Mediterranean	2	14	3	21	9	64	14	99
Eurasia	3	19	6	38	7	44	16	101
Insular Pacific	8	44	8	44	2	11	18	99
North America	3	13	7	30	13	57	23	100
South America	3	14	5	24	13	62	21	100
Column totals	20	18	36	32	56	50	112[a]	100

Data are given for number (*N*) and percentage of societies. See Appendixes A, B, and C for discussion of variables used in this table.
[a]No information for 44 societies.

By referring to Neumann's analysis of the feminine archetype, I do not mean to imply that images associated with inner processes are universally present in the human collective unconscious, as Neumann believed. I am simply suggesting that some people choose to focus on female reproductive functions and project their images of these functions onto the cosmology. Other people choose to ignore these functions and focus instead on imagery associated with males in coming to terms with the sources of creative power.

For this study, 112 creation stories were categorized according to the three attributes that have been discussed (i.e., sex of the creative agent, place of origin, mode of creation). The stories were then classified as feminine, masculine, or mixed on the basis of the attributes they emphasize. Where at least two attributes alluded to feminine symbolism, the story was classified in the feminine category. Where at least two alluded to masculine symbolism, the story was classified in the masculine category. Where the three attributes were mixed in a story (suggesting both masculine–feminine and inner–outer), the story was classified in the masculine–feminine category.

Using these criteria, 50% of the 112 tales fell in the masculine category, 32% in the mixed, and 18% in the feminine. Table 3.1

presents the geographical distribution of the tales. Over half of the tales from Africa, the Circum-Mediterranean, North America, and South America are masculine. Very few masculine tales are found in the Insular Pacific, where the largest percentage of feminine tales was recorded. Ritual emulation by men of female reproductive functions is common in these societies. In New Guinea and Australia, for example, rituals are reported in which men bleed their penis to simulate menstruation or perform genital operations on themselves to simulate the vaginal opening. The fact that many feminine origin tales are found in societies of the Insular Pacific is, thus, consistent with the ritual focus on female reproductive functions. The greater percentage of masculine origin tales in the other parts of the world may be explained by the historical importance of environmental circumstances separating males from females.

Male parenting and creation symbolism

Having shown that creation stories display an internal regularity in structure, in which female figures are associated with nature and natural creation processes, and male figures are associated with the sky and magical creation processes, the next question is whether these associations are related to behavior. There is a puzzling contradiction between belief and reality in the notion that people are made magically by a masculine supreme being. An examination of the role of fathers in societies with masculine origin symbolism helps resolve this contradiction. In these societies earthly fathers are distant, controlling figures. They are removed from biological maternity and have little to do with the handling of infants. This finding, presented in Table 3.2, suggests that gender symbolism in origin stories reflects sex roles in behavior.

Fathers spend more time with infants in societies having feminine creation symbolism (see Table 3.2).[5] In the majority of these societies (63%), fathers are in frequent contact with infants. On the other hand, in the majority of societies having masculine origin symbolism fathers are, at best, occasionally involved with infants. In the majority (72%) of the societies with couple (meaning mixed masculine and feminine) origin symbolism, the father is in occasional to frequent contact with infants.

Table 3.2. *Relationship between types of gender origin symbolism (A05) and proximity of fathers to infants (Inf 23A)*

Proximity of father to infants	Feminine (1)[a]		Couple (2)		Masculine (3)		Row totals (N)
	N	%	N	%	N	%	
No close proximity, or rare instances of close proximity (1–2)[a]	1	6	9	28	16	34	26
Occasional or irregular close proximity (3)	5	31	12	38	23	49	40
Frequent or regular close proximity (4–5)	10	63	11	34	8	17	29
Column totals	16	100	32	100	47	100	95[b]

Data are given for number (N) and percentage of societies. $\chi^2 = 12.83$ ($df = 4$); $p = 0.01$. Pearson's $R = -0.30$, $p = 0.002$. Appendix B gives reference for Inf 23A.
[a]Numbers in parentheses refer to values used in computing Pearson's R.
[b]No information for 61 societies.

In societies with feminine origin symbolism, childrearing is characterized by nurturance and love from both parents. Mothers or siblings may be the most involved in childrearing, but the father is not disassociated from his children. His behavior ranges from friendly play to frequent bodily contact. In general there is close cooperation and sharing of responsibilities between husband and wife. Cooperation is stressed in all social relations. Among the Lepcha, for example, peacefulness is taught to the young, and competition or individuality is not allowed to interfere with group cohesion. This is seen especially in the husband–wife relationship. Men relieve their wives of childcare duties; they nurture their children, holding them in their arms or laps; and on long journeys they will carry children on their backs.[6]

Egalitarianism and sharing between husband and wife among the Semang were described in Chapter 1. Childcare responsibilities are dispersed throughout the family group, whatever that group might be. Children are loved and cherished by all the adults of the Semang camp. Perhaps because men do not band together for hunting or warfare, the Semang male is more involved with his family. Men do not have separate houses and they spend their leisure time in the company of their families. When women group to gather food, men will either accompany the women or, sometimes, remain behind in the camp with the smaller children. During fruit gathering, an activity central to the Semang food quest and ritual life, complete families will travel together. Thus, men are closely involved in all family and childrearing activities.[7]

Among the Tikopia there is a general spirit of rivalry, and cooperation is not stressed to the same degree. Friction between husband and wife is not uncommon, but amicable relations generally exist. Couples are closest while bringing up their children, and fathers play an important role in childrearing. Although the father's duty is to provide food and shelter for his children, he is expected to take his turn in looking after them and usually does so with interest and pride. The affection of a father for his daughter is said to be often greater than that for his sons, and mothers favor their male children.[8]

A more complete separation of parenting roles, along the lines found in Tikopia, is typical of societies in which the masculine and feminine contributions to creation receive equal emphasis. In these societies, as a rule, fathers are remote from the care of infants but are actively involved in the socialization of young children. The father's role is not so much to nurture as it is to meet his children's materialistic needs. Ashanti children, for example, are nurtured by their mothers and grandmothers. Ashanti fathers are expected to feed, clothe, and educate their children and, later, to set them up in life. Ashanti fathers win their children's affection by caring for their material and educational needs. In return, fathers expect obedience, deference, and good behavior.[9]

In the case of the Alorese, who trace their origins to a series of brother–sister incestuous unions, both parents are equally uninvolved in rearing children. Consistent nurturance of the child ends on the fourteenth day after birth; thereafter care is sporadic, inconsistent, and undependable. Older siblings are responsible for carrying and feeding the child. The father does not provide for the child, he is often absent, and his behavior toward children is unplanned and unsystematic. The role that he plays, usually later, is "uniformly despotic; he is in a position to subordinate the child's independence to his own ends."[10] For Alorese children, there is little opportunity to form strong attachments to either parent.

Fathers in societies with exclusively masculine origin symbolism are distant, controlling figures who are inactive both in the care of infants and in the socialization of young children. The Amhara, for example, trace their origins to the magical actions of a Supreme Being. It is the Amhara woman's job to conceive and the man's job to control and dominate. For the first 2 years, the Amhara baby is never out of touch with the body of the mother or some other woman. Fathers rarely fondle the baby until it is weaned. After this it is only a "special occasion" when the father lets the infant ride on his shoulders. Fathers, whether natural or adopted, expect complete obedience from their children. It has been said that "reverence for one's fathers is perhaps the key legitimating principle in the structure of Amhara morality. This is the outgrowth and foundation of a social system which makes children devoted servants of their fathers and keeps men under their fathers' control until they are fully adult." Amhara men consider all women to be biologically, intellectually, and morally inferior. Amhara women, however, do not necessarily accept this judgment. In the case of some types of women, such as upper class or older women, men admit that their judgment concerning women may not be valid.[11]

Suspicion, competition, sexual antagonism, and rigid sexual segregation characterize many of these societies. The disassociation of the father from children is in large part a disassociation from women. Masculinity and the male collective are often well developed. Among the Comanche, masculinity is expressed through the military complex, which colors all tribal values. Comanche law is described as a struggle for status among individual males. Competition for "bravery ranking" is a major male pastime and includes, among other things, stealing women from their husbands.[12] Males are too busy proving their maleness to spend time with children.

The Azande are not much different. The person dearest and most loved by the Azande male is himself. The Azande are jealous of skill and talent, competitive, and frequently suspicious that witchcraft is working against them. Family life is characterized by the inferiority of women and the authority of elders. Women play no part in public life and are looked upon as childbearers and servants. The father exercises great control over his sons, who treat him with the utmost respect. Daughters are considered inferior beings, not to be admitted into companionship with their fathers. They are part of the background, where they work and eat separately with the female members of their father's household. [13]

The cycle for Mundurucu babies is one of initial total dependence on the mother, followed by a period of care by several women, displacement by a new sibling, and the awakening of interest by the father. Mundurucu fathers show little or no interest in their children until they are able to walk. Very little solicitude is shown toward the mother, who is considered to be in a state of social marginality from the onset of labor until a few days after the child is born. This is because children may be stillborn, deformed, or may die after only a few hours of life. Infanticide is practiced if children are born with serious birth defects and if twins are born. Since animals have multiple births, twins are killed, because it is believed that they are a reversal of man's differentiation from animals. [14]

To summarize, in most cases in which fathering is absent or barely stressed in behavior, maternity is absent in the projection of the beginning of things. The nurturant father, on the other hand, is buttressed by the female creator. In these cases the reproductive functions of women are celebrated both in myth and behavior. In the absence of the female creator, fathers are involved with children in infancy and early childhood either as disciplinarians or not at all. When their major role is to discipline and control, fathers are not unlike supreme beings. They are distant, controlling figures who are removed from biological processes.

The role of environment

A basic assumption underlying the approach taken in this book to the origins of sex-role plans is that the authority relationship between the sexes is based in part on a people's concept of the source of supernatural power and on how they choose to engage this power for their own ends. The question before us now is why people become oriented toward feminine creative symbolism, with its corresponding emphasis on locating power in the earth, water, and natural reproductive functions, as opposed to masculine creative symbolism, with its emphasis on locating power in the sky, animals, and magical acts. The answer lies in the way people interact with their environment.

In nonindustrial technologies, humans are enmeshed in a complex web of powers and forces that are believed to be present in the society itself, in each individual, in animals, in plants, and in all the phenomena of nature. People depend on these powers for their sense of well-being and their survival. In generating ideas about the sources of power, people work with subjective images inspired by the ease and consistency in their quest for survival. For example, dependence on large game moving in migratory herds or the fluctuation of food between abundance and scarcity produces different pressures than those experienced by the Mbuti and the Semang in their bountiful forest environment. The Mbuti address the forest gently and the Semang offer the blood sacrifice to ensure themselves a relatively constant food supply. Because their survival is not as much at risk, their perceptual link to the nonhuman environment is mainly positive and imbued more with connotations of protection than of destruction and danger.

Peoples who inhabit less predictable habitats, however, develop a different ideological and ritual relationship with the nonhuman world. Consider, for example, a society that relies on large game for food and, perhaps, clothing or items for domestic use. In these cases the hunter and the hunted are engaged in a game of skill in which both have the power to outwit the other. In addition, there are the other animals who prey on the wounded and the carcasses of the dead. Such animals do not always distinguish between men and animals; they are carnivorous predators, as are men. Thus, there is a game of skill established that involves animals and men in a competitive struggle for sustenance. In such instances power does not come readily to humans; power must be acquired, controlled, and manipulated for human purposes. In these instances, also, power is likely to be construed as having both positive and negative connotations.

In societies dependent on animals, women are rarely depicted as the ultimate source of creative power. The latter is usually attributed either to an animal deity or to a supreme being. When large game are hunted, regardless of the contribution of meat to the overall diet, males engage in an activity whose outcome is unpredicatable and entails danger. Whether or not men spend part or most of their time in hunting activities is not as important as the

Table 3.3. *Relationship between types of gender origin symbolism*
(A05) and game hunted (Sub 05D)

Type of game hunted[a]	Feminine		Couple		Masculine		Row totals (N)
	N	%	N	%	N	%	
Small game, fowl, or several types of game hunted	13	72	20	61	23	48	56
Large game hunted mainly	5	28	13	39	25	52	43
Column totals	18	100	33	100	48	100	99[b]

Data are given for number (N) and percentage of societies. $\chi^2 = 3.48$ $(df = 2)$; $p = 0.18$. Appendix B gives reference for Sub 05D.
[a]Regardless of contribution to food supply.
[b]No information for 57 societies.

psychological energy expended in this effort. This energy is not directed inwardly toward nurturing children or family but toward acquiring and using powers beyond man's dominance. The major source of power is perceived as residing in a supreme being who resides in the sky or in animals.

There are 99 societies for which information on type of game hunted and an origin story was available. In 43 of these 99 societies, large animals are the predominant type of game hunted. In all but 5 of these 43 societies, couple or masculine origin symbolism is present. Table 3.3 displays this association between gender symbolism in origin stories and type of game hunted. The table shows also that most (72%) of the societies with feminine origin symbolism hunt small game or several types of game. Thus, we can conclude that hunting large game influences a people's orientation to the sources of power.

In addition to affecting their orientation to power, hunting large game also affects the role of fathers in nurturing infants. When large animals are hunted, fathers are more distant, that is, they are not in frequent or regular proximity to infants. There are 113 societies for which information on type of game hunted and father's proximity to infants was available. Of these 113 societies, large game are hunted in 41. In most (78%) of these 41 societies, fathers

Table 3.4. *Relationship between fathers' proximity to infants (Inf 23A) and type of game hunted (Sub 05D)*

Fathers' proximity to infants	Small game, etc.		Large game mainly		Row totals (N)
	N	%	N	%	
No close proximity or rare instances of close proximity	11	15	16	39	27
Occasional or irregular close proximity	34	47	16	39	50
Frequent or regular close proximity	27	38	9	22	36
Column totals	72	100	41	100	113[a]

Data are given for number (N) and percentage of societies. $\chi^2 = 8.54$ ($df = 2$); $p = 0.01$.
[a]No information for 43 societies.

are occasionally or rarely involved with infants. On the other hand, in those societies where small game or several types of game are hunted, there is a somewhat greater probability that fathers will be in frequent or regular proximity to infants (see Table 3.4).

These observations suggest the genesis of origin symbolism diagrammed in Figure 3.1. In this diagram, masculine and feminine origin symbolism are depicted as being the ultimate consequences of certain environmental factors. In particular, it is postulated that a concern with hunting large game results in an outer orientation to the sources of power. This would be especially true where gathering is less important, because virtually nothing perceived as crucial to human sustenance would come from the earth. On the other hand, an inner orientation, resulting in feminine origin symbolism, is postulated when large animals are absent or not hunted and when plant food is more important. When there is equal emphasis on plant food and hunting, inner and outer symbolism are both represented.

Origin stories are symbolic manifestations of an outer, inner, or dual orientation to nature. Proximity of the father to children is

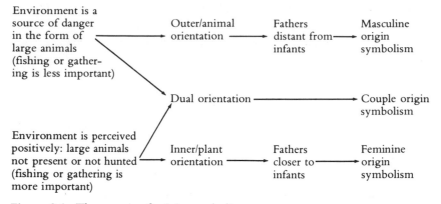

Figure 3.1. The genesis of origin symbolism.

the behavioral manifestation of the same cognitive phenomenon. Moreover, the father's role in childrearing is affected by the mode of securing food. Thus gender symbolism in origin stories is a joint consequence of sex roles in childrearing and the way in which the environment is exploited in the pursuit of food. Statistical analysis of the postulated causal chain presented in Figure 3.1 supports this conclusion.[15] Environmentally induced vulnerability (as in the hunting of large game) results in an outer orientation manifested first in the distancing of fathers from infants and second in beliefs about outer power. On the other hand, the sense of security gained from a lush environment, where food is derived from the earth, results in an inner orientation manifested in nurturing fathers and beliefs about inward power.

Environment, origin beliefs, and history

The scenario just presented in the previous section for the construction of origin beliefs was simplified by submerging questions of what happens over time as a people's subsistence economy changes and becomes technologically more advanced. For example, when a hunting economy changes to plant cultivation, is feminine origin symbolism adopted, or is masculine symbolism retained? Firm data are not available for answering such questions, but speculation based on certain types of information is certainly in order.

Table 3.5. *Gender origin symbolism (A05) and dominant mode of subsistence (Econ)*

Subsistence mode[a]	Feminine		Couple		Masculine		Row totals	
	N	%	N	%	N	%	N	%
Animal economies								
Hunting	0	0	0	0	7	100	7	100
Animal husbandry	2	22	0	0	7	78	9	100
Fishing	1	9	2	18	8	73	11	100
Plant economies								
Gathering	3	27	5	46	3	27	11	100
Semi-intensive agriculture (fruit trees and/or vegetable gardens)	5	46	4	36	2	18	11	100
Shifting cultivation of fields	6	17	14	39	16	44	36	100
Advanced agriculture	3	11	11	41	13	48	27	100
Column totals (N)	20		36		56		112[a]	

Data are given for number (N) and percentage of societies. $\chi^2 = 25.01$ ($df = 12$), $p = 0.01$. Appendix B gives reference for Econ.
[a]No information for 44 societies.

First, it is clear from the information presented in Table 3.5 that there is, by and large, an association between plant and animal subsistence economies and type of origin story. In this table, subsistence economies are ordered by whether the predominant mode for acquiring food emphasizes animals or plants. Almost all of the animal-oriented economies are characterized by masculine origin beliefs, whereas the plant economies are characterized by feminine, couple, or masculine symbolism. The simpler plant economies (gathering and semi-intensive agriculture) tend toward feminine or couple origin symbolism, but the more advanced plant economies (shifting cultivation and advanced agriculture) are split nearly evenly between those displaying exclusively masculine symbolism and those displaying feminine or couple symbolism.

Such results suggest that in plant economies, increasing technological complexity encourages a masculine orientation. Before accepting such a proposition, however, it is essential to consider the circumstances under which people exchange a foraging for a settled agricultural way of life. If people move from a predominantly hunting to an agricultural subsistence economy, the chances are that masculine origin symbolism will prevail as people hold on to their old identity. On the other hand, if plant cultivation was an indigenous development growing out of the gathering activities of women, it is reasonable to suggest that the core of women who gathered plants and slowly began to till the earth would have become the logical focus for equating maternity, fertility, social continuity, and the social good. This kind of development seems to have characterized the historical past in such societies as the Iroquois and the Ashanti (see Chapters 1 and 6).

If the transition to agriculture was a consequence of migration or conquest, people face the decision of whether to adopt or reject foreign supernatural symbols along with the new technology. The choice is clearly a function of circumstances. For example, when the early Hebrews entered Canaan, they temporarily adopted the Canaanite fertility cult as they adopted the agricultural ways of their neighbors. Later the Hebrews rejected the fertility symbolism, with its focus on the feminine, in an effort to strengthen their identity as the "chosen people" in the new land (see Epilogue). On the other hand, when the Azande moved as a group of warrior/hunters into the land they now occupy, they adopted agriculture from the people they conquered. The exclusive emphasis on animals and masculine symbols in Azande thought suggests that these people retained the orientation of hunters as they adopted agriculture (see Chapter 9).

Symbolic orientations are clearly vulnerable to circumstance. Origin stories may be part of ancient tradition or borrowed by one people from another. It is unusual to find recorded descriptions of the manner in which people come to think of their origins. Two such examples, one from the Navaho of the American Southwest and the other from the Dahomeans of West Africa, provide some insight into the kinds of circumstances leading people to borrow origin concepts.

Katherine Spencer provides a provocative reconstruction of the probable adoption by the Navaho of their origin myth. Once a hunting–gathering people, the Navaho are thought to have adopted agriculture under the impetus of Pueblo contact sometime after they settled in the Southwest. Thus, agriculture represents a second phase in the history of the Navaho economy. Hunting, gathering, and agriculture are all represented as functioning parts of the economy in the Navaho origin myth. Sheep, goats, and the horse, on the other hand, which were added to the Navaho economy later and represent still a third phase in this economy, are not incorporated in the origin myth as part of the economy.

The Navaho origin story also ignores the matrilineal emphasis of Navaho social organization, with the exception of the frequent assumption that women are clan progenitors. Spencer believes that the omissions of matrilineal descent and animal domestication from the Navaho origin story may be due to their relatively later development among the Navaho. She thinks that their origin myth may have come from similar myths widespread in the Southwest or that this story may have been adopted directly from the western Pueblos, before the institution of matrilineal descent or animal domestication.[16]

The Navaho example illustrates that culture contact at a certain stage in a people's technological and social development may influence the codification of their mythological charter, which remains relatively unchanged thereafter. Another example is provided by the story of how the people of Dahomey of West Africa came to worship Mawu-Lisa, believed to be the creator of the universe and the Dahomean people. The Mawu-Lisa cult underlies the dual-sex ideology that is so evident in Dahomean life. This cult, it is said, was introduced into the kingdom of Dahomey in the early eighteenth century and had "a civilizing" influence. Mawu-Lisa is variously conceived as a pair of twins, one female and one male, or as "an androgynous, self-fertilizing being." Mawu is female, the earth, the west, the moon, the night, and the rising sun. Lisa is male, the sky, the east, the sun, the day, and the setting sun. Together, Mawu-Lisa expresses the equilibrium between opposites and the unity of the world.

According to the story of how the Mawu-Lisa cult became part of Dahomean religion, the cult initially was part of the culture of the original inhabitants of the Abomey plateau and was not represented in the culture of the conquerors who formed the great Da-

homean kingdom. The conquerors believed that their clans originated from the mating of a female with animals or vegetables. The
original inhabitants, on the other hand, claimed descent from people who came down from the sky or who came out of holes in the
ground and the mountain sides. These clans are credited with
founding the cult of Mawu-Lisa.

The Dahomeans tell the following story about the adoption of
the Mawu-Lisa cult by the conquerors. The wives of the conquerors were giving birth to animals. These women became en-
vious of the indigenous women, who were giving birth to humans. The wife of the conquering king eventually asked one of the
indigenous women what made it possible for her to give birth to
humans. The answer was that by offering sacrifices to Mawu,
Lisa, and to the other cult beings, human beings would bear human beings. W. J. Argyle suggests that the borrowing of the
Mawu-Lisa cult took place amid technological developments, including the possible introduction of maize, and expansion on the
Abomey plateau that gave rise to the kingdom of Dahomey.[17]

The Navaho and Dahomean examples suggest that migratory
movements into areas where agriculture was adopted may have
changed an outer-oriented group of hunter/warriors into agriculturalists with a revised mythological charter in which both masculine and feminine symbolism are represented. However, migratory movements into areas of scarce resources, such as described
for the Yanomamo or the Azande (see Chapters 2 and 9), may
have accentuated masculine-oriented origin myths despite the
adoption of agriculture.

Vulnerability and dependency underly this discussion of the different ways in which people come to construe the sources of creative power. People seek to explain what they fear and to enlist the
aid of the supernatural in their behalf. Whether the supernatural is
conceived in predominantly masculine or feminine terms rests ultimately on what people feel they need. If animals are in decline,
the symbolism will surely be dressed in the sex of those who hunt.
If the earth is the focus for dependence, then powers of the inner
together with the fertilizing power of rain will be the subject of
propitiation. If human rather than animal babies are wanted, then
the gods will be humanized. From their dependence people select
their symbolism.

The environmental context

Reflections of social life and thought in origin stories

Recognizing the many complexities swept under the statistical rug by cross-cultural generalizations, several conclusions can be drawn from the associations described in this chapter. First, there is a conjunction between culturally shared fantasies about the role of the sexes in creation stories, sex-role behavior in childrearing, and mode of acquiring food. The pursuit of large game results in an outer orientation and the pursuit of food drawn from the earth or water in an inner orientation. The phrases "man the animal" and "mother earth" make a great deal of sense in the light of these findings, if one understands that man means male. Where males pursue animals, fathers are more distant from childrearing and power is conceived of as being "beyond man's dominance." When gathering is emphasized in the absence of the pursuit of large animals, fathers are closer to childrearing and notions about creative power turn to feminine or couple symbolism. By themselves these results are fascinating, because they call to mind the familiar association of female with inner and male with outer.

There is a diverse body of literature on the correspondence between a father's role in the care of infants and a people's concept of first creation. For example, in an analysis of the earth diver origin myth found in North American Indian mythology, Alan Dundes notes that as early as 1902 Washington Matthews proposed the idea that the emergence myth was a projection of man's experience with the phenomenon of human birth.[18] Later, in *Male and Female,* Margaret Mead suggested that the more men are removed from the phenomenon of human birth, the more the male imagination contributes to the "cultural superstructure of belief and practice regarding child-bearing."[19] More recently, the contention that religious beliefs are a projection of early human experience and childcare customs can be found in the psychocultural model of the relationship between personality and culture postulated by John and Beatrice Whiting.[20]

In a more philosophical vein, Dorothy Dinnerstein reflects on the monotheistic, all-powerful, parental male figure of Jehovah: "He was created single to represent unified, coherent natural and moral principles; parental because we still needed to feel externally protected and disciplined; and male because on the deep mental

73

levels tapped by religion, a father – so long as he is a figure whose presence in prerational infancy was much less important than the mother's – is necessarily a more understandable, less magical authority: more of a fellow "I" to the human self in its ambivalent growth – across a lifetime and across millennia – toward autonomy."[21]

Anthropologists argue that origin myths establish "who one is," "what is," and "why one behaves and acts in accordance with custom."[22] In analyses of specific myths, anthropologists have shown that myth themes reflect many aspects of social life. In the most thorough analysis of this type, Katherine Spencer finds 47 correspondences between themes in the Navaho origin myth and Navaho social behavior. She also finds 13 myth themes that are not reflected in Navaho social life and 21 key social traits that are not represented in the myth. The correspondences, Spencer says, demonstrate what "has already come from such diverse anthropological sources as Boas, Malinowski, and Radcliffe-Brown," namely, that "a people's literature reflects their way of life, manners, and customs."[23] The discrepancies, she suggests, may be due to the probable adoption by the Navaho of their origin myth from their Pueblo neighbors, into whose territory they migrated.[24] Another possibility suggested by her is that the discrepancies arise because some Navaho social practices have not yet been completely incorporated into their origin myth. This latter possibility suggests that origin myths represent reflections of the past as well as rationalizations for the present.[25]

The parallel between themes in origin stories and everyday life has also been noted by Victor Barnouw in a comparison of the Chippewa and Navaho origin tales. The Chippewa tale focuses on the aggressive actions of a single male figure, but the Navaho origin legend emphasizes collective action, in which women figure as prominently as men. Barnouw suggests that the themes of aggression in the Chippewa tale reflect feelings of hostility, which probably occurred in the often-isolated Chippewa family groups. The theme of oral frustration, also evident in the Chippewa tale, may be related to the former scarcity of food in the Chippewa region.[26] The importance of women in the Navaho tale and the relative absence of themes of aggression, which Barnouw notes, is repeated in the importance of Navaho women in everyday life and the emphasis on cooperative social interaction, as described by Laila Hamamsy.[27]

It is clear, then, that origin stories reflect some aspects of social life. The relationship shown in this chapter between proximity of fathers to infants and a people's concept of their divine origins provides statistical support for this point of view. The role of food source suggests that divine and secular concepts of birth are part of a people's adaptation to their environment. This interrelationship between natural environment, sex-role behavior, and world view provides the central theme in the chapters to follow. In these chapters, sex-role plans are discussed in terms of the integration or segregation of the sexes in everyday life and the relative balance of power between the sexes in political and economic activities.

The next two chapters focus on the forces that divide the sexes in everyday life. Sexual separation, as opposed to integration, is necessary for the development of sexual inequality and male dominance. Obviously, the sexes must be conceptually and physically separated before one sex as a group can exclude or dominate the other. However, this is not to suggest, nor should it be assumed, that sexual segregation automatically implies sexual inequality. As will be seen, there are examples of societies in which the sexes are separated but the balance of power between the male and female worlds is equal.

4 · Plans for the sexual division of labor

Within anthropology there has been a long-standing disagreement as to whether the sexual division of labor is imposed by cultural patterning, differences in physical strength, the greater expendability of men, and/or the constraints of childbearing and nursing. The disagreement persists because, depending on the kinds of activities examined, a persuasive argument can be made for both the biological and cultural patterning of work. For example, hunting and the processing of tough and hard raw materials are almost universally strictly male activities. There are no counterbalancing technological activities that are universally assigned exclusively to women. More often than not, however, gathering, processing vegetal foods, cooking, and other household duties are the woman's job. From these facts alone it is tempting to argue that the sexual division of labor is patterned by the biological and reproductive differences between men and women.

Yet there are other activities that require considerable strength and are inconsistent with the demands of maternity. In some societies these activities are performed by women either separately or in conjunction with men, in others they are the job of men alone. For example, carrying burdens, long-distance trading, or agricultural tasks may be the sole responsibility of either sex or may be shared by both. The assignment of these kinds of tasks in a particular society can only be interpreted within a cultural framework.

In this chapter the sexual division of labor is treated as a behavioral manifestation of a people's sex-role plan. The question of origins is addressed by examining the environmental and cultural context of sexual segregation and integration. Plans for the sexual division of labor, it will be argued, are formed from a people's adaptation to their environment. As such these plans must be viewed as part of a more general cultural configuration. Sexual segregation is associated with the outer/animal orientation described in the last chapter; a more balanced division of labor is found with the inner/plant orientation and with the dual-sex pattern.

The kinds of activities that are universally allocated to males

In most societies for which we have information, men are the warriors, hunters, and processors of raw materials related to weaponry and tools. Women have sometimes acted as full-time warriors and hunters, wielding the same weapons as men and displaying the same success (see discussion of the Dahomeans that follows). Such examples, however, are few and occur under special circumstances.

In a study of the sex assignment of 50 work activities in the 186 societies of the Standard Cross-Cultural Sample, George P. Murdock and Caterina Provost identify 14 activities that are performed strictly by males in nearly all societies. These activities are of two general kinds: 1) hunting and butchering, and 2) processing of hard or tough raw materials (such as smelting of ores, metalworking, mining, and quarrying).

There are no technological activities that are strictly feminine, though cooking and the preparation of vegetal foods come close. Murdock and Provost explain the occurrence of the strictly masculine tasks on the basis of the greater physical strength of males and their superior capacity for mobilizing it in brief bursts of excessive energy. They also suggest that females are attached to the household by "burdens of pregnancy and infant care."[1]

Douglas R. White, Michael L. Burton, and Lilyan A. Brudner provide a different explanation for the strictly male tasks. Although they do not deny the existence of human sexual dimorphism, they note that there is plasticity in the development of physical strength, so that cross-culturally there is considerable diversity in the degree to which males are stronger than females. In addition, they observe that many of the strictly male tasks require relatively little physical strength. Danger, long distance travel, and "economies of effort," they suggest, more than physical strength or the constraints of child care, explain the existence of strictly male activities. Other anthropologists have also commented on the importance of danger and travel. Judith K. Brown, for example, has argued that given the great importance attached to bearing children, it would be inefficient for a society to expose nursing mothers or childbearing women to danger. Ernestine Friedl points out that men are the expendable sex because they are not the bearers of new additions to the work or warrior force.[2]

White, Burton, and Brudner take the argument a step further by introducing the notion of efficiency in the utilization of learned skills: "There are economies of effort in having the same persons perform adjacent tasks in production sequences, since adjacent tasks often require similar technological skills, and are often performed in similar contexts." Thus, the performance by women of tasks that are consistent with nursing and child care (in many but not all cases) and the performance by men of tasks that are consistent with travel and danger are a consequence of efficiency considerations – not of intrinsic features of the tasks.[3]

It is also helpful to understand that strictly male activities provide males with a means for defining and displaying the adult male gender identity. Usually people define their sense of self as male or female by what they do. The female gender identity is automatically defined, at least for tribal peoples, by childbearing and nursing. What comes to women naturally and provides them with a set of discernibly female activities comes to men more artificially. Perhaps because women have ways of signaling their womanhood, men must have ways to display their manhood.

Stressing the importance of the male role for male gender identity, Margaret Mead says: "The recurrent problem of civilization is to define the male role satisfactorily enough . . . so that the male may in the course of his life reach a solid sense of irreversible achievement, of which his childhood knowledge of the satisfactions of childbearing have given him a glimpse."[4] The male role is often defined as what the female role is not. If female activities are associated with the qualities of reproduction, male activities are associated with the opposite qualities. As femaleness is linked to fertility and growth, maleness is linked to infertility and death. Sometimes these sex-linked attributes are projected onto animate and inanimate objects in the environment. For example, in a New Guinea highland society, certain foods are identified with the "juicy, soft, fertile, fast-growing" qualities of women and other foods are identified with the "dry, hard, infertile" slow-growing qualities of men. Men in this society publically avoid the female foods (which they may eat in secret) in order to preserve their gender identity and, likewise, women publically avoid the male foods.[5]

The equation between hard:soft–infertile:fertile–male:female is present in many societies. The hard:soft–male:female equation is implied by the kinds of manufacturing activities assigned to men as compared to those assigned to women. As noted before, raw materials that are hard or tough are processed strictly by males. Soft and pliable raw materials are more often (though not exclusively) processed by females. Only men work in metal, stone, bone, and wood. Women, more often than men, make baskets and mats, do loom weaving, make pottery, and spin.[6]

These observations are presented in order to stress how the importance people attach to childbearing and to demarcating the boundaries between maleness and femaleness can be reflected in the universal assignment (with very few exceptions) of men to some tasks. However, these are only a few tasks when compared with all that have been observed. In the next sections we will want to understand the reasons for sexual segregation in tasks that do not involve travel and danger.

The cultural patterning of work

Beyond the few tasks that are assigned to men alone or to females mainly there is considerable diversity in the cultural patterning of male and female work rhythms. Margaret Mead describes this diversity in five Insular Pacific societies. Among the Samoans, Mead remarks, "work is scaled to age and status rather than to sex." She says it would be hard to form from the Arapesh and the Balinese sexual division of labor "any picture of biological difference in rhythms for the two sexes," because in both societies men and women perform many of the same tasks. Among the Manus and Iatmul, on the other hand, she found definite sex differences in the rhythm of work. Manus men perform the heavy tasks and trade on long voyages; women carry on more of the routine activities of life. Iatmul women work steadily in groups performing the ordinary, monotonous tasks that can easily be interrupted by the demands of child care. Iatmul men's work is almost entirely episodic, requiring sudden spurts of energy followed by a period of rest. Of the five groups, Mead notes that only the Iatmul conform to the Western picture of "man as the lineal descendent of a nomadic hunter, capable of strong output of effort, but demanding long periods of recuperation," and "of women as better fitted by nature for the routine tasks of everyday life . . ."[7]

The variation Mead described for five societies is repeated cross-culturally. For example, the percentage of technological activities performed by women alone in the societies of this study may range from as little as 9% in some societies to 73% in others (see Table 4.1). In those cases where women are responsible for almost three-quarters of all work, one can hardly argue that women's work is constrained by lack of physical strength or by the demands of childrearing.

Sexual separation is so extreme in some societies that almost all work activities are defined as either male or female, with the result that the sexes form sexual ghettos. For example, today's Egyptian peasants say "there is no man who is not a farmer, and no woman who is not a housekeeper and cook. A man cooking or sewing, or a woman ploughing or irrigating the land is something unheard of in our village."[8] The Mundurucu sexual division of labor is strictly observed and very few tasks overlap. Husbands and wives rarely engage in joint work of any kind. The sexual division of labor assigns all women of a household and of the village a role complementary to the productive efforts of the men. This is a society in which men associate with men and women with women.[9]

The Kikuyu division of labor in food production is also strict. Males tend the livestock and females manage the household. A man who indulged in any female activity, such as cooking, washing, or hauling wood and water, would scandalize the women and make it very difficult for himself to find a wife. Agricultural duties are almost equally divided between men and women, although a given activity is performed by only one sex.[10] The same occurs among the Bambara where, both within and across categories of activities, there is a fairly rigid sexual division of labor. For example, in the construction of huts (a communal endeavor), only men perform the masonry work and only women gather water. Men plaster the outside and women the inside. In farming, men do most of the planting and weeding, and women harvest and prepare most of the food for sale or consumption. Hunting, metal-work, and observing communal religious ritual are activities re-

Table 4.1. *Average percentage of sexually integrated and segregated work activities in 156 tribal societies*

	Average percentage	Lowest percentage	Highest percentage
Sexually integrated technological activities (AH 85)	9	0	35
Technological activities performed predominantly or exclusively by women (AH 84)	38	9	73

The sex assignment of the technological activities coded by Murdock and Provost for each of 156 societies of the Standard Cross-Cultural Sample are used in computing percentages. Sexually integrated activities are those coded by Murdock and Provost (1973:204) as being "performed by both sexes with approximately equal participation or with a roughly equivalent division of subtasks." Sexually segregated activities are those coded as being performed "predominantly" or "exclusively" by females. See Appendix B.

stricted to men; the preparation and sale of food are restricted to women.[11]

Sexual segregation in tribal societies is more common than sexual integration. Whereas the percentage of female segregated work activities may range from 9% of all technological activities in some societies to 73% in other societies, the percentage of sexually integrated tasks ranges from 0 to 35% (see Table 4.1). Sexual segregation in work activities is most pronounced in economies dependent mainly on the processing of animals for food. In animal economies women perform more work activities alone and their labor accounts for 55% of all technological activities as compared with plant economies, where female labor accounts for approximately 44% of all activities (see Table 4.2). Thus, ironically, where hunting or animal husbandry constitutes the main subsistence focus, women do more work than men.

Sexual segregation in animal economies is part of a cultural configuration in which fathers are distant from the care of infants and the symbol of the all-powerful male is projected into the cosmol-

Table 4.2. *The sexual division of labor in different subsistence economies*

Subsistence mode (Econ)	1) Predominantly female technological activities (AH 84)[a]		2) Sexually integrated technological activities (AH 85)[a]		3) Average % of all technological activities in which women participate[b]
	N	%	N	%	
Animal economies					
Hunting	12	51.4	12	4.4	55.8
Animal husbandry	14	43.9	14	10.6	54.5
Fishing	15	42.6	15	10.1	52.7
Plant economies					
Gathering	14	37.2	14	6.8	44.0
Semi-intensive agriculture (fruit trees and/or vegetable gardens)	15	32.0	15	9.5	41.5
Shifting cultivation of fields	43	38.7	43	7.6	46.3
Advanced agriculture	43	33.5	43	11.0	44.5
Column totals (N)	156		156		

Data are given for number (N) and average percentage of societies. 1) $F = 7.0$; $p = 0.000$; 2) $F = 2.2$; $p = 0.04$.
[a]See explanation in Table 4.1.
[b]Average percentage of all technological activities in which women participate is the sum of the percentages in columns 1 and 2.

ogy. Women are solely responsible for the care of infants and for much of the labor. Although men labor less, the centrality of masculine or animal symbolism in cosmology suggests that men are considered the generators of power. In their capacity as childbearers, women are often equated with the animals men control. Men carve a separate domain for themselves by taking public responsibility for female and animal fertility.

In plant economies, the roles of men and women in symbolism and in the division of labor reverse the pattern described for animal economies. Feminine or dual-sex symbolism is represented in cosmology, fathers are involved with the care of infants, and women contribute less to the labor pool in comparison with their contribution in animal economies (see Table 4.2). Two patterns for the sexual division of labor can be discerned in these economies. The first is the sexually integrated pattern and the second is the dual-sex pattern.

In societies with a relatively high percentage of sexually integrated tasks, distinctions by sex, though present, are less important in social life. For example, the sexual division of labor among the Lepcha, an agricultural people living in the Himalayas on the southern and eastern slopes of Mount Kinchenjunga, can be contrasted with sexual segregation in animal-oriented societies. A high percentage of work activities among the Lepcha are integrated (28% as opposed to the overall average of 9% for the 156 societies noted in Table 4.1). Although many activities are customarily practiced by men or by women only, members of the other sex are not prohibited from doing them if they feel so inclined. For example, only women spin and only men weave baskets; but there is no reason why a man should not spin if he wants to and knows how, and some women do weave baskets and mats. Women who are willing and able may perform any task. Men are expected to be better tree climbers than women, but many women are more efficient tree climbers than their husbands. The husband feels no humiliation at his wife's superiority, nor is he ridiculed by others. If anything, he is considered lucky in having an exceptionally able partner. The one activitiy prohibited to women is killing animals.[12]

Lepcha fathers are closely involved with the care of children. Indeed, all adults respond to the demands of infants and young children. Fathers often carry their children on their backs, especially on long journeys. Men nurse children, holding them in their arms or on their laps. Pacificity is taught to the young. The characteristic deemed the most undesirable in children is inability to cooperate with others.[13]

The Lepcha emphasize the female's role almost exclusively in their conception of origins. Their story of creation, which, it is said, takes 7 whole days in its telling by heart, begins as follows:

Under this world is an ocean; under that ocean is another earth of twelve superimposed stories, and under that there lives Itpomu, the Creative Mother, and her husband Debu. Their first children were

83

. . . Narzong-nyou and Komsithing. After them were born . . .,
all of whom are the present earth;. . .
    The first children of Itpomu and Debu were Komsithing and
Narzong-nyou; although they were brother and sister they married,
and as a consequence all their children were devils and snakes and
lizards.[14]

Female deities occupy center stage in Lepcha mythology. The
chief supernaturals are the deities Itpomu and her daughter Narzong-nyou. Itpomu is somewhat distant; she is never invoked directly, but her creations are sacrificed and prayed to. The chief
goddess is her daughter, who is believed to live in the country and
to have been responsible for its geography, flora, and especially
fauna. She is also responsible for a great number of institutions, as
is her elder brother and husband, but he is considered a foreigner
because after he and his wife separated as a result of their incest, he
went off to Tibet.[15]

    Thus Lepcha cosmology casts women in the role of generators
and relegates men to the status of foreigner. This centrality of the
female in origin cosmology is not uncommon in societies where
there is a relatively high percentage of sexually integrated activities
and a relatively low percentage of sexually segregated activities
(see Table 4.3).

    Sexual integration is also consistent with an emphasis on coop-
eration rather than competition in human affairs. Societies with
more sexually integrated activities place little value on competition (see Table 4.4). The Lepcha, for example, judge their fellows
in their social roles and not as individuals. Similarities rather than
differences among individuals are the focus of attention. This
stress on the resemblance of individuals makes for a low development of the ego, little internal competition, and the minimization
of the most obvious contrasts – such as between rich and poor,
between men and women, and between adults and children. As
Goeffrey Gorer says, the "Lepcha recognise no social goals which
can only be achieved at the expense of others."[16]

    Thus sexual integration is part of a cultural configuration that
glorifies the role of women in the generation and control of
power. The elevation of the female to the status of control means
also that there is more cooperation than competition in human
affairs. The involvement of the father with the care of infants carries the spirit of cooperation into the socialization of the young.

Table 4.3. *Gender origin symbolism (A05) and the sexual division of labor*

Origin symbolism	1) Predominantly female technological activities (AH 84)		2) Sexually integrated technological activities (AH 85)	
	N	%	N	%
Feminine	20	36.0	20	11.6
Couple	36	37.3	36	9.1
Masculine	56	40.8	56	6.6
Column totals (N)	112[a]		112[a]	

Data are given for number (N) and average percentage of societies. 1) $F = 1.9$, $p = 0.16$; 2) $F = 5.5$, $p = 0.006$.
[a]No information for 44 societies.

Table 4.4. *Emphasis on competition (Coma) and the sexual division of labor*

Training boys to be competitive	1) Predominantly female technological activities (AH 84)		2) Sexually integrated technological activities (AH 85)	
	N	%	N	%
No emphasis on competition or strong emphasis on cooperation	5	31.6	5	18.2
Moderate emphasis on competition, some competitive games	70	36.0	70	9.2
Strong emphasis on competition	41	41.1	41	8.5
Column totals (N)	116[a]		116[a]	

Data are given for number (N) and average percentage of societies. 1) $F = 3.4$, $p = 0.04$; 2) $F = 4.1$, $p = 0.02$. Appendix B gives reference for Coma.
[a]No information for 40 societies.

Constructing sex-role plans

A third cultural configuration:
the dual-sex orientation

The patterning of the division of labor discussed previously presents two logical extremes – one in which the focus is on competition and maleness, another in which the focus is on cooperation and femaleness. A third configuration joins the male and female in a relationship of complementarity and duality in symbolism and behavior. The sexual division of labor in these cases is balanced, by and large, and competition may be the prevailing ethic.

The Iroquois, Ashanti, and Dahomeans, discussed in previous chapters, are obvious examples of the dual orientation. As described in the last chapter, nineteenth-century Dahomean social structure and creation cosmology were founded on the principle of the duality of the sexes. This principle was a pervasive feature of Dahomean culture, manifested in many different ways. In politics, every official in the kingdom had his female counterpart, or "mother," resident in the royal compound. It was the duty of these women to know intimately all the administrative affairs of her male counterpart and to keep constant check upon his operations.[17]

All that was inside the palace was opposed to everything outside. This distinction between inside and outside was made explicit by the Dahomean king. More than 8,000 people lived "inside" the palace, most of whom were women. These women were part of a system of control exercised by the king over his ministers of the "outside." The minister of the "outside" could only approach the king in the palace in the presence of his female counterpart of the "inside." His "mother" was as much his representative to the king as she was the king's representative to him.[18]

The same dual-sex organization existed throughout the army. The army was divided into two wings, the right and the left. Each wing was further divided into a male and female part. Every male, from the highest-ranking officer to the last soldier, had his female counterpart in the palace.[19] These women constituted an effective fighting force, and some observers considered them superior to the men.[20]

In 1845 it was estimated that the king's army consisted of 12,000 soldiers, 5,000 of whom were women. In the second half of the nineteenth century there were two armies: a standing army of male and female warriors and a reserve army of all adult men and women capable of bearing arms. In wartime, one group of Amazons (the name given to Dahomean female soldiers by European travelers) was charged with guarding the palace while another waged war. They wore uniforms just as the men did: "Sleeveless tunics, with blue-and-white stripes, reached to the knees; baggy breeches were held in at the waist by a cartridge belt."[21]During military campaigns, the Amazons were organized along the same lines as the male army, into three groups. The elite corps, the Fanti company, consisted of the famed elephant huntresses, the boldest and toughest of the Amazons. They constituted the royal bodyguard and the main body of the Amazons. Then there were left and right wings of the army, commanded by female officers.

Amazons were recruited from free Dahomeans and captives. They were forced to be celibate, which may explain why only eunuchs were allowed at the palace where they lived. They could not marry until they reached middle age and had received the king's consent.[22] This was the device by which the king protected himself against military plots. By surrounding himself with these women, he insulated himself from male competitors and maintained his position as absolute monarch. By denying these women access to males, he reduced the likelihood of devious schemes being hatched between a woman and her lover. And, of course, he kept his female warriors from being burdened by pregnancy. The king's concern was clearly not to produce children but to protect himself. Hence women were expendable.

In a sense, these Amazons were like powerful nuns who bore arms for their earthly king and gave him absolute devotion. Denied childbirth and childrearing, and skilled at handling instruments of destruction, these women clearly fell into a masculine and not a feminine mode. The Amazons said about themselves, "We are men, not women."[23] Contrary to what adherents of the matriarchy theory might like to think about them, they were not feminists fighting for the rights of women, nor were they rulers. They were warriors in the service of their king.

The importance of the dual-sex ideology and the central role of females in the Dahomean polity and army caused astonishment in the men who observed or wrote about them. The following, somewhat startled, incredulous description of Dahomean women is not at all uncommon:

The fact is that in very few communities of state level were women called upon to play so large a part in services vital to functioning of the polity. The gift of the female sex for absorbing detail, retaining information on facts of everyday life in which commonsense is anchored, have been tested and not found wanting.

The recognized excellence of administration and the eminent role played in it by the female element does not seem fully to account for the extent to which Dahomean women were drawn into public life up to its highest levels. This suggests that behind the duality device as such there must have been active some motivation stemming from a mental attitude that transcended considerations of practical efficiency.[24]

The mental attitude of which this observer of the Dahomeans speaks, which transcends "considerations of practical efficiency," underscores again the importance of gender ideology and associated world view in motivating sex-role behavior.

Many examples of the operation of the dual-sex ideology can be found in West Africa. In addition to the Ashanti and the Dahomeans, the Igbo of midwestern Nigeria provide still another example. Kamene Okonjo labels West African political systems in which the major interest groups are defined and represented by sex "dual-sex systems." In these systems each sex manages its own affairs, and women's interests are represented at all levels. Describing the operation of the dual-sex system among traditional political units of midwestern Nigeria, she says that in each there were separate male and female political religious institutions, giving the sexes their own autonomous spheres of authority and an area of shared responsibility. Women settled disputes among women and made decisions and rules affecting men. Women had the right to enforce their decisions and rules by reverting to sanctions similar to those employed by men. Ultimate authority and policy making affecting the female sphere rested in the hands of the female monarch, who was the crowned and acknowledged head. She lived in a palace and ruled from a throne. She was known as the *omu*, and was theoretically the acknowledged mother of the community. The male monarch, known as the *obi*, was, in theory, the acknowledged head of the whole community.

The sexual division of labor

In practice, however, the *obi* was concerned more with the male section of the community and the *omu* with the female sector.[25]

Okonjo says that the "dual nature of the system aimed at a harmonious and effective division of labor by which both sexes would receive adequate attention to their needs." She notes that there is no historical record of conflict between an *obi* and an *omu*, nor of any clash of functions. The male and female cabinets, she says, were meant to ensure "complementarity in their parallel functions."[26]

Sex-role plans and configurations of culture

In this chapter, three types of cultural configurations with their underlying plans for the integration or separation of the sexes have been described. These configurations orient sex-role behavior beyond what is determined by the demands of childbearing or male physical strength. Sexual integration is much less common than sexual segregation. A relatively high proportion of sexually integrated tasks usually means that feminine supernatural symbolism is part of a people's cosmology and that cooperation is stressed in behavior (see Tables 4.3 and 4.4). Hence, sexual integration is suggestive of a cultural configuration not unlike the inner/plant orientation described in the last chapter (see Figure 4.1).[27]

Sexually segregated societies are of two kinds – those marked by a dual-sex ideology and those in which the outer/animal orientation provides the major cultural focus. The outer/animal orientation is marked by the primacy of masculine symbolism and competitive interaction. The dual-sex orientation, on the other hand, brings the inner and the outer, the feminine and the masculine, into a relationship of balanced complementarity.

The material presented in this chapter suggests that the sexual division of labor cannot be reduced to biological givens or to differences in physical strength. Such argumentation wrests human behavior from the web of significance in which it is embedded. A full understanding of the sexual division of labor requires unraveling the kinds of configurations described in this chapter.

Why hunting and warfare are usually the jobs of men cannot be explained simply on the basis of practicality or male prowess. Because women bear new life, the job of taking life falls to men. If

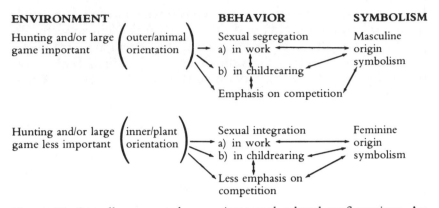

Figure 4.1. Sexually segregated versus integrated cultural configurations. Arrows indicate significant correlations (see Appendix C, Table C.5, and Appendix D, Table D.1).

killing were part of femaleness, the conceptual distinction people make between life giving and life taking would be violated. It is not that women cannot hunt or go to war; rather, it is that motherhood, gentleness, and forgiveness do not mix well with predation, toughness, and warlikeness. Conceptual distinctions demarcating femaleness from maleness, as Mary Douglas says, help people create a semblance of order (see Chapter 5). The duality expressed by the male and female principles in belief systems like Mawu-Lisa in Dahomean culture establishes in the human world the equilibrium between opposites that underlies the conception of order in the universe.

5 · Blood, sex, and danger

Separatist attitudes, such as the notions that women should be secluded during menstruation and that sexual intercourse pollutes men, enforce the physical separation of the sexes. Such attitudes vary in number and intensity from society to society. In some societies, menstruating women are barely noticed. In others, menstruating women are secluded in special huts where they occupy a position of social marginality because they are thought to harbor a terrific, usually destructive, force. Or, in a different expression of the same underlying plot, sexual contact with a woman is thought to sap male strength, weaken a woman's nursing child, or endanger the whole community.

Such fantasy enactment, on the surface irrational in the extreme, has been variously interpreted as signaling the inferiority of women, or indicating castration anxiety in men, or offering a means for symbolically controlling danger. An example of the first kind of argument, applied to the restriction of menstruating women, is found in Frank Young and Albert Bacdayan's hypothesis that menstrual taboos "are institutionalized ways in which males in primitive society discriminate against females."[1] William Stephens, on the other hand, hypothesizes that "the extensiveness of menstrual taboos observed in a primitive society is determined (to a significant extent) by the average intensity of castration anxiety felt by men in that society."[2]

The discussion in this chapter regarding the occurrence of menstrual taboos and other intersexual avoidance practices follows the third line of argument. This argument is best exemplified by the work of Mary Douglas, who treats concepts of pollution and danger as a system of meaningful symbols in which the actual relationship between the sexes plays a negligible role. Douglas thinks that pollution beliefs serve as analogies for the social order. She says that we cannot possibly interpret rituals concerning bodily

91

emissions "unless we are prepared to see in the body a symbol of society, and to see the powers and dangers credited to social structure reproduced in small on the human body."[3]

Following the framework suggested by Douglas's analysis of pollution beliefs, I argue that beliefs about the virulence of the power inherent in female bodily or sexual functioning is neither a reflection of castration anxiety nor of sexual inequality. Rather, the presence of such beliefs provides us with a clue to the presence of critical human concerns. By projecting these concerns onto women, people provide themselves with a stage on which to control the dangerous forces they face. Beliefs about the danger of menstrual blood symbolically reverse the equation of femaleness with life and growth discussed in the last chapter. By attaching to femaleness characteristics that we ordinarily associate with the destructive functions performed by males in hunting and warfare, these beliefs make women, in a sense, like men. Similarly, as we shall see, there are beliefs about the growth-giving aspects of male blood that reverse the equation of maleness with destruction and make men like women.

The body as symbol

Mary Douglas says that ideas about separating, purifying, and demarcating "have as their main function to impose system on an inherently untidy experience." It is only by exaggerating certain differences, such as between male and female, "that a semblance of order is created."[4] Presumably, the need for imposing order grows out of a people's experience with disorder. If we accept this assumption, and Mary Douglas's suggestion that we see in the body a symbol of society, we would expect that danger attributed to bodily emissions replicates real dangers experienced beyond the confines of society.

In untamed and "inaccessible" territories, Mary Douglas says, men seek power "not available to those who stay in the control of themselves and of society."[5] Generally men, not women, wander beyond the confines of society to confront danger in pursuit of power. And yet within society the bodily emissions of women in some cases connote power and danger. Mary Douglas's equation of body with society suggests that such beliefs mirror the danger that surrounds the social body. By observing certain taboos in connection with menstrual blood, women harness the danger within in order to turn its power to work for the social good. Men work toward the same goal when they observe taboos in order to meet with success in hunting, warfare, and other quests for power that take them beyond the realm of control.

The idea that a people's sense of danger is projected onto the female body is suggested by Mary Douglas's comparison of the Mbuti and the Hadza of East Africa. Like the Mbuti, the Hadza are gatherers and hunters. Comparing principles of classification between these two groups, Mary Douglas remarks that whereas among the Mbuti "neither sex, age, nor kinship order their behavior in strictly ordained categories," among the Hadza there is an extraordinarily intense consciousness of sexual difference, which divides the sexes into "two hostile classes, each of which is capable of organizing itself for defense or virulent attack against the other."[6] This opposition between the Hadza sexes is more pronounced during the dry season, when camps are bigger and large animals and humans congregate near the few available sources of water. During the wet season, however, food becomes both abundant and evenly dispersed, and the sexes live together relatively harmoniously in small, widely scattered camps, subsisting on roots and small game. In these small wet-season camps, men and women are not segregated greatly. Only the large camps of the dry season seem to stimulate sexual segregation and mutual hostility between the sexes.[7]

It is common for the relationship between the sexes among the same group of foragers to change, depending on seasonal activities or a switch from nomadic to sedentary life.[8] In foraging societies, when food is abundant and dispersed, small family groups wander with relative ease in their environment and the sexes are integrated in most activities. This ease disappears during the season when the food supply fluctuates or is concentrated in certain areas.

The Hadza dry season brings animals and people into competition for the same water resources. During this season Hadza men hunt large game, which implies danger, and they gamble in camp, which conveys a concern with chance. In the concentrated settlements of the dry season, the Hadza believe that contact with menstrual blood is dangerous. This is the wedge that drives the sexes apart – as is the case in most societies in which sexual separation is rigid. When a Hadza women menstruates, she avoids certain activities, which would be polluted by her contact. In addition, her husband of the moment, whoever he may be, must abstain from his ordinary activities lest he endanger the rest of the camp's chance of success in hunting. In contrast to the Hadza, the Mbuti have no conception of pollution, "of death, nor of birth, nor of menstruation."[9]

The sexual segregation and taboos restricting the activities of Hadza men and women during the dry season may well be the means by which the Hadza handle their perception that the odds are stacked against them, that their lives are at the mercy of random blows inflicted by nature. We can only speculate why people handle their fear at such times by separating the sexes and deeming menstrual blood powerful and dangerous.

To many peoples, blood means the source of life and the signal of death. A people's experience with blood must be more negative than positive when their lives are threatened by starvation, thirst, or by the hungry animals they hunt. Little information exists on the mortality rate of hunters. If, as in warfare, hunters risk death, then they must be extraordinarily cautious. A hunter who has had recent contact with a menstruating woman possibly carries the smell with him, warning the animals of his presence. Unfortunately, we have little information on how hunted animals are affected by the smell of menstrual blood.

Restrictions separating the sexes are more elaborate in concentrated settlements. When humans congregate in larger settlements, the smell of menstrual blood must be more obvious. It is a frightening smell because it is reminiscent of death. Being a fluid that flows from the body, menstrual blood is like the fluid that drains from the newly dead. Both types of fluids represent the loss of a vital essence. The more people experience death in nature, the more likely they are to view menstrual blood as dangerous.

Such a response to menstrual blood is illogical, because blood in women signals their readiness to bear life, whereas the blood drawn by hunters signals death. However, by killing animals, men also bring life in the form of animal protein – a food with a high prestige value wherever men hunt. If the blood that flows from women can only be equated with life, then why is it so often equated with danger? Perhaps the answer lies in a rather simple proposition. If blood is associated with life and death in the experience of males, a balance is achieved by associating female blood with life and danger. If humans do strive to achieve such a balance, we would expect, to the extent that men have more experience with blood and death, that the blood of women would be endowed with corresponding connotations.

The Ashanti of West Africa (see Chapter 1) specifically equate menstruation with "killing an elephant" and childbearing with being a warrior. Like the Dahomeans, the Ashanti are a West African kingdom in which there is extraordinary sexual parallelism in many aspects of thought and behavior. This can be seen in the treatment of a girl at her first menstruation and a woman at childbirth.

When the Ashanti girl reaches puberty, it is said "the *Bara* state has stricken her. She has killed an elephant." This is an occasion for elaborate ceremonials and exchange of gifts. A mother's first act, upon learning the news from her daughter, is to inform the villagers, the Sky God, the Earth Goddess, and the ancestors. Taking some wine and spilling it on the ground, the mother says:

Supreme Sky God, who is alone great, upon whom men lean and do not fall, receive this wine and drink.

Earth Goddess, whose day of worship is a Thursday, receive this wine and drink. Spirit of our ancestors, receive this wine and drink.

This girl child whom God has given to me, to-day the Bara state has come upon her.

O mother who dwells in the land of ghosts, do not come and take her away and do not have permitted her to menstruate only to die.[10]

The onset of menstruation signifies that a girl is ready to make her contribution to the continuation of the lineage through the bearing of children. However, although the blood denotes the possibility of life, it also reminds people of death. The advent of puberty means that the child of a departed ancestor will soon die in order to be reborn into the world of the living. People say, "A birth in this world is a death in the world of ghosts; when a human mother conceives, a ghost mother's infant is sickening to die."[11] Menstrual blood implies power, and there are many taboos in connection with it. During the puberty ceremonial, a girl is taken to the river, where she is disrobed and immersed three times with the words: "We quench the *bara* fire at its source."[12] Menstrual blood is thought to nullify all supernatural powers possessed by persons, spirits, or objects. These powers, if rendered inactive by contact with a menstruating woman, have to be "recharged, as it were, by propitiation, extirpation, and augmentation rites, to placate them and build them up anew."[13]

If a woman dies during childbirth, she is treated like a warrior who has lost an important battle. A ceremony is conducted that only pregnant women attend. The goal of the ceremony seems to be to chastise the woman who has died, and hence has failed in her primary duty, and to prevent other such failures. During the ceremony the other pregnant women of the village get a plantain leaf and say "Bang! (imitating a gun) be gone with your evil, you have been unable to bring forth, you have been unable to fight, you have fought only to die." Then each woman takes a knife and addresses the body: "We told you to fight but you could not fight, when our turn comes to fight we swear the oath we shall not pass out."[14]

Thus, the Ashanti impose hunter and warrior imagery on female reproductive functions. By phrasing the natural rhythms of life giving and life taking in the same terms, the Ashanti establish a symmetry between male and female. In other societies, the natural rhythms of females are imposed on the male body to achieve a different kind of symmetry. Among the Arapesh of New Guinea, Mary Douglas says, the male genital organ is incised at puberty to achieve symmetry with the female reproductive system.[15] This symmetry is evident in attitudes regarding male and female sexual power. Male and female sexual power is manifested in blood, which each sex seeks to control in the interest of fertility and growth. The female nourishes the fetus with "good blood," but her menstrual blood is considered dangerous. The male has equivalent blood in his penis, which he draws to feed his newborn child as women feed the fetus with blood in the womb. Female menstruation is regarded as strengthening because it discharges from the women's body dangerous fluids received from men in intercourse. Similarly, men emulate this natural purifying discharge by artificially letting blood from the penis.

Another kind of symmetry is established by beliefs that menstrual blood saps male energy and draws the power from his weapons. The symmetry established by this conception can be likened to positive and negative charges, in which the negative force believed to be inherent in menstrual blood has the power to obliterate male physical strength. In order to recharge themselves with the requisite energy, men avoid female bodily fluids. As a consequence, mutual avoidance is observed between the sexes to the point of rigid sexual separation in many activities.

Mary Douglas argues that pollution beliefs – be they beliefs about the danger of menstrual blood, about contact with the dead, or about the danger of certain foods – prevent threatened disturbances of the social order.[16] In the world view of many tribal peoples, the disturbances most feared are those believed to influence childbearing and food production. Often people blame the occurrence of such disturbances on their own acts. For example, an adulterous woman may believe that her sexual transgression has endangered the lives of her unborn and living children; or a fratricide is thought to emit a putrid odor that frightens off the herd and puts the vital resources of the tribe at risk; or a diminishing population is attributed to rampant jealousy and destructive sorcery. Such views of the close tie between humans and the forces of nature provide coherent principles of social control. Pollution beliefs help people to regulate their universe by enforcing conformity. By controlling their own actions, people give themselves a sense of evening uncertain odds.[17]

The body in society and nature: the Andaman Islanders

Radcliffe-Brown's classic ethnography of the Andaman Islanders, inhabitants of small islands covered by dense tropical forest in the Bay of Bengal, illuminates the linkage humans establish with nature in the relative absence of other disturbances, such as those associated with warfare and hunting. The Andaman Islanders live in an area inhabited only by small game, and warfare is virtually nonexistent.[18] The main pressures they face come from nature. The Andamanese construe their world as one in which dangerous powers or forces are "present in the society itself, in each individual, in animals and plants and the phenomena of nature, and in the world of spirits.[19] The people depend on these powers they have invented and on the ceremonials by which they transform these powers for human use. All things taken from the jungle or the sea, either for food or for making tools and weaponry, are believed to be dangerous unless approached with ritual precaution.[20]

Sources of danger become sources of strength and well-being when controlled ritually. Ritual demarcates people and food, or people and society. Every problem or special state the Anda-manese encounter involves eating (or not eating) and painting the body to signify an individual's relationship to nature and society.

In ritual, the Andamanese reaffirm their sense of balance in the universe. The colors red and white are ceremonially employed to signal various states. White signifies a state of well-being, which is associated with fine weather (brightness in the day), goodness, and happiness. Light is associated with euphoric, and dark with dysphoric, conditions. Light, fine weather, and white are associ-ated with honey, because in the season of fine weather honey is plentiful. There is a special connection between honey and a spe-cies of large snake, which comes to be representative of fine weather and states of well-being. When men or women want to express their sense of good feeling, they paint themselves with a white zig-zag pattern to represent the snake. A man who is suc-cessful in the day's hunting will have his face ornamented with this pattern.[21]

Red symbolizes blood and fire. Blood is identified with the warmth of the body and with life; blood and fat are sometimes spoken of as the two vital principles. Red is associated with

excitement, vitality, mental and bodily activity, and with energy or force in general . . . When a person is sick . . . in need of vitality, of energy . . . his body is daubed with the red paint that is a symbol of the things that he needs . . . By a simple mental process he comes to believe that by applying the paint to his body he increases his energy and vitality, and so helps himself to get rid of the sickness.[22]

Applying paint to the body increases an individual's energy, vi-tality, and sense of personal force, qualities that are an important part of the cultural evaluation of personhood. Red and white paint are also used to purify one who has committed homicide. Such a person is entirely cut off from social life for a specified period and lives in a condition of extreme danger because of the blood he has shed. During this time he may not touch food with his hands, and at the end of the period of isolation the hands are purified by ap-plying white and red clay.[23] It is interesting to note that a newly menstruating girl is also isolated and forbidden to eat with her fingers. She is, however, for a time afterward forbidden to use red or white clay.[24] Perhaps this is because of the power and force that are welling within her. This is suggested by the belief that if a man were to touch a girl during her first menses or for some time after, his arm would swell up.[25] When boys are initiated, they are painted red and rubbed with turtle fat.[26] This, it would seem, is the means by which boys are supplied with the vitality that comes from within girls. Both women and men are painted during mourning ceremonies, before or after eating, for ceremonial dances, at marriage, and to cure illness. Women decorate their husbands and take great pride in the designs they create. Only at initiation is differential treatment accorded to the sexes.[27] On other ceremonial occasions, for example, men and women wear exactly the same ornaments.[28]

At first menstruation, the birth name of a woman is dropped and she is called by a flower name. She is given a flower name because she is, as it were, "in blossom, and only when her body ripens to its fruit is she a complete women."[29] A girl is isolated at first menstruation and required to bathe in the sea. At every recurrence of the menstrual period, a woman must abstain from eating certain foods.[30] This is the extent of the Andamanese fear of menstrual blood, a fear that is handled more in connection with food taboos than by restrictions against women.

Beyond preparing a girl to become a mother, the Andaman Islanders do not clothe sexual differences with images of danger. Among the forest dwellers in particular there is considerable integration between the sexes. At certain times of the year when they do little hunting, the forest-dwelling men will join women in gathering roots and fruits. When honey becomes plentiful, it is collected jointly by men and women, although only men climb trees and cut the honeycombs down.[31] When the favorite fruit becomes ripe, men and women collect it together. Among the coast dwellers men hunt and fish, and women collect fruits, roots, prawns, crabs, and small fish. Women provide firewood and water and cook for the family. When food is prepared for communal camp eating, the cooking is done entirely by men.[32]

Community affairs are regulated entirely by the older men and women. The possession of certain personal qualities make some men more influential than others. Women may occupy a position of influence similar to that of the men.[33] Women do not exercise influence in the hunting sphere, but they have much influence in settling disputes between individuals or local groups. Certain men, and possibly some women, have additional influence be-

99

cause they possess supernatural powers.[34] Numerous spirits are thought to inhabit the jungle, sea, and sky. These are both male and female spirits, and all of them have supernatural powers. Whenever anyone dies, he or she becomes a spirit. Natural phenomena are also personified. Some tribes believe that the sun is the wife of the moon and the stars are their children. Others believe that the moon is female, the sun male.[35] There is no consistency in these beliefs, except that males and females are equally represented in them. Male and female symbolism is also represented in the numerous tales of how the first man and woman came about.[36]

For the Andamanese, the main source of danger comes from mishandling nature and violating the laws of society. What is taken from nature to provide for the people's well-being is handled gingerly. A man who takes the life of another is considered to be in a state of social marginality until ritually purified. The Andamanese clearly do not handle their concerns by attributing danger to women. To return to the proposition presented at the outset of this chapter, the reason that the Andamanese do not attribute danger to female reproductive functions may be that men do not fear bodily harm in the enactment of the male role. Hence, there is no need to project on the female anatomy the dangers men experience in reality.

Fluctuating food, warfare, and fear of fluxing women: the Bellacoola

In contrast to the Andamanese, the Bellacoola (of the northwest coast of North America) were confronted with very real threats to survival: famine and warfare. Famine is a central theme in Bellacoola catastrophic stories. In these stories, famine is preceded by signs of disorder in the cosmos. For example, in one story it is said: "One winter, long ago, the sun, instead of stopping at its usual place, continued far beyond its proper course." This event was followed by a prolonged famine five years later, in which the berries flowered but did not ripen and few fish entered the river.[37]

Before the establishment of British rule, there was considerable warfare among the Northwest Indian tribes. It appears probable that at least several villages of the Bellacoola were engaged in warfare every few years, before 1860. Scarcity of food seems to have been the most frequent cause for warfare, and the tribe that had accumulated the greatest food supply was the object of attack. The abundant supplies of salmon available to the Bellacoola made them tempting victims for less fortunate and more belligerent neighbors. Attack meant that a revenge attack had to be carried out. There was no assurance that the latter would be successful, because the Bellacoola had no organized mechanism for mounting a warfare expedition. If somebody's relative had been slain, revenge would motivate him to join in the expedition. Otherwise, only the influence of the expedition's leader would entice men to join. This so-called leader had little authority over his men, who could desert at any time. This lack of martial ability sometimes led the Bellacoola to place themselves under the protection of other groups, which could only have enhanced their sense of insecurity.[38]

The insecurity faced by the Bellacoola is reflected in attitudes regarding menstrual blood and female sexual fluids. The avoidance of female sexuality as well as menstrual blood seems to have been one of the ways the Bellacoola adapted to uncertainty. In 1880 (the period on which the following description is based), the Bellacoola depended mainly on fish. During certain times of the year the river teemed with salmon, enabling the country to support its relatively large population. Throughout the year salmon was the principal article of diet.[39] This dependence was reflected in the rigidly enforced restrictions concerning the river and its fish. Most important, no menstruating woman could bathe in the river, lest a speck of her blood blind the fish. When the fish were running in the river, women were not allowed on the bank nor to repair the nets.[40] After the year's first salmon catch, the men had a feast and brought what was left home for the women to eat. It was believed that the salmon would not be offended if the women ate only the leftovers.[41]

The Bellacoola concept of menstrual blood reflected the powers of nature. Both the blood and nature were endowed with the capacity to destroy and to protect. At first menses the adolescent girl was subject to many restrictions. She could not go near the river lest the salmon be offended and avoid the Bellacoola.[42] Neither could she pick berries, because no more would grow in the valley; she could not touch anyone nor allow anyone to touch her; she could not pass in front of any man; she went to bed before everyone else and was the last to arise. If she disobeyed these and other restrictions, she would die.[43] She was "both feared and respected,

101

possessed of supernatural power, and yet baneful." Many Bellacoola stories describe how girls during their first menses were able
to vanquish supernatural beings; one tells of how they "once saved
mankind when the sun came too close to the earth."[44] First menstrual blood was the most dangerous, but all menstrual blood carried some danger because it was considered a powerful *human* sub-
stance, and, therefore, a potent protection against supernatural
beings. It was valuable as a defense against evil monsters, but it
was equally deadly to shamans and other human beings with supernatural powers.[45]

Shamans had the power to cure and ask assistance of any supernatural being when this was believed necessary. Like a menstruating woman, a shaman's power was internal, involuntary, and had
to be controlled. Because power was concentrated in both, they
had to observe strict taboos so as not to endanger themselves and
others. However, a shaman had to be particularly careful to avoid
a menstruating woman, whereas the reverse did not seem to be the
case. The death of a shaman was frequently accompanied by some
convulsion of nature. Because of the personal danger involved,
many people took certain precautions to avoid becoming shamans. A man would hold "intercourse with his wife from below,
so that her flesh, impure through its liability to menses, can form a
barrier to the coming of supernatural power."[46] If a man wanted
to become a shaman, he signified his wish by sleeping on the right
side of his wife. Thus, there was a close connection between the
supernatural powers bestowed on shamans and the powers inherent in menstrual blood.

Sexual segregation among the Bellacoola was based, at least in
part, on the desire to separate blood as life from blood as death.
Contact with menstrual blood or the internal force of women
through sexual intercourse was avoided by Bellacoola men about
to embark on a hunting or warfare expedition. Contact with menstrual blood was believed to endanger a man's success, and sexual
intercourse to sap his energy. In seeking to subdue and conquer
external sources of power, men avoided internal sources.

The Bellacoola were a prosperous people who lived in large village congregations. Wealth distinctions existed among them, and
in warfare it was not uncommon to take prisoners, who became
slaves. There were no leaders with overall authority.[47] A man

could attain prominence through the potlatch system and come to be known as a "chief" or be granted a special seat near the fire in the houses. The advice of such men was generally followed in subsistence, hunting, and warfare matters, but they lacked executive authority.[48] A woman was rarely established in a "seat," although she could be when a chief had no sons or other near male descendants. A woman who was thus established had the same status as a male chief.[49]

Like many other foraging societies, however, influence depended mainly on personal prestige and valor, which was validated by the public display of wealth in giving potlatches. Power was also exercised by shamans, who could be male or female. Both male and female personages were amply represented in the supernatural realm. Boas, who wrote extensively on ancient Bellacoola mythology, stated that "in the upper heaven resides the supreme deity, a woman who interferes comparatively little with the fates of mankind."[50] This woman, who rules the upper heaven, is called "our woman," or she who is "afraid of nothing." She is associated with blue, white, and black and it is said that her infrequent visits to the earth cause sickness and death. She is also described as a great warrior.[51] McIlwraith, who reconstructed Bellacoola life for a later time period, remarks that this deity was then no longer important in Bellacoola belief.[52]

The idea of a powerful female deity fits with the Bellacoola conception of femaleness as a receptacle of great danger and power. The power of menstrual blood seems to have come first on the Bellacoola ideological power scale. Menstrual power could neutralize the supernatural and vanquish the power that supplied food in nature. As a consequence, menstrual blood was perceived as needing to be controlled so that it would not destroy unwittingly. The Bellacoola maintained the balance of power between themselves and their universe through the taboo system, which separated men and fish from the natural functions of women, including female sexuality. The taboo system and associated ritual seems to have provided them relief from their sense of human vulnerability and dependence in the face of superior forces. This method of maintaining the balance of power resulted in sexual separation that was based more on fear than on practical necessity.[53]

Pollution of menstrual blood and sexual intercourse

Several considerations have been raised so far that elaborate on the theme of body as symbol of society in connection with the function of menstrual taboos and sexual separation before hunting and warfare. Most important, blood as life is separated from blood as death; male hunting and warfare are equated with menstruation and childbirth. By imputing danger to the female body, people make public the dangers men face. Attributing danger to the female body may also serve pragmatic ends. For example, the perception of women as dangerous may mirror the hostile relations with groups from which wives are acquired. Or belief in the danger of sexual intercourse may reduce interpersonal conflict during times of scarcity.

Analysis of heterosexual avoidance practices in many societies suggests that imputing danger to the female body symbolizes many things. Mary Douglas argues that beliefs about menstrual pollution "give scope for playing out interpersonal conflicts" and reflect structural dimensions of the social order. At the interpersonal level, she says, fastening on the danger of menstruation is a way of separating male and female social spheres, asserting male superiority, or blaming family disasters on rival co-wives. At the social level, she says, menstrual pollution beliefs may be used to lay claim to a special relation. She cites the Hadza belief that the husband of a menstruating woman must observe the same taboos as his wife and argues that this serves to define the married couple where no other mechanism for publicizing the marital relationship exists and where marital ties are unstable. In addition, she argues, menstrual pollution beliefs reflect the structure of the larger social order. For example, the sexual symmetry established by beliefs regarding male menstruation among the Arapesh expresses the duality evident in the Arapesh social structure.[54]

Some of Douglas's ideas and others expressed in this chapter can be examined by determining the context of restrictions on menstruating women in a large number of societies. The most frequent types of menstrual restrictions that can be observed are: 1) No sexual intercourse is allowed; 2) Menstruous women must observe personal restrictions regarding dress, movement, and contact with things or people; 3) Menstruous women are not allowed to have contact with male ritual equipment or weaponry; 4) Men-

Table 5.1. *The number of menstrual taboos (H16)*

Number of menstrual taboos	No. of societies[a]	%
No menstrual restrictions	8	7
One restriction present	26	24
Two restrictions present	25	23
Three restrictions present	17	15
Four restrictions present	15	14
Five restrictions present	19	17
Column totals	156	100

[a]No information for 46 societies.

struous women are not allowed to cook or handle food; 5) Men-struous women are secluded in special huts.[55] The number of such restrictions observed in a particular society varies from none in some to all five in others. Seven percent of the societies for which information was available have no such restrictions and 17% have all five (see Table 5.1).

Menstrual taboos clearly separate men from women and, as such, may be understood as an assertion of separate male and female social spheres. A high number of menstrual restrictions certainly makes sexual integration in work impractical. This is evidenced by the negative association between menstrual taboos and the number of sexually integrated work tasks.[56]

If menstrual restrictions are the means by which men assert their superiority, as Mary Douglas and Frank Young suggest, we would expect there to be more restrictions in societies where males are clearly dominant and women subordinate. However, this is not so. There are nearly as many restrictions in societies where the sexes are equal as in societies where sexual inequality prevails (see Table 5.2). Other kinds of dominance relations, however, are associated with the number of menstrual restrictions. When men engage in frequent or endemic warfare, there are more restrictions against menstruating women. The same is true when at least some wives are acquired from hostile groups (see Table 5.3). Such findings confirm the earlier suggestion that the bodily danger faced by men is reproduced in small on the female body. These findings can also be construed to mean that women taken

Table 5.2. *Male dominance (MD) and the number of menstrual taboos (H16)*

Male dominance[a]	Average no. of menstrual taboos[b]	No. of societies[c]
Sexes are equal	2 (2.30)	33
Males display dominance and women exercise power	3 (2.69)	39
Sexes are unequal	3 (2.72)	29

$F = 0.72$, not significant.
[a]This measure of sexual inequality is discussed in Chapter 8 and Appendix F.
[b]Average numbers of menstrual taboos are rounded off. Actual averages are in parentheses.
[c]$N = 101$. No information for 55 societies.

Table 5.3. *Warfare (War), marrying women from hostile groups (Wie), and the number of menstrual taboos (H16)*

	Average no. of menstrual taboos[a]	No. of societies
Warfare or fighting		
Reported as absent or occasional	2 (2.03)	33
Reported as frequent or endemic	3 (2.87)	63
Column total (N)		96[b]
Wives taken from hostile groups		
Reported as present at least for some wives	3 (2.95)	38
Reported as absent	2 (2.31)	59
Column total (N)		97[c]

War: $F = 6.5$, $p = 0.01$; Wie: $F = 3.8$, $p = 0.05$. Appendix B gives reference for War and Wie.
[a]Average numbers are rounded off. Actual averages are given in parentheses.
[b]No information for 60 societies.
[c]No information for 59 societies.

Table 5.4. *Scalp taking (Scal) and the number of menstrual taboos (H16)*

Scalp taking	Average no. of menstrual taboos[a]	No. of societies[b]
Absent	2 (2.49)	55
Incidental	3 (2.92)	12
Active	4 (3.86)	7

$F = 2.65$, $p = 0.08$. Appendix B gives reference for Scal.
[a]Average numbers of menstrual taboos are rounded off. Actual averages are in parentheses.
[b]$N = 74$. No information for 82 societies.

for wives in dangerous territories are believed to carry the danger with them.

Regarding the argument that menstrual restrictions express a symmetry between male and female, it is interesting to note that there are more menstrual taboos in societies where scalping is actively pursued by men (see Table 5.4). This suggests that taking scalps can indeed be likened to menstruation, as was suggested in the case of the Papago (see Chapter 2). Papago men adopt scalps as their children and use them as fertility symbols. The scalp's power is treated in much the same way that people treat the power inherent in menstrual blood. It is reasonable to suggest in such cases that blood is the tie that binds the childbearing woman to the "ripe" man who has acquired a scalp.

When men go to war they are engaged in the task of acquiring something for society, as women give something when they bear children. Male behavior, such as that described for the Papago scalpseeker, should not be interpreted as motivated by "womb envy."[57] As Mary Douglas suggests for the Hadza, the observance of similar taboos by male and female or the imposition of male or female rhythms on members of the opposite sex provides a visible bond between father and mother, husband and wife. Such bonds and practices also establish a balance between life-giving and life-taking forces.

To complete this discussion, we can consider beliefs regarding pollution of sexual intercourse. In some societies men avoid sexual contact with women because they believe that female genitals are dangerous. Such beliefs help people to regulate their universe by enforcing sexual repression during times of scarcity. For example, the Lele were observed by Mary Douglas to ban sexual intercourse as part of a fertility ritual performed during the dry season of 1953, when hunting failures were common and tension ran high. The ritual was specifically performed to bring animals to the hunters' arrows. Part of the ritual included the announcement that the village was "tied," which meant that sexual intercourse was banned until the ritual was completed with a successful hunt.[58]

Sexual repression in reaction to a diminishing food supply is common in tribal societies. When the food supply is low and stomachs are tight, people either resort to practices like those described by Mary Douglas for the Lele or they surround sexuality with danger. The relationship between a fluctuating food supply and sexual pollution beliefs shown in Table 5.5 suggests that people conserve sexual energy in societies where the food supply is uncertain. Sexual repression curtails the expenditure of inner energy when outer sources of replenishment are unreliable. Belief in the contaminating powers of women, of course, limits human reproduction. As Shirley Lindenbaum says, "Fear of pollution is a form of ideological birth control." Such fears often decline with the introduction of new technology and food sources.[59]

Male and female worlds

Sexual segregation or integration is tied to environmental circumstances or to fear. When people live in an environment where the energy vital to human survival is constant and responsive to human needs, they attribute life-giving qualities to women and to the supernatural. There is no sense of danger attached to sexuality or to menstruation. The Mbuti sing to their forest and the forest provides them with food and shelter. The Mbuti girl's first menstrual period is treated as a time of rejoicing and flirtation rather than as a time for segregation and the observance of strict taboos. The Semang (see Chapter 1) respond to the god of thunder and lightning by throwing their blood against the wind. This blood is poured into the umbels of the fruit tree to make the fruit grow. The Andamanese also attach mainly positive connotations to the

Table 5.5. *Average number of sexual pollution beliefs (A11) and nature of the food supply (Sub 13)*

Nature of the food supply	Average no. of sexual pollution beliefs[a]	No. of societies[b]
Food supply is constant	1 (0.9)	27
Food supply fluctuates but storage techniques insure against periods of famine	1 (1.2)	58
Food supply fluctuates and no storage techniques insure against famine	2 (1.5)	26

$F = 3.2$, $p = 0.05$. Appendix B gives reference for Sub 13.
[a]Based on counting presence of following beliefs: 1) sexual intercourse is prohibited during menstruation; 2) sexual intercourse is considered polluting to males (at times other than during a woman's menstrual period); 3) men avoid or fear female genitals. Average numbers of sexual pollution beliefs are rounded off. Actual averages are in parentheses.
[b]$N = 111$. No information for 45 societies.

sources of energy. In these groups blood is more a source of life than a harbinger of death.

Nature was bountiful for the Bellacoola but not constant. The Bellacoola depended on the river and its fluctuating supply of fish to support a relatively large population. The power of menstrual blood came first on their ideological power scale. Menstrual power could neutralize the supernatural and vanquish the power that supplied food in nature. Thus, menstrual blood was perceived as needing to be controlled, so that it would not destroy unwittingly. Controlling the power inherent in menstrual blood meant that women were separated from men and from the main source for food. In such a way the Bellacoola relieved their sense of human vulnerability in the face of superior forces.

Sexual separation for whatever reason creates two worlds – one male and one female – each consisting of a system of meanings and a program for behavior, almost like separate and distinct cultures. The male world focuses on such exclusively male activities as war-

109

fare and hunting and is supported by an ideology that projects power outward onto those aspects of nature and supernature that men follow – the stars, the sky, animals, otiose deities. The female world focuses on such exclusively female activities as childbirth and food gathering and is supported by an ideology that projects power inward onto those aspects of nature and supernature that contribute to growth – the earth, the water, the female creator, nature deities.

Sexual inequality is irrelevant in societies in which these two worlds are balanced. Sexual inequality becomes relevant when one world expands and the other fades away. Not surprisingly, given the evolution of technology and the global expansion of the male-oriented Western world, the past several centuries have seen the fading of the female world and the ascendancy of the male world in many tribal societies. How and why this happens is the subject of the chapters in the next section.

PART III

The women's world

My child, the obi is the head of the men, and I am the head of the women. I and my cabinet represent the women in any important town gatherings and deliberations. If decisions arrived at are such that the womenfolk are to be told about them, I get a woman to sound the gong to assemble the women. On less important occasions, my cabinet members pass the word around among the women by word of mouth.

> Igbo female monarch speaking to Kamene
> Okonjo, a sociologist

We are not so happy as we were before. . . Our grievance is that the land is changed – we are all dying.

> Igbo women speaking to British colonial
> officials

6 · The bases for female political and economic power and authority

Until recently, the prevailing consensus among anthropologists was that male dominance is universal. It has been noted, for example, "that all contemporary societies are to some extent male-dominated," and that "sexual asymmetry is presently a universal fact of human social life."[1] The more extreme expression of this underlying premise contends that "male supremacism" is "well-nigh universal" and "not a shred of evidence, historical or contemporary, supports the existence of a single society in which women controlled the political and economic lives of men."[2]

This consensus is a reaction to the nineteenth-century argument proposed by Johann Bachofen and Lewis Henry Morgan that there was a time in human cultural evolution when women ruled. Bachofen based his beliefs on archeological remains indicating the importance of female goddesses and queens and on the mythology of ancient civilizations in which females were depicted as powerful. Morgan based his argument on his knowledge of societies like the Iroquois where, he argued, women were in charge of the economic arena, descent was reckoned through women (called *matriliny*), and women played a crucial role in ritual and political activities.

Because the matriarchy theory has been resurrected as a historical fact by contemporary feminists, anthropologists have searched for societies "in which women have publicly recognized power and authority surpassing that of men."[3] Finding no society in which women occupy the main positions of leadership, anthropologists argue that male dominance is universal.

There is a certain bias to this point of view, a bias that is understandable given the Western equation of dominance with public leadership. By defining dominance differently, one can show that in many societies male leadership is balanced by female authority. For example, among the Ashanti, Iroquois, and Dahomeans, al-

113

though women were not as visible as men in external public affairs, their right to veto male actions suggests a bipartite system of checks and balances in which neither sex dominated the other. Alice Schlegel makes this point when she notes that the power of Iroquois women to make or replace political appointments, to veto warfare, and to control appropriations is "like many of the powers vested in contemporary positions of centralized authority, from the United States presidency on down to the local level!"[4] Karen Sacks adds that to view male and female authority in societies like that of the Iroquois as unequal rather than different reflects a "state bias" in Western anthropological interpretation of prestate politics.[5]

The chapters of this section examine the bases for female political and economic power or authority. Power refers to "the ability to act effectively on persons or things, to take or secure favourable decisions which are not of right allocated to the individuals or their roles." Authority is defined as "the right to make a particular decision and to command obedience."[6] Economic power or authority refers to the ability or right to control the distribution of goods, food, or services beyond the household level. Political power or authority refers to the ability or right to control or influence group decision making, including the assignment of leadership roles beyond the household level.

Females *achieve* economic and political power or authority when environmental or historical circumstances grant them economic autonomy and make men dependent on female activities. Female economic and political power or authority is *ascribed* as a natural right due the female sex when a long-standing magico-religious association between maternity and fertility of the soil associates women with social continuity and the social good. The rights and duties attached to this emphasis give women formal power and control at the local level as well as the right to influence male actions and decision making beyond the local level. Male power and authority, on the other hand, is part of the social and ritual equation of hunting, warfare, fertility, social continuity, and the social good. The rights and duties associated with this emphasis give men formal power and control at the local and nonlocal levels. These rights and duties, however, do not necessarily exclude women from the realm of control.

Bases for female power and authority

The ascribed bases for female economic and political authority

Irrespective of cultural configuration, of the ascribed or achieved bases for female power, women rarely hold the focal leadership roles. Women either delegate leadership positions to the men they select or such positions are assigned by men alone. In those cases where women delegate such authority, they retain the power to veto the actions of those they have selected. A question frequently asked of anthropologists is why women would choose to delegate leadership rather than seize such authority for themselves.

The answer lies in the proposition, presented in Chapter 4, that it is more efficient for women to delegate than to monopolize power. Since women are the potential bearers of new additions to the population, it would scarcely be expedient to place them on the front line at the hunt and in warfare. In addition, there are such questions as: What would there be for men to do if women hunted, warred, or ruled? How would men acquire the "reason for being" that comes to women automatically? In certain sectors of our own society and others, these questions are easily answered: Men gamble. Because men must sometimes gamble with their lives, power and prestige are the incentive that motivates them to hunt and defend territory and are the reward for being very nearly expendable in terms of the group's ultimate survival.

In many societies, as bearers of children and nurturers of plant life, women occupy a focal position in the realm of final authority. "Whether the male chief is big or small," say the women of a West African female solidarity group, "what matters is that he was given birth by a woman."[7] Such women protest a chief's action by treating him like a child. They either rely on shame or ridicule to get their way or, if pushed to an extreme, will march scantily clad with bared breasts while men stand by in a state of embarrassed silence and passivity, as if they had been overcome by a superior military force. This strategy can only be employed successfully among peoples who believe in the power and invincibility of womanhood.

The power and invincibility of womanhood underlies the operation of the "women's world" in West African dual-sex political systems. The importance of this world in the governance of everyday life is illustrated in the following statement made by the *omu* ("mother") of one of the Igbo political units in midwestern Nigeria mentioned in Chapter 4. In an interview with the *omu,* or Obamkpa, Kamene Okonjo asked, "Our Mother, what part do you play in the running of this town?" She replied:

My child, the *obi* is the head of the men, and I am the head of the women. I and my cabinet represent the women in any important town gatherings and deliberations. If decisions arrived at are such that the womenfolk are to be told about them, I get a woman *(onye oga)* to sound the gong *(ekwe)* to assemble the women. On less important occasions, my cabinet members pass the word around among the women by word of mouth.

If there is drought, we curse whoever caused it. If there is sickness and people are dying, my cabinet goes naked in the night with live brands to curse whoever brought it. If there is sickness in the next town, I do something with my cabinet to insure that sickness does not enter this town. There are medicines we make at the entrance to the town. These are just a few of my duties. I am the mother of the people, you know, and I have to insure in any way I can that they enjoy continued good health and happiness.[8]

In dual-sex political systems like Obamkpa each sex has its own autonomous sphere of authority and an area of shared responsibility. The relationships of the greatest solidarity are among men and among women. In other societies the village-level relationships of the greatest solidarity are among women or among persons related through women. Societies in which the primary solidarity relations involve women are frequently referred to as *matrifocal.* Comparing matrifocal societies in Southeast Asia, Nancy Tanner finds a commonality in the female role. Women are generally the producers and control economic resources. Kinswomen are in frequent contact through mutual aid groups. Women are decision makers and are at least as assertive as men. In all cases, women occupy central kin positions. The role of "mother" is ritually elaborated and is more important than the role of wife. Although the financial contribution of men, be they husbands, brothers, or sons, is important, women can effectively support and care for their children with very little input from men.[9]

The most persistent male–female bond in matrifocal societies is between mother and son. Sons are welcomed when they return from their external pursuits, but husbands are barely tolerated. Among the Atjehnese of Sumatra, Tanner says, husbands and fa-

116

thers do not figure in women's image of the hereafter. Paradise is thought of as a place of abundance where women are reunited with their children and mothers.[10] In another Sumatran society (the Minangkabau), Tanner notes that heaven is thought to be beneath the sole of a mother's foot. The mythical queen mother of this group is referred to by a term that, literally translated, means "Own Mother." Her importance is celebrated in women's ceremonial dress, in weddings, and in parades. She had no husband, and her brother is not mentioned; her son, however, plays an important role in the tales about her.[11]

The importance of women in the Seneca origin myth and their centrality in Iroquoian ritual, economic, and political affairs were noted in Chapter 1. During the two centuries of the Colonial period, Anthony F. C. Wallace says, the Iroquois were a population divided into two parts: sedentary females and nomadic males. The men were absent in small or large groups for months or even years on hunting, trading, war, and diplomatic expeditions. Although their activities were peripheral to the village affairs (which women largely ran), men were responsible for the economic and political welfare of the Six Nations.[12]

Iroquoian female power was part of a centuries-old tradition – based first on custom and later codified in the Constitution of the Five Nations – in which women were officially proclaimed the progenitors of the people and the owners of the land and the soil. Although they bore a resemblance to the Hebrew tribes in the minds of early missionaries, the Iroquois were not a migrating people; they did not move en masse from one territory to another. For centuries they remained settled in the general area where they first cultivated what they called "the three sisters" (corn, beans, and squash). The power of women and their title to the land evolved naturally from cultural circumstances in which wandering men followed game and stationary women developed early agriculture.

During the early Colonial period, the Iroquois could be described as matrifocal at the village level and patrifocal at the level of League and intervillage affairs. Before the establishment of the League and the tribal units that united to form the League, the Iroquois could perhaps be described as matriarchal, if this term is redefined to mean female economic and ritual centrality and not female rule. Archeological excavations of pre-Iroquoian village

117

sites show that they were unfortified, suggesting that if there was an emphasis on warfare, it lacked major economic motivation, and conquest was an unknown objective. In these sites, horticulture clearly takes precedence over fishing and hunting, which would have been male activities. Houses contained several hearths and appeared to be early prototypes of the longhouse, in which families related through women lived. One can infer from this evidence that the village was the primary sociopolitical unit and that matrifocality superseded patrifocality.[13]

When matrifocal activities override the importance of male activities and correspond to the largest sociopolitical unit, the use of the term *matriarchy* is appropriate in order to signify the greater importance of females. The evidence for the primacy of matrifocality among some of the prehistoric Iroquoian ethnic units is strong. The same possibility is posed by the peripherality of the male in the Southeast Asian societies mentioned previously. Unfortunately, in these cases and in so many others where female economic and ritual centrality is evident, we do not have the archeological evidence that would allow for the reconstruction of prehistoric patterns showing that the primary domain of influence may have once coincided with a group of economically self-sufficient women. If prior matriarchies did exist, they were probably a consequence of the evolution of plant domestication from the plant-gathering activities of women. This would have given women economic and ritual centrality and, hence, a primary voice in decision making.

As with the Iroquois, the position of Ashanti women can be traced to a long-standing ritual tie with the soil, which may have been based on indigenous early farming. The basis of the Ashanti regard for women (described in Chapter 1) can be seen in their ritual interconnection of earth–life–ancestors–blood–females. The Ashanti believe that the lineage – and the clan that incorporates several lineages – is synonymous with blood and that only women can transmit blood to descendants.[14] It is said that some Ashanti originated from the earth. The earth is believed to be filled with the spirits of the departed forebearers of the clan. These spirits are thought to be the real landowners, who still continue to take a lively interest in the land from which they had their origin or that they once owned. The Golden Stool (the male symbol of leadership), which is believed to have originated from the sky, cannot come into direct contact with the earth; it is always placed upon an elephant's skin. The feet of the king of Ashanti can never touch the ground, "lest a great famine should come upon the nation." He is always followed by a servant bearing a spare pair of sandals, in case the band across the instep of those he is wearing breaks.[15]

There is a sacred grove in a forest that is marked as the most hallowed spot in all Ashanti territory. At this spot, it is said, some clan forebearers belonging to certain ruling clans "came forth from the ground, and settling near by, increased and multiplied, learned to use fire and other arts, till eventually, compelled by increasing numbers, they scattered and became the clan or 'blood' from which the rulers of the united nation later chose their kings and queens."[16] Near this spot there are a number of mounds containing "ancient pottery" and "neolithic instruments." R. S. Rattray says that the whole of this area must "at some remote period, have been the site of a great settlement, larger by far than any Ashanti towns or villages of the present day." The names of the people supposed to have come from the ground of the sacred grove were given to Rattray by the Queen Mother. Some of them are the forebearers of the royal Oyoko clan. The notion that the forebearers of certain clans came forth out of a hole in the ground is a belief in many parts of Ashanti. Rattray thinks that the Ashanti adopted these beliefs from an indigenous people, because the Ashanti "are a people from the North and not the indigenous inhabitants of the country they now occupy."[17]

If the Ashanti did come from another land, they did so long ago, probably in a series of uncoordinated movements of related groups of people in response to the introduction, via maritime trade with the Americas, of new food crops.[18] Yams play an important part in Ashanti ritual and daily diet. Yams could have been introduced from the Americas or domesticated in West Africa.[19] Whether or not the Ashanti acquired yams or participated in the cultural tradition responsible for their domestication, all the evidence suggests an ancient tradition of farming. This tradition may account for their deification of the earth; or the personification of the earth may have been the motivation for domesticating plants. If people believe, as the Ashanti do, that the earth is the repository and the origin of their important ancestral spirits, they are likely to pay more attention to products of the earth.

To conclude, the ascribed basis for female power and authority in the secular domain is found in a ritual orientation to plants, the earth, maternity, and fertility. This orientation is probably part of a historical tradition that began when the detailed knowledge of wild plants led to simple farming. More than likely, women were responsible for this development. Dorothy Hammond and Alta Jablow say that there is little doubt that farming in the form of horticulture developed from the practice of gathering, and therefore it was the invention of women.[20] The invention of domestication undoubtedly gave women the right to control the fruits of their efforts just as men controlled the product of the hunt.

Peoples who carried their crops with them as they emigrated or who remained in an area where their ancestresses first experimented with plant domestication probably maintained the web of meanings that mediate female social and ritual authority. To break the equation of maternity with fertility of the soil would, in the minds of such peoples, threaten the wellspring of plant and human life. Maternity and fertility of the soil are equated because as women bring forth new life from their bodies, plants burst forth from the earth. The earth spirit is female; certain crops are revered and associated with children or women. It is said in some societies, for example, that yams are "like women, they give birth to children."[21] Yams are used in much of Ashanti ritual. Before tilling the soil, a farmer offers mashed yams sprinkled with the blood of a fowl to the earth spirit. Like the Ashanti, the Iroquois respected and revered the female virtues of food provision and the fertility of the earth, especially for corn, a crop that the Iroquois grew early in their culture history. In both societies, female secular power and authority are inseparable from the system of meanings in which the past is tied to the present, and the sources of life are tied to the reproductive and productive functions of women.

The case of the Abipon: female power and the hunter/warrior
configuration

It would be misleading to assume that female economic and political rights are based solely on female social and ritual principles like those described in the previous section. In many societies it is clear that female influence is based on a sexual division of labor that gives women access to rights and duties and brings them economic self-sufficiency. Often, in these cases, men are absent for long periods engaged in hunting, warfare, trading, or migrant labor. In the absence of males, the regulation and conduct of local affairs may be in the hands of women.

The Abipon represent one of the most striking examples of female power in the face of male absence. While men hunted and warred, Abipon women did most of the work.[22] Women were also almost solely responsible for the rites of propitiation involving the Abipon celestial supreme being called "Grandfather." The Abipon deserve attention not just because they exemplify female power in an outer-oriented society. Our knowledge of the Abipon comes largely from the work of Martin Dobrizhoffer, a Jesuit missionary who lived among them from 1750 to 1762. His book, published in 1784, is described as "one of the most famous monographs ever written on any South American tribe."[23] Thus, Dobrizhoffer's description affords a rare glimpse of tribal life before prolonged European contact.

The Abipon were one of many aboriginal tribes of the Gran Chaco, a vast plain in the center of the South American continent between the fringe of the Matto Grosso Plateau and the Argentine Pampa. This area is described as depressed, a dry country hardly suitable for human settlement were it not for the lagoons and water holes scattered throughout.[24] The Spanish settled in the area during the sixteenth century, not because it had any special appeal, but because it was on the route leading to the silver and gold of western South America. For the Indians, the most important consequence of this contact was the introduction of the horse.

The Abipon may have been the first Chaco Indians to turn equestrian.[25] Acquisition of the horse enabled them to fight the Spaniards on an equal footing. It also changed the aboriginal economy. Agriculture was abandoned and the Indians became expert cattle, sheep, and horse raiders. The Abipon stole thousands of cattle and horses from Spanish ranches. Dobrizhoffer reports that from some raids a warrior would come back with at least 400 horses, and that 100,000 horses were captured by the Abipon within about 50 years.[26]

Warfare and hunting consumed the lives of men. They were as successful in killing Spaniards, taking heads, scalping, or capturing slaves as they were at acquiring horses. They eluded Spanish retaliation because they were continually moving from place to

121

place. Competition was evident and there were clear distinctions between superior and lesser sorts. Dobrizhoffer refers to noblemen and noblewomen. Personal ornamentation signified distinctions in wealth. Men wore necklaces, women tattooed their faces, breasts, and arms. The number and variety of tattoo patterns indicated a woman's status. A woman with only three or four black lines on her face was either a captive or of low birth.[27] Their wealth, social distinctions, and warlike nature might suggest that the Abipon would treat women as chattel, as did other equestrian societies described in the nineteenth century. For example Hoebel, who reconstructs the life of the equestrian Comanche in 1870, writes that women, horses, and dogs were classified as private property.[28] This was emphatically not so with the Abipon. Abipon women were neither subordinated nor considered inferior. They were fierce, dominant, and, in their own sphere, as aggressive and competitive as were Abipon men.

The activities of Abipon men and women usually did not overlap, except in the ritual sphere, where women were perhaps more important than men. Females were powerful both collectively and individually. In a vivid description of the cooperative work of the female collective, Dobrizhoffer says:

Above a hundred women often go out to distant plains together to collect various fruits, roots, colours, and other useful things, and remain four or eight days in the country, without having any male to accompany them on their journey, assist them in their labours, take care of the horses, or guard them amidst the perils of wild beasts, or of enemies. Those amazons are sufficient to themselves, and think they are safer alone. I never heard of a single woman being torn to pieces by a tiger, or bitten by a serpent, but I knew many men who were killed in both ways.[29]

Although they frequently operated as a collective, this did not prevent women from engaging in bloody battles among themselves. A quarrel between two women or two sets of women who had independently arrived at separate decisions about certain events could degenerate into a blood bath in which all women participated. Men stood by, calmly watching these fights without interfering, because this was women's way.[30] Women would also, at times, inflict their blows on men and engage in ceremonial wrestling with other women. After a chief's son was born, the strongest woman in the camp would lead a group of girls in whipping all the men. The same strong woman would challenge all the "stout women" to wrestle.[31]

Dobrizhoffer uses the term *horde* to designate the group of families following a *cacique* or chief. A horde consisted of extended families, any group of which might leave a horde whenever it suited them to join some other chief. A chief was usually a man judged to be properly noble and warlike. His main task was to be the war leader. The position could be inherited or achieved through skill and valor. Females could and did become chiefs. Dobrizhoffer remarks:

I must not omit to mention that the Abipones do not scorn to be governed by women of noble birth; for at the time I resided in Paraguay, there was a highborn matron, to whom the Abipones gave the title Nela-reycate, and who numbered some families in her horde. Her origin, and the merits of her ancestors, procured her the veneration of others.[32]

Since families could break away from a horde and join another whenever they chose, it would appear that the "chief" was not powerful in the sense of controlling the actions of others. Much more influential were the "jugglers" (shamans). They were believed to have innumerable powers – to inflict disease and death, cure, forsee the future, cause rain and tempests, call up the spirits of the dead, change into a "tiger," and handle snakes. Their power was acquired in a vision quest from a supernatural relative, or sky-being, called "Grandfather," who was associated with the Pleiades. Jugglers accompanied all hunting and war expeditions. They advised on where to hunt and how to conduct a battle.[33] A juggler could be of either sex, but females may have outnumbered males. Dobrizhoffer, at least, seemed quite impressed with the number of female jugglers: He says that they "abound to such a degree, that they almost outnumber the gnats of Egypt."[34]

Female jugglers formed groups, often led by an old woman. Their major task was to consult the "evil spirit," take charge of certain ceremonies in connection with "Grandfather," and conduct all mourning ceremonies. The highest-ranking female juggler was responsible for inaugurating a new chief. A female juggler was in charge of the ceremony that welcomed the Pleiades back when this constellation became visible in the southern sky during the month of May. It was believed that when the Pleiades

123

could not be seen it was because "Grandfather" was sick. During the welcoming ceremony an old woman danced with a gourd rattle while "military trumpets" blared at intervals. She rubbed the thighs of some men with her gourds, and in the name of "Grandfather" promised them swiftness in hunting and warfare.[35]

It is not known what happened to the Abipon. In 1750 Dobrizhoffer says they numbered about 5,000. In 1767 they had been reduced to 2,000. According to Metraux, after the expulsion of the Jesuits the Abipon disappeared and ceased to play any historic role.[36] The advance of the military posts in the Chaco during the nineteenth century restricted their hunting grounds and forced numerous bands into submission. Many were slaughtered and others were absorbed into the Creole population.[37]

The achieved bases for female economic and political power

In foraging societies like that of the Abipon, women achieve power when social survival rests on their economic self-sufficiency as well as on the hunting activities of men. Although hunting is the most prestigious activity in these cases, the gathering activities of women often supply the bulk of the food. In addition, hunting success may depend on the knowledge women supply of the whereabouts of animals.

For example, Patricia Draper, who accompanied !Kung women of the Kalahari Desert in Africa on gathering expeditions, describes the dependence of male hunters on the information women bring back about the "state of the bush." Although !Kung women do not hunt, they act as intelligence agents for the men. If on a gathering expedition women discover fresh tracks, they send an older child to deliver the report to the men in camp. Since women are skilled in reading the signs of the bush, upon their return to camp, men query them about evidence of game movements, the age of animal tracks they may have encountered, the location of water, and the like.

All !Kung agree that meat is the most desirable and most prestigious food. But the hunters cannot always provide it, and the vegetable food gathered by women is the staple, contributing about 60% to 80% of the daily food intake by weight. In addition to demonstrating how important women's gathering activities are to male hunting, Draper challenges the common point of view that gathering is a monotonous routine requiring no more than sub-normal intelligence. Successful gathering among the !Kung involves the ability to discriminate among hundreds of edible and inedible species of plants at various stages of growth. This kind of intelligence is fully as important to !Kung survival as the physical strength, dexterity, and endurance required for success in hunting.[38]

The foraging !Kung are described by Draper as sexually egalitarian. Draper says that !Kung females are autonomous and participate in group decisions because they do not need the assistance of men at any stage in the production of gathered foods. Nor do they need the permission of men to use any natural resources entering into this production. !Kung men and women live in a public world, sleeping and eating in a small circular clearing, within which all activities are visible. There are inherited positions, such as the "headman," among the !Kung, but these are said to be essentially empty of behavioral content.[39]

There are many similar examples of the self-sufficiency and autonomy of women in foraging societies. In some cases, women take over the hunting activities of men. Descriptions of female hunting in several North American Indian societies have been provided by Regina Flannery, Ruth Landes, and Louise Spindler. In the cases cited by them, certain females adopted "masculine styles" that they learned from men and performed out of necessity. When she lived among the Eastern Cree of the James Bay region of Canada during the summers of 1933 and 1935, Regina Flannery came to know several old women reputed to have been excellent hunters in the old days. They hunted either because of the illness or death of their male relatives or, as the women said but no man ever admitted, because of "just plain incompetence of the men at hunting."[40] While living among the Mescalero Apache in the mountains of southeastern New Mexico, Flannery was told by a "shriveled-up, decrepit old woman" that in the past "young married women might go hunting with their husbands, not merely to accompany them, but actually to take part in the chase." Flannery found it hard to believe that such a woman "was once active and skilled enough to rope a buffalo, wind the rope around a tree, and kill the animal with an axe." However, she received corroborating information from others that in the past this was not an uncommon feat for women who, if they needed food, would kill whatever animals they came upon.[41]

Ruth Landes and Louise Spindler were informed about similar customs by Ojibwa and Menomini women. Landes describes Ojibwa women who, learning the appropriate skills from male relatives, became successful hunters and trappers.[42] Spindler says that in aboriginal Menomini culture, "a woman who fished well, raced well, hunted well, or danced like a man was highly respected." She refers to such a woman as a deviant who chose to "perform a wide range of male activities which might appeal to her" rather than to stay "at home, performing women's tasks, and listening by the hour to the tales of her grandmother." In recent years, she adds, women have continued to fill male roles, such as judge, advisory council members, political offices, and consultants in the mill office.[43] Thus, these North American Indian women are depicted as having deviated from the feminine lifestyle to adopt the masculine style. They do so largely for pragmatic reasons, and some women achieve great success in the male role.

In more advanced, agricultural societies, female trading activities have provided women with economic autonomy and, in some cases, with a significant power base. Women traders predominate in West Africa, the non-Hispanic Caribbean, and parts of mainland Latin America. Ester Boserup suggests an association between female farming and female trade. She says that where market trade is dominated by men, men do most of the agricultural work. On the other hand, she says, "where women are actively engaged in producing the crops, and particularly when they are farmers on their own account, they also take the crops to the market where they may also sell articles which they have not produced themselves."[44]

Many exceptions to this generalization can be cited. Boserup notes that Vietnamese men regard trade as debasing for men and think that women are more economical and thrifty. Philippine men regard themselves as being too sensitive for the coarse language and aggressive behavior necessary in trading activities and let their wives handle small-scale market trade, leaving large-scale trade to foreigners.[45]

In a survey of the role of women as traders, Sidney Mintz notes that who trades may be related to "civil security" and to which sex produces the marketable commodity. For example, Afikpo Igbo women, who unlike Igbo women of midwestern Nigeria do not

126

enjoy equal status with men, are discouraged from engaging in long-distance trade due to lack of "civil security." Afikpo Igbo men engage in long-distance trade, leaving women to run the internal market system in which they market their agricultural produce.

An important economic innovation, increasing the capacity of Afikpo Igbo women to deal as equals with men, was the introduction of cassava processing and cultivation, apparently from Yoruba groups of Western Nigeria. Since men would only grow yams, and all other crops were cultivated by women, cassava cultivation fell to women. Men rejected cassava cultivation as beneath them. Control over the production and marketing of cassava, which gained rapid acceptance as a subsistence crop, became a major source of economic independence for women. Mintz cites Ottenberg, who comments on the reaction of women to cassava cultivation:

Nowadays women do not care if the husband does not give them any food, for they can go to the farm and get cassava. If a woman has any money she buys [rents] land and plants cassava. The year after she does this she can have a crop for cassava meal, which she can sell and have her own money. Then she can say, "What is man? I have my own money!"[46]

Thus, female trading activities may be inspired by events surrounding Europeanization. In a lengthy description of Haitian marketing, which is monopolized by women, Mintz suggests that Haitian women took over marketing because men were in danger of conscription by Haiti's military regimes after independence in 1804. At least as important, he remarks, was the gradual accumulation of land by an expanding peasantry and the concentration of males in agricultural production. The acquisition of land may have been "land enough to free women from cultivation but not land enough to produce a yield sufficiently large to make it profitable for the peasant cultivator to go regularly to market himself."[47]

Full-time Haitian market women are not restricted by familial obligations or by rigid patterns of male authority. Many Haitian market women are single or live in common-law relationships that permit them maximum mobility. These women are nomadic and their husbands remain sedentary. Many of the most active rural trading women are away from their homes for 4 days in 7. It has been said "that some Haitian farmers are left at such a loss by their marketer wives' absence that they 'fast stoically for two or three days' until their spouses return.''[48] Though market women may use their profits to help their husbands' agricultural efforts, Mintz says that these husbands have no recognized claim on their wives' capital.[49]

To conclude, female economic power is sometimes a result of a sexual division of labor in which women achieve self-sufficiency and establish an independent control sphere. This sphere need not be supported or legitimized by a system of magico-religious or legal titles. However, in the absence of such titles, female power is more vulnerable to change. This can be seen in female trading, especially in the face of "Westernization." Mintz notes that the traditional predominance of female traders in Africa, for example, is threatened by the opportunities available to men to expand commercial activities in the European economy and by the exclusion of women from export commodity activity.[50] Similarly, in Haiti there are upper limits to the expansion of female trading activities because the larger Haitian economy is male dominated and controlled, giving women little or no opportunity to reinvest their capital in new forms of production.[51] The effects of Western culture on the public power and authority of tribal women are examined in more detail in the next chapter.

The ascribed and achieved bases for female public power and authority and increasing technological complexity

The previous discussion of the bases for female economic and political power and authority can be related to the cultural configurations described in Chapters 3 and 4. In these chapters the discussion focused on environmental circumstances leading to an inner/plant as opposed to an outer/animal cultural configuration. Feminine or couple origin symbolism was associated with plant economies, whereas masculine symbolism was associated with animal economies. Since feminine symbolic principles are more evident in plant than in animal economies, we would expect a corresponding greater representation of women in the secular power activities of plant economies.

This expectation is supported by the data presented in Table 6.1. Females wield political and economic power in a higher proportion of plant than animal economies. The data presented in

Table 6.1 show, however, that in the more advanced plant economies females are less likely to wield such power, just as feminine
origin symbolism is less likely to be represented in these economies, as was shown in Chapter 3 (see Table 3.5). Thus, technological complexity appears to inhibit the expression of feminine political, economic, and symbolic power.

These facts can be interpreted in several ways. First, there is
Eleanor Leacock's argument that in foraging and precolonial simple agricultural societies, the sexes were equal and women
functioned publicly in making economic and social decisions.
Drawing on propositions advanced by Engels, Leacock argues
that with increased technological specialization, production for
consumption changes to production of commodities for exchange. The latter form of production, she says, takes the direct
control of produce out of the hands of the producers and creates
new economic ties that undermine the collectivity of joint households. Women lose control of their production because they are
relegated to individual households, where they become the private
dispensers of services and producers of children. This process,
Leacock says, was thwarted where women "were organized to
maintain and protect their rights."[52]

Confining her discussion to Africa, Ester Boserup presents a
similar argument in saying that the simultaneous introduction by
Europeans of intensive agricultural techniques and cash crops undermined traditional female farming and, hence, female control of
production. Although women continued to cultivate food crops in
some societies, Boserup says, this activity was no longer accorded
the same social significance. The prestige of men was enhanced
because they were introduced to the technology of the colonial
society and became the intermediaries between the old and the
new traditions. Where men were recruited into industry and
women remained the primary producers for village households,
female production did not necessarily mean female economic
power. As men became more dependent on the colonial economy,
women, in turn, became more dependent on men. Thus, as Kay
Martin and Barbara Voorhies say in their summary of Boserup's
argument, "As males begin to consistently exchange goods and
services for part or all of the domestic necessities, the cultivative
labor of women diminishes in scope and importance."[53]

130

Table 6.1. *Relationship between female economic and political power or authority (Stata) and type of subsistence economy (Econ)*

Subsistence mode	Females have no economic or political power or authority (scale score 1-4)		Females have economic power or authority (scale score 5)		Females have political and economic power or authority (scale score 6-7)		Row totals	
	N	%	N	%	N	%	N	%
Animal economies								
Hunting	3	27	4	36	4	36	11	99
Animal husbandry	5	42	3	25	4	33	12	100
Fishing	2	17	0	0	10	83	12	100
Plant economies								
Gathering	3	25	0	0	9	75	12	100
Semi-intensive agriculture (fruit trees and/or vegetable gardens)	4	33	1	8	7	58	12	99
Shifting cultivation of fields	13	34	6	16	19	50	38	100
Advanced agriculture	8	22	9	25	19	53	36	100
Column totals	38 (29%)		23 (17%)		72 (54%)		133[a]	

See appendixes B and E for discussion of the female power (Stata) measure. This measure forms a Guttman scale. Data are given for number (N) and percentage of societies.
[a] No information for 23 societies.

These arguments are compelling and to a large degree correct, as will become evident in the discussion of the effect of colonialism on traditional female power in the next chapter. However, these arguments do not explain why women hold political and economic power or authority in 53% of the advanced agricultural societies (see Table 6.1). Leacock, Boserup, and Martin and Voorhies do not distinguish between the ascribed and achieved bases for female public power. The introduction of cash crops or intensive agricultural techniques surely must have a differential impact on secular female status, depending on whether this status is ascribed or achieved. Where female power is a natural right accorded women and part of a long-standing cultural configuration, it is less likely that technological complexity will greatly undermine the importance of women. In these kinds of societies the organization by women to protect their rights is facilitated by cultural tradition. On the other hand, in societies where women have traditionally achieved power, it is more likely that technological complexity will have the effect described by Leacock and Boserup.

If female power is related to feminine symbolism and in situ cultural development, we can assume that the authority of women is an integral part of the fabric of a people's social identity and, as such, less easily destroyed by colonial influence. If females live in a world where power is determined by might as opposed to right, it seems reasonable to suppose that the outside influence that disturbs the relative access of males and females to scarce or valued resources will have a corresponding effect on the relative balance of power between males and females. In some cases the balance of power may shift in favor of females. This happened in some areas of Africa where the outlawing of warfare by colonial administrations gave women greater opportunity for trade and, hence, access to wealth than their husbands and brothers had.[54] In most cases, however, in the absence of a historical tradition extolling the right of women to control, it is logical to assume that women will lose access to strategic resources in the face of increased technological complexity for the reasons advanced by Leacock and Boserup.

The data of this study support these suggestions. First, Leacock is right that women are more likely to function publicly in making economic and social decisions in foraging than in nonforaging so-

131

Table 6.2. *Relationship between gender origin symbolism (A05)
and female economic and political power or authority (Statb) in
foraging and nonforaging societies*

Origin symbolism	Females have no political power or authority (scale score 1–5)		Females have economic and political power or authority (scale score 6–7)		Row totals (N)
	N	%	N	%	
Foraging societies					
Feminine or couple (1)[a]	2	29	5	36	7
Masculine only (2)	5	71	9	64	14
Column totals	7 (33%)	100	14 (67%)	100	21[b]
Nonforaging societies					
Feminine or couple (1)[a]	12	34	26	68	38
Masculine only (2)	23	66	12	32	35
Column totals	35 (48%)	100	38 (52%)	100	73[b]

Data are given for number (N) and percentage of societies. Foraging societies: Pearson's $R = -0.07$, not significant. Nonforaging societies: Pearson's $R = -0.34$, $p = 0.002$. Numbers in parentheses indicate values used in computing Pearson's R.

[a]Feminine and couple categories are lumped in order to contrast symbolism that includes the feminine with symbolism that does not. See discussion of these categories in Chapter 3.

[b]$N = 94$. No information for 62 societies.

cieties. Women enjoy economic and political power or authority in 67% of the foraging societies of this study as compared with 52% of the nonforaging societies (see Table 6.2). The dimension of symbolism does appear to affect the impact of technological complexity. Among the more technologically advanced nonforagers, women are more likely to hold economic and political power or authority if feminine symbolic principles (in origin stories) are also present (see Table 6.2).

A long and stable association with one place is also important. Women play a more prominent role in societies described either as "aboriginal" to the area or as having "migrated long ago" than

Table 6.3. *Relationship between migration (Mig) and female political power or authority (Statb)*

Reported experience of migration	Females have no political power or authority (scale score 1–5)		Females have economic and political power or authority (scale score 6–7)		Row totals (N)
	N	%	N	%	
People said to be aboriginal to area or to have migrated centuries ago (1)	13	33	31	61	44
People reported as being recent migrants within past 100–150 years, or people labeled as migrating conquerors (2)	27	67	20	39	47
Column totals	40	100	51	100	91[a]

Data are given for number (N) and percentage of societies. Pearson's $R = -0.28$, $p = 0.004$. Appendix B gives reference for Mig.
[a]No information for 65 societies.

they do among peoples believed to be recent migrants to an area (see Table 6.3). Migration clearly has a negative effect on the expression of female power and authority in many societies (see Table 6.3). However, as the following chapters argue, the experience of migration, like technological complexity, has a differential impact on peoples with a tradition of ascribed female power as compared with peoples without such a tradition.

To conclude, women exercise economic and political power in the majority of foraging societies. In gathering and fishing societies especially, women wield secular power. Technological complexity is likely to undermine the political and economic autonomy of women if the traditional sex-role plan does not incorporate feminine symbolic principles. Ancient metaphors for female power give women a basis upon which to organize to protect their rights during social disruption. Sometimes, in the face of unrelenting external pressure, such as that exerted by a male-dominated colonial power, the traditional symbols that define the women's world may fall. As people combat such outside influences, the power of women may disintegrate as new metaphors for sexual identities replace the old. Some examples of the effect of European colonialism on the women's world are presented in the next chapter.

7 · The decline of the women's world: the effect of colonialism

The evidence marshaled by anthropologists showing the effects of Western colonialism on traditional female power and authority is impressive. The work of some writers has led to the conclusion that "the penetration of Western colonialism, and with it Western practices and attitudes regarding women, have so widely influenced women's role in aboriginal societies as to depress women's status almost everywhere in the world."[1] In this chapter two case studies showing the manner in which European influence eroded the bases of traditional female authority are presented.

In one case, the Igbo of southeastern Nigeria, the struggle was between Igbo women and British administrators, with Igbo men playing a passive but supportive role. In the other case, the Iroquois, the struggle was between Iroquoian women and the followers of a charismatic Iroquoian male who, aided by Quaker missionaries, sought to revitalize Iroquoian life and institute a new sex-role plan. In both cases women resisted the forces of change. Igbo female resistance led to the "women's war," in which thousands of women marched against the British and destroyed property. Iroquoian female resistance led to witchcraft accusations, resulting in the execution of some women for following traditional female patterns. The killing and wounding of approximately 100 Igbo women and the token executions among the Iroquois broke the spirit of resistance.

Another, less direct consequence of Western colonialism can be traced to the population movements inspired by Western penetration into tribal territories. These movements had variable results. The introduction of the horse and musketry in the Americas, for example, enabled some foraging and horticultural peoples to turn to the full-scale hunting of buffalo. The evidence in these cases suggests that the balance of power between the sexes changed because of increased dependence on hunting and warfare.

135

Although the introduction of the horse made a new and abundant food source available to some, others faced with the European expansion were not so lucky. Either to escape European domination or because they were pushed by their more powerful and expanding tribal neighbors, some peoples fled into marginal territories, where the scarcity of food forced them to eke out a precarious existence. Although we cannot reconstruct the devolution of female power in these cases, those to be examined suggest a causal relationship between scarce resources and the oppression of women.

The case studies in this chapter highlight the direct and indirect effects of "Westernization" on a people's traditional sex-role plan. By no means offering a complete review of what is known about these effects, the descriptions that follow reveal at least some of the dynamics involved in the development of male dominance, sexual inequality, and the devolution of female power. This is a difficult process to reconstruct fully because of the absence of good historical data. The material presented suggests certain hypotheses that will be applied, in the chapters of the next section, to a more general examination of the development of male dominance and sexual inequality.

The Igbo women's war

In 1929 Igbo women in southern Nigeria staged a riot that involved an area covering 6,000 square miles and touched the lives of 2 million people. Known to Igbo women as "the women's war," the riots (also referred to as the Aba riots) are an example of women mobilizing by the thousands to protect their own interests. The way in which Igbo women acted on this occasion provides us with an example of female resistance to Western colonial practices that disregarded the "women's world."[2]

The Igbo of southern Nigeria are to be distinguished from the western Igbo, described in Chapter 4, who have a constitutional village monarchy and a dual-sex political organization. They are also different from the Afikpo Igbo, mentioned in the last chapter, among whom female status is low. In southern Nigeria female solidarity and mutual support played a conspicuous part in the operation of local village affairs. Sylvia Leith-Ross refers to these women as the economic and political equals of men.[3] Each village and town of the area had a women's council to protect female interests, headed by a spokeswoman known for her wisdom and discretion, who was nominated by consensus. In the smaller villages, all married women attended the council's meetings, which were announced by the spokeswoman, who went "round the village beating two short sticks or a light wooden drum and calling out a short phrase in which she announces the time and place of the next council."[4] All but pregnant women, mothers suckling their babies (because of the noise and distraction), and very old women (who would take no useful part in the discussions) attended the meeting. In large villages or towns where the presence of all married women would make the council too large, spokeswomen from each compound were nominated and attended meetings as representatives of the other women.

Men were not allowed at these meetings, but they approved of them because they understood the women's wish to preserve the peace of the town and because they felt that women had "a greater sense of abstract justice." It was thought that, unlike the men, the women would not be biased by personal prejudice or long-standing feuds when they must decide to mete out punishment for some offense. In the past the councils had both spiritual and temporal power. All rulings were thought to be sanctioned by Ajala, the earth spirit, and could be enforced by "war" or "spoiling" a person's property. This meant corporal punishment, public humiliation through ridicule, or destruction of the offender's property. All punishment was carried out by the women. In addition to its judicial functions in keeping the peace and punishing offenders, the council decided upon sacrifices to be made to Ajala, consulted a diviner about the planting of women's crops, and passed certain "laws" protecting crops from theft or damage by livestock. All such laws "were unquestionably obeyed by the men, as if they recognized that it was both the right and the responsibility of the women to safeguard the fruits of the earth, i.e., of Ajala."[5]

There was no system linking women's councils across villages, districts, or provinces. They were strictly organized to deal with local matters. However, the markets linked women over a wide area in a kind of bush telegraph system. Women visited two or three different markets a week. There they heard the news and gossip of the whole province and sent messages "to right and left, immediately passed on from woman to woman, from one market to another. One hears over and over again the remark: 'I will speak of it in the market.'"[6] These women's councils, women's traditional right to punish offenders by "war" and "spoiling" property, the system of communication, and an overwhelming sense of sisterhood are the keys for understanding the magnitude and vigor of "the women's war."

The women's war began in 1929 in a place called Oloko. The British had recently introduced a system of taxing men and had decided that in order to assess the taxable wealth of all the people, it would be necessary to count women, children, and domestic animals. When Okugo, the chief of Oloko, attempted, under instructions from the local British officer, to count the goats and sheep belonging to Nwanyeruwa, an important woman in the village, she yelled, "Was your mother counted?" at which point they seized each other by the throat. A meeting of women was called, where it was decided to send a palm leaf, the symbol of trouble and a call for help, to all the women in the area. Women poured into Okugo's compound from around the countryside and proceeded to "sit" upon him. To "sit" upon a man is a pidgin English term referring to the punishment inflicted by women on any man who has broken their laws. It has the same meaning as "spoiling" a person's property. The crowd mobbed the chief, damaged his house, demanded his cap of office, and forced the district officer to arrest him and charge him with assault. "The women," said this officer with some embellishment, "numbering over ten thousand, were shouting and yelling round the office in a frenzy. They demanded his cap of office, which I threw to them, and it met the same fate as a fox's carcase thrown to a pack of hounds. The station between the office and the prison . . . resembled Epsom Downs on Derby Day."[7]

Despite assurances from chiefs and administrative officers that women were being counted for purposes other than taxation, the trouble spread to Aba, an important trading center. There some 10,000 women, calling themselves "the trees which bear fruit" and "scantily clothed, girdled with green leaves, carrying sticks," converged upon the town. They attacked and looted the European trading stores and the bank, broke into the prison, and released prisoners. After 2 days of rioting, troops arrived and dispersed the crowds without serious casualties.[8]

The decline of the women's world

In another part of Igbo land crowds of women gathered, be-
decked in the symbols of war. "Dressed in sackcloth, their faces
smeared with charcoal, sticks wreathed with young palms in their
hands, while their heads were bound with young ferns," they
burned the Native Court and sacked and looted the European
store and other property. They declared that the district officer
"was born of a woman, and as they were women they were going
to see him." When the women mobbed police and military
troops, 18 were killed and 19 wounded. In another incident, elsewhere, 32 women were killed and 31 wounded after a mob of
women made threatening and obscene gestures against the troops,
calling them sons of pigs, and striking at the district officer with
their sticks.[9]

The trouble that broke out in early December was under control
by the twentieth day of that month. Igbo men did not participate
in the rioting. With a few exceptions, they acted as passive but
consenting parties to the behavior of their wives.[10] Children were
nowhere in evidence during the riots. The rioting was carried out
solely by adult women, who sent round the palm leaves to rally
their comrades and beat the drums to convey the message of war,
just as the drums are sounded to announce a council meeting. Un-
willing women were forced to join. One woman, whose daughter-in-law was killed during the rioting, testified as follows:

We met a crowd of women heading to Utu-Etim-Ekpo. The women
stopped us. There were plenty too much women, a very large crowd.
They were coming along the road and beating their laps and lifting their
heads towards the sky and waving their sticks. All had sticks; big sticks. I
was afraid of them. They took away my basket and forced me to join
them . . . "You are a woman, you must join us." They looked quite
different from any other crowd of women I have ever seen. They had
nkpatat (wild fern) round their heads. There were no children with them.
As they had no children with them that also made me afraid. I do not
know where any of the women came from. I was very much afraid of
them and did not look at their faces.[11]

The riots were a testimony to the vigor and solidarity of Igbo
women. Although the threat of taxation was the immediate cause,
they were really fighting to preserve "the spirit of womanhood."
Speaking to the subsequent Commission of Inquiry, the women
said, "We are not so happy as we were before . . . Our grievance

139

is that the land is changed – we are all dying."[12] Taking these words literally, the British did not understand their meaning. In fact, the women were right – their way was dying, their spirit and ties to the land were slowly being crushed by the new ways brought by the Europeans. The power of the women's councils had been eroded by the institution of a Native Court system composed solely of Igbo men. During the riots these courts were sacked and burned in 16 Native Administration centers. When giving evidence, the women "uttered a flood of criticism against the corruption and injustice of the chiefs and courts."[13] The commission promised that the Native Courts would be reorganized to reflect more faithfully the Igbo system of justice, and that women would sit as judges.[14]

In 1934 this promise had not been fulfilled. The women's councils had lost more power because the government forbade the women to "war," which had been their major means of enforcing their rulings. In rising to defend what they called the "women's world," Igbo women lost the women's war. Believing themselves to be inviolable, the women were shocked at the carnage leveled against them. Despite their assertions of being prepared to die, they firmly believed that the soldiers would not fire on women, that they had no bullets, and that women were never killed in war. As rioters, they compared themselves to vultures, which in Ibibio (a neighboring tribe) means the "messengers of God." One woman said to the commission:

I was surprised to see the soldiers fire as we were women we call ourselves vultures as we did not think soldiers would fire at us. Vultures go to market and eat food there and nobody molests them nobody will kill vultures even in the market, even if it kills fowls. We only fling sticks at them if they take our chop and so we thought soldiers will not harm us what we may do.[15]

European education, Christianity, and the desire for European goods also contributed to the end of the "women's world." A fitting epilogue is delivered by Sylvia Leith-Ross, a concerned British woman, who wonders how long it will be before education can "give the girls something as important, as satisfying, as pervasive, as the land gave to their mothers."[16] And so a new sex-role plan is imposed by the conquerors on the conquered.

Handsome Lake and the decline of the Iroquois matriarchate

The world of the Iroquois women declined in importance during the nineteenth century because of the revitalization of the Iroquois male role, which had deteriorated during the Colonial period. The drastic changes in Iroquois sex-role behavior have been referred to by Anthony F. C. Wallace as the "decline of the Iroquois matriarchate." These changes were codified in the religion of Handsome Lake, a Seneca prophet, which was largely a religion devoted to providing new rights and duties for men. The story of Handsome Lake exemplifies the emergence of sexual inequality brought on by a male religious figure as an adaptive response to extreme circumstances threatening to destroy the spirit of Iroquoian males. During the period of Handsome Lake and thereafter, Iroquoian women held power in name only.

The era of Iroquoian women ended when the White Roots of the Tree of Peace – the symbol of the Iroquois League laid down in their constitution – were hacked away by a series of disastrous wars and treaties in the late eighteenth century, leaving the Iroquois people with "a shrunken homeland, a reduced standard of living, and a demoralized society."[17] Early in the nineteenth century, Iroquois men found themselves no longer able or needing to range over thousands of miles to hunt, fight, and negotiate treaties and attend councils. In these circumstances, the religion of Handsome Lake took root.[18]

Handsome Lake had followed the life of the traditional Iroquoian male. He had undertaken the long hunting, warring, and diplomatic journeys characteristic of the Colonial period, and he had become one of the 49 chiefs of the great Council of the Six Nations by nomination of a clan matron. Later in life, after the reservations came into being, and he and his contemporaries were cooped up in a little slum in the wilderness, exposed to pushy white people, including Quaker missionaries living in the same village, he began to have a series of visions while lying as a drunken invalid in the house of his brother.[19]

The body of Handsome Lake's separate utterances of anecdote, parable, revelation, prophecy, apocalyptic, and law, laid down with divine sanctions, came to be known as the Great Message.[20] A mixture of Christian moral admonitions with comments on the

141

traditional Iroquoian way of life, the Great Message was "born of a miscegenation of Quaker with old Seneca stock."[21] The Great Message sought to eliminate drinking and witchcraft and taught that men were to practice agriculture in the white man's style and that husband and wife were to cleave together.[22] The main injunction regarding sex roles was, in essence, that men were to toil in the fields and women were to conceive and obey. In addition, old women were not to exercise power over their daughters nor to interfere between a daughter and her husband. Women who did not follow this way, who continued to do their own planting (as many older women did), were in danger of being accused of witchcraft and being executed.[23]

Many women adopted the new way quickly. Others resisted the changes and sought to reassert their traditional powers. Some mothers advised their daughters to use contraceptives and abortion and to leave husbands who took up the new ways. Handsome Lake attacked these women, saying, "The Creator is sad because of the tendency of old women to breed mischief." Handsome Lake accused such women of witchcraft and threatened them with execution. In a study reporting these and other developments, Joan Jensen notes that Handsome Lake made many such accusations among the Senecas and, though he opposed them, some executions did occur. Jensen says:

One old woman was reported cut down while at work in her corn field in 1799. Another was reported executed on the spot after a council decided on her guilt. Four of the "best women in the nation" narrowly escaped execution at Sandusky when the executioners refused to carry out the sentence. Probably not many old women died but the lesson was clear.[24]

The codification of a new sex-role ideology was not the main thrust of Handsome Lake's teachings, but it was an important by-product. Handsome Lake was mainly concerned, as Anthony F. C. Wallace notes, with stabilizing the nuclear family by strengthening the husband–wife relationship. This meant weakening the traditional bond between mother and daughter. Although he did not challenge the matrilineal principle as it operated formally in determining clan membership and in granting women the right to nominate chiefs, Handsome Lake made it clear that the nuclear family, rather than the maternal lineage, was to be the moral and economic center of Iroquoian life.[25]

Like all prophets, Handsome Lake's admonitions did not arise out of an ideological vacuum, which is to say that he taught what many had begun to believe. Quaker influence in his village had been responsible for the institutionalization of many of the reforms he sought before his first visions in June of 1799. During this time Quakers urged men in the village to experiment with the plough and to keep domestic animals because game was growing scarce. Eventually, the greater yield produced in part of a field ploughed by men (the rest being prepared in the traditional manner by women with a hoe) challenged the ancient belief that only women could make crops grow. When Handsome Lake began to travel and preach, there is no doubt that the spreading of his message was aided by the support he received from Quakers for promulgating in Iroquoian terms what was basically a Quaker message.[26]

The salvation of Iroquois males could only have been achieved at the expense of the classic matrifocal system. Men forced to be sedentary had to find something else to do or relive through whiskey the power and prestige they had once experienced on the trail. The part played by Quakers in the rearrangement of sex roles is ironic, given that Quakers came from one of the most sexually equal of Protestant sects. But this may help explain the success of the Quaker influence. The separate–but–equal style of Quaker men and women in their own religious observances would have been compatible with Iroquoian basic beliefs. The Quakers did not come to the Iroquois with the idea of dominating them in the realm of religion. Rather, they were concerned with preserving a disintegrating culture. The retention of certain formalities of the old way and the sheer necessity for the new way explain this peculiarly successful interaction between two different but very similar peoples.

Female power and movement onto the Great Plains: the Lords of the Plains and the Sacred Buffalo Hat

When the horse was introduced in North America by the Spanish, the Great Plains of North America teemed with buffalo, an extremely rich source of food and derivative byproducts. Buffalo could only be effectively exploited when it was possible to move easily across the great dry stretches between the water sources in search of herds and to transport enough meat to the base camp to sustain the tribe through the winter. The introduction of the horse, and later the gun, resulted in many population movements onto the Plains as former foragers or horticulturalists gave up their traditional ways of life. Mobility and the prizes won in the hunt greatly transformed these cultures, but, as E. Adamson Hoebel says, "the past – as always – left its imprint."[27] There are a few hints of the consequences for traditional female power of the movement onto the Plains.

The history of the Comanche, whose defense of the prairie country south of the Arkansas River for over a century earned them the title "Lords of the South Plain," provides some clues about the evolution of male dominance, for which the Plains Indians are notorious. Before acquiring the horse from the Spanish and turning to buffalo hunting in the south, the Comanche probably lived a life similar to that of the Western Shoshone, who subsisted mainly by gathering.[28] Among the Western Shoshone, plant harvesting was the main subsistence activity, since game was relatively scarce.[29] Seed gathering instead of hunting determined the economic routine, and women were more important economically than men.[30] The economic importance of women, Steward says, offset any tendency toward male dominance, since "there were virtually no noneconomic activities which either sex would use as a social lever." Other factors contributing to sexual equality, in Steward's account, were the practice of polyandry, couples living with the wife's parent for several years after marriage, and the absence of gang rape, a practice often found among bison-hunting people.[31]

Because of the scarcity of food, it was physically impossible for Western Shoshonean families to remain in one place for very long or for more than a few families to remain in permanent association. The most important sociopolitical unit was, consequently, the biological family and the small winter village, consisting of a loose aggregate of families. The village had a single headman whose title meant "talker," which designated his most important function. His task was to keep informed about the ripening of plant foods in different localities and to give directions to families who wished to engage in joint expeditions to gathering locations. He was little more than a family leader or village adviser.

Villages amalgamated into bands in other parts of Shoshone territory when a fertile environment permitted large villages or when transportation was so improved that large groups could live together and either bring their foods to a central point or travel as a body in search of them. Bands were formed just before the coming of the white man among the Northern Shoshone. The introduction of the horse caused a tightening of band organization. Political control was centered in chiefs, whose authority varied somewhat with their personalities. This authority was increased immeasurably by the arrival of the white man.[32]

The Comanche, who resembled the Northern Shoshone in language and culture, are believed to have migrated south in the late seventeenth century to be near a source for horses. Horses were a symbol of wealth and prestige, a cause for war, and a way of acquiring wives. The owner of a large herd was in a position to give more generous gifts to a prospective wife and her family. Horses also were an informal medium of exchange. They could be presented as gifts in exchange for services rendered and as fees to medicine men. They were frequently used in settlement of controversies between individuals and thus had legal as well as monetary significance.

Comanche men, it is said, "loved their horses more than they loved their wives . . . or child, or any other human being." A man kept his favorite horse close to him at all times so that he could tend it, pet it, and adore it. Killing another man's favorite horse was akin to murder. In short, favorite horses were like dearly loved people.[33]

The Comanches were organized in family groups and bands. The latter were autonomous, loosely organized units that roamed in a vaguely defined territory within the Comanche country. The organization of the band was similar to the political organization of the Shoshone. The band ranged in size from a single family camping alone to the small camp of related persons to a large group of several hundred people. The family headmen, of which there was at least one for each group, were known as the peace, or civil, chiefs. When the large band was functioning as a unit, it contained several peace chiefs, one of whom was recognized as the head chief of the band. The rest formed an advisory council to the leader.[34]

The basic principle of Comanche political organization was the constitutional separation of civil and military leadership. Both positions were achieved by virtue of an individual's qualities as a leader. When a man emerged as a civil chief, he became a kind of revered patriarch. He was "father" to all the band and the people were his "children." He had no formal authority and his influence was limited to internal and civil matters only. Like the "talker" among the Western Shoshone, he "spoke the custom" because he was reputed to have "the finest sense of social fitness."[35]

Important policies affecting the tribe were determined in council. The council was loosely organized and arrived at decisions through consensus. All of the old men of the tribe who had shown exceptional ability as warriors, leaders, or guides were members. The council considered such matters as moving the camp, undertaking a tribal war, making peace, forming alliances with other tribes, selecting the time and place of the summer hunt, and deciding on community religious services. Women sometimes attended the meetings and on rare occasions were permitted to speak, but such occasions appear to have been exceptions to the normal pattern.[36]

The life of the Comanche male revolved around warfare and raiding. War was regarded as the noblest of pursuits, one that every man should follow. Boys were taught that success in war brought the respect and admiration of men, women, and children, and that the most worthy virtue for a man was bravery. Death in battle was said to be glorious and to protect one from all the miseries that were inevitable to old age.

Before the introduction of the horse, Plains warfare was sporadic and less bloody. The horse furnished the Plains tribes with both a motive and the ability for war. Raiding rather than trading was the major method for replenishing and adding to one's herds. The introduction of the horse also increased the pressure of the whites on the eastern frontier, setting in motion a chain reaction of tribal displacements that caused Indian groups to compete for the same resources, leading to constant warfare between these groups.

The decline of the women's world

As warfare became the pattern of life, the young and physically able men achieved higher status, and the war chiefs who led raiding parties for additional horses became political leaders. The old peace chief ideal still survived, but it was overshadowed by the ideal personality type of warrior.[37]

In this setting, the legal position of women became largely that of chattel. Wives were bought with horses and treated like property. Upon marriage a woman passed to her husband's group and the husband had the right to kill or torture his wife. It was also the right of a brother to kill his sister. Other categories of property consisted of horses and dogs.[38]

Although absent in the realm of public activity, female power continued to maintain a role in the Comanche conception of the supernatural and in their mythology. The Comanche believed that power resided in animate beings (usually animals), who would bestow it on those who sought it (usually men). The beings in whom power resided were called "guardian spirits" and were believed to speak human language and possess the ability to assume various forms. Guardian spirits were referred to as "givers of power," which are "outside" man's "realm of dominance."[39] Comanche men engaged in a perennial search for this power, which often required some sort of covenant before being bestowed. The ultimate source of all power was the "Great Spirit" (at least it was called that by early missionaries). The Great Spirit was the prime mover in the creation of the Comanche, although the actual performance of this task was delegated to a secondary spirit. The Great Spirit was equated with the sun. Next, after the sun, the earth was worshipped as "Mother because it was the receptacle and producer of all that sustains life."[40] The earth was thought of as the mother of men and animals. These deities, although active in the affairs of men, gave no personal power, since this could only be received by guardian spirits.

Although buffalo meat became the dietary mainstay, Comanche men did not forget their gathering heritage. Women did most of the collecting, but men knew what was growing about them and how to use it. Both Comanche men and women were knowledgeable of the plant environment, particularly of those plants valuable to the tribe.[41] The importance of the earth as mother, the receptacle and producer of all that sustains life, was not forgotten. However, as warfare intensified and buffalo herds were depleted, the Comanche became predominantly oriented to a military–buffalo complex, from which women were virtually excluded.

The Cheyenne Indians, one of the most notable of the western tribes inhabiting the Great Plains, provide a very different picture of change in traditional female status resulting from adoption of the horse. Before moving onto the Plains, the Cheyennes resided near Lake Superior. They migrated westward toward the end of the seventeenth century, and early in the eighteenth century they became closely associated with sedentary village tribes of the upper Missouri River, such as the Mandan and Hidatsa. These tribes were "old-time gardeners" who lived in permanent villages constructed of large, semisubterranean earth lodges. They were organized into matrilineal clans, and marriage was matrilocal. During the eighteenth and early nineteenth centuries, the Cheyennes lived in earth-lodge villages and grew corn, beans, and squash. They were first exposed to the horse around 1760. By 1830 they had abandoned the village life of gardeners for the nomadic life of hunters.[42]

The history of the Cheyenne after they adopted the horse suggests that the female social and ritual principles, which undoubtedly existed before the acquisition of the horse when they were mainly horticulturalists, were transformed but retained in the buffalo–horse period. The two most important Cheyenne sacred symbols and associated ceremonies are devoted to male and female power. The Sacred Medicine Arrows symbolize male power and the identity of the tribe; the Sacred Buffalo Hat is the living symbol and source of female power and fertility.

The Sacred Medicine Arrows, the male power symbol, represent for the Cheyenne their symbolic insurance for survival. When turned against the buffalo, the Medicine Arrows make them confused and helpless. When carried against an enemy, they cause the foe to become blinded and befuddled. Thus, the Medicine Arrows symbolize central anxieties: "failure of the food supply and extermination by enemies."[43]

The Medicine Arrows also symbolize the collective existence of the tribe. They are "the embodiment of the tribal soul." In them resides a spiritual power that belongs to all the people and is revered by all. They are never neglected, because to do so would mean that the tribe would decline in prosperity. The ceremony called the "Renewal of the Sacred Arrows" brings the entire Cheyenne tribe together. During this ceremony, from which women are excluded, the norms of proper conduct as formulated by Sweet Medicine, the Cheyenne mythical culture hero, are restated. The authority of the tribal chiefs is reaffirmed, especially the authority of the head chief, who, because he possesses the sweet medicine bundle given to the tribe by Sweet Medicine, is the living incarnation of the long-dead creator of the Cheyenne way, Sweet Medicine.[44]

Is'siwun, the Sacred Buffalo Hat, is the symbol and source of female renewing power. It was through the Buffalo Hat that the Sun Dance first came to the Cheyenne. In the Sun Dance a Sacred Woman offers what is known as the Sacred Woman's sacrifice. This involves ritual intercourse with the male Pledger of the Sun Dance. Through this act woman symbolically joins with man in bringing about the renewal of the Cheyennes and their world. Thus the Sacred Buffalo Hat is the symbol of reproduction and "world creation." The word *is'siwun* means a herd of buffalo. In the context of the Sacred Buffalo Hat the term also means a group of female bison. The Buffalo Hat is formed from the horned scalp of a female buffalo, and traditionally Is'siwun's power guaranteed a plentiful supply of buffalo for the people.[45]

Cheyenne life reflects the dignity accorded women in the sacred ceremonies. Women possessed great influence among the people. They discussed affairs with their husbands, were great persuaders and cajolers, and generally had their way. Cheyenne tradition credits a woman with the founding of the tribal Council of the Forty-Four. This council is described as the "keystone of Cheyenne social structure" and the oldest of their formal institutions.[46] Traditions of women chiefs exist, as well as accounts of women possessing great supernatural powers. Female influence has been reported to have been present in many a council session, though ordinarily men alone spoke in the tribal councils. According to George Bird Grinnell, a longtime observer of the Cheyenne, women were, "in fact, the final authority in the camp."[47]

The respect and mutual affection that existed between Cheyenne husband and wife is reported by many sources. There is no evidence that women were treated as property or routinely maltreated by their husbands.[48] In a moving autobiographical statement, a Northern Cheyenne woman, named Iron Teeth, whose

95 years spanned almost the entire period of white contact with her tribe before 1930, describes the life she led with her husband. She hunted buffalo with him and, in general, their relationship was one of partners sharing equally in the work of the family.

Iron Teeth hunted small game alone and searched for wild horses, which she would tame and break herself. She talks about the exploits of other women in battle and in self-defense against marauding Indians. These women received the vocal and ceremonial respect given to acts of extraordinary bravery.[49]

Iron Teeth herself was a fierce, tough woman who was dedicated to her husband and five children. Her description of her life suggests that the backbone of the Cheyenne way lay in the family. As she sat at age 95 on an Indian reservation in 1929 telling her story, her emotional energy was clearly still with her husband, who had died long ago at the hands of white soldiers, and with the children she had mothered. Speaking of a hide scraper made from the horn of an elk, a gift from her husband after they were married, and on which she had made marks to keep track of the ages of their children, she said:

Throughout seventy-four years it has always been a part of my most precious pack. There were times when I had not much else. I was carrying it in my hands when my husband was killed on upper Powder River. It was tied to my saddle while we were in flight from Oklahoma. It was in my little pack when we broke out from the Fort Robinson prison. It has never been lost. Different white people have offered me money for it. I am very poor, but such money does not tempt me. When I die, this gift from my husband will be buried with me . . . Red Pipe was the only husband I ever had. I am the only wife he ever had. Through more than fifty years I have been his widow. I could not sell anything he made and gave to me. I used to cry every time anything reminded me of the killing of my husband and my son. But I now have become old enough to talk quietly of them. I used to hate all white people, especially their soldiers. But my heart now has become changed to softer feelings. Some of the white people are good, maybe as good as Indians.[50]

In sum, the position of women among the Cheyenne was changed, not debased, by the acquisition of the horse. The reason for the change was partially due to the horse–buffalo complex and partially due to the hostile forces confronting the Cheyenne on the

Plains. The Sacred Medicine Arrows, the embodiment of Cheyenne identity, symbolized male dominance over men of other tribes and over animals. No females dared look at these divinely given symbols, and even today it is reported that a devout woman excuses herself from the presence of men who are speaking about the Arrows.[51]

The emphasis on the Arrows could be interpreted as an enactment of male dominance, or it could be understood as necessary for Cheyenne psychosocial survival. The Cheyenne conceived of the universe as a mechanical system with a limited energy quotient, which progressively diminishes as it is expended. Ceremonies like the Renewal of the Sacred Arrows produced a recharge and readjustment of the parts so that the whole could again operate at its full potential. Because Cheyenne male power and energy were equated with "the tribal soul," and because this soul was in danger during the long years of Plains warfare, greater effort was devoted to renewing and reaffirming the male portion of the Cheyenne world. It would be more appropriate to view such a process as a strategy for survival rather than as a display of male dominance, sexual asymmetry, or sexual inequality.

There is a practice found among the Cheyenne that can only be described as forcible male domination of women. In view of all that has been said about the easy and loving relationship between the Cheyenne sexes, this practice strikes a jarring note. Known as "putting a woman on the prairie," an outraged husband of a "strong-willed, flagrantly adulterous" woman has the right to invite all the unmarried members of his military society to a feast on the prairie, where his wife is raped by each. One woman was forced into intercourse with 40 or more of her husband's associates. The right to put a woman on the prairie is observed infrequently. Though referred to as a right by Hoebel, who describes this practice, he notes that it is not always honored by a woman's close relatives, who may kill the men involved in gang rape. The men who participate in gang rape are ashamed. The practice is an anomaly in Cheyenne ideals for the husband–wife relationship. Hoebel suggests that the practice originates from frustrations bred from the self-control and sexual repression that Cheyenne men observe in order to conserve their energy to pass on to their children and to use in warfare.[52]

The women's world

Two different patterns emerge from the preceding descriptions of the Comanche and Cheyenne. Both groups experienced a tightening of the male collective and the exclusion of women from formal group decision making. In both cases this appears to have been an adaptive response to the Plains horse–buffalo–warfare complex and the growing threat posed by the encroachment of white hunters and soldiers. Among the Comanche the forcible subjugation of women was included in the new adaptation to the Plains life-style. Among the Cheyenne the status of women was not lowered but changed and transformed in their struggle for survival against hostile Indians and whites. However, the seeds for Cheyenne male dominance were clearly present.

These differences can be attributed to the nature of the pre-horse background. The Comanche came from a loosely organized, amorphous cultural background in which there were no ascribed bases for power. The sexes were more equal primarily because of economic circumstances, which made gathering more important than hunting. The Cheyenne, on the other hand, came from a sedentary, agricultural background where they may have shared traits with societies known to have well-developed female social and ritual principles (i.e., the Mandan and the Hidatsa). When the Cheyenne abandoned the life of agriculture for that of horse nomadism, the bases for female power and authority were transformed to fit the exigencies of the new life. There is evidence that agriculture was not completely abandoned by Cheyenne women. Iron Teeth says that when she was a little girl corn was planted every year before going on the summer hunt. This statement is corroborated elsewhere by Cheyenne women born early in the nineteenth century who said that they commonly planted corn patches, as their mothers before them had done, and had taught them to do.[53] If this was the case, then the traditional economic centrality of Cheyenne women may have persisted after the horse was acquired.

The movement of foragers into marginal territories

Unlike the Comanche and the Cheyenne, who left their traditional territory to embrace a more promising existence, the expansion of the Europeans pushed other foragers into marginal territories where food was scarce and fear ruled social life. In these cases one can observe processes similar to those described for the Comanche and Cheyenne. Men band together in secret to conduct power and fertility ceremonies, from which women are excluded. In addition women are debased and treated as objects against which men unleash physical and sexual aggression.

The Aranda of Australia, the Shavante of lowland South America, and the Northern Saulteaux of Canada provide examples of foragers ruled by fear. The assumption of male dominance is evident in these groups. Men display aggression toward women, which is acted out in institutionalized rape or in the ever-present threat of rape. All power and fertility ceremonies are conducted by men, and females are excluded from public decision making. These groups appear to be run by men for the purposes of men alone.

There is evidence of a time among the Aranda when women played a more prominent role in tribal affairs. No such evidence is recorded for the Shavante or Northern Saulteaux, among whom male dominance is more pronounced. This may be because the Aranda were observed in the late nineteenth century, before the exigencies of European contact had completely eroded the traditions of the past. The Northern Saulteaux and the Shavante, on the other hand, were observed in 1930 and 1958, respectively, when deculturation due to marginality and migration was more advanced.

"However kindly disposed the white settler may be," say observers of the Aranda, his presence introduced "a disturbing element into the environment of the native, and from that moment degeneration sets in."[54] The chance of securing European-made articles in return for services rendered to the settler attracted the native to the vicinity of white settlements. Young men neglected the ways of their fathers and disease caused rapid depopulation. Those groups of Aranda natives who continued to follow the old way of life were those who roamed in territories where the climate was too dry and the water supply too meager and untrustworthy to attract the Europeans.

Protected from European contact by virtue of their ecological marginality, the Aranda roamed in small local groups, each of which claimed a given area of the country. Consisting mainly of individuals describing themselves by the name of some animal or plant, the local groups were headed by a man who was more a ritual than a political leader. The duties of the ritual leader included overseeing the sacred storehouse, usually a cave or hole in the ground in which were hidden the sacred objects of the group, and determining when men should perform the sacred ceremonies, many of which were conducted to increase the supply of plants and animals. No woman, child, or uninitiated man could come near the sacred storehouse or handle the sacred objects under pain of death. Women were also excluded from the performance of most of the sacred ceremonies.[55]

Churinga was the name given to the sacred objects that women were never allowed to see. These objects were associated with the spirits of totemic animals. The mystery attached to these objects, it was said, had its origin in the "desire of the men to impress the women of the tribe with an idea of the supremacy and superior power of the male sex."[56] There is evidence that in the past these objects and the ceremonies associated with them were not taboo to women. In many myths and tales there are accounts of how women in the far-distant past handled the sacred objects and performed sacred ceremonies exactly as the men do now. It is probable that such traditions indicate the existence of a time when men and women were more nearly equal than they are now.[57]

Male dominance, if defined as the forcible control by men of women, is acted out in the Aranda rape ceremony, which marks a girl as marriageable. At age 14 or 15 the girl is taken out into the bush by a group of men for what is known as the vulva-cutting ceremony. A designated man cuts the girl's vulva, after which she is gang raped by a group of men that does not include her future husband. When the ceremony is concluded, the girl is taken to her husband and from then on no one else has the right of access to her.[58]

The Shavante responded to the cruelties perpetrated by Europeans against them by fleeing into Brazilian virgin territory – an area that did not interest the colonizers once it had been reported that there was no mineral wealth to be found. There is a Shavante tale that describes how in the old days they lived next to the whites. When a settler seduced one of their women, the Indians became afraid that they would be killed and their women taken. They therefore fled by night and crossed a big river, which served as a dividing line between them and white contact.

The decline of the women's world

Whether this myth is true or not, there is good evidence that the Shavante are migrants who avoided European contact by settling in an inhospitable territory and by developing the art of aggression to the point that they were greatly feared and largely left alone.[59] Hunting and warfare are activities that interest the Shavante male above all else. Boys are trained in men's houses in the virtues of cooperation, manliness, and bellicosity. The Shavante have ceremonies of aggression in which initiated men ritually attack uninitiated boys. In the most important ceremony of all, women are ritually raped in a demonstration of the twin powers of sexuality and aggression.[60]

The Shavante roam their land comparatively unmolested because it is generally considered poor country and is the most sparsely populated in Brazil. It consists of open savannah and jungle, and the Shavante prefer the open country. The thrill of stalking and pursuing their game is heightened when they are in the open. Hunting is the activity that most interests men, on which they spend most energy, and about which they talk unceasingly. Although hunting can be successful in the jungle, the Shavante remain on the savannah even if this means going short of water in the dry season. They think of the jungle as alien and ugly and are contemptuous of people who make it their home. During the wet season they keep to the savannah even when the land is so waterlogged that they walk perpetually in a foot or more of water.[61]

Factionalism and hostility are fundamental facts of Shavante life. All those who do not fall within the initiated men's class are objects of hostility. Shavante men display a we/they mentality in which all human beings who are not part of the initiated men's club are enemies and the potential object of hostility. These attitudes foster in men a state of constant warfare readiness – it prepares men to fight when and if they must. While waiting for the imagined attack, they sharpen their teeth on women.

Like the Shavante, Northern Saulteaux men acted as if they were the victims of an oppressor against whom they must struggle continually in order to survive. Whereas the Shavante conceive their enemy in the form of hostile humans (food for the Shavante is not a problem), the silent enemy among the Northern Saulteaux (and the Aranda also) was the shortage of food and the ever-present possibility of famine. Recognition and status among the

155

Northern Saulteaux were bolstered by acquiring power from the superhuman "masters" of the animals they hunted. Without this power, a satisfactory human life was thought impossible. Every species of animal was believed to be controlled by a spiritual boss or owner who must not be offended. The most feared of all animals was the snake, even though the only species of snake in their environment was the harmless garter snake. They projected their sense of inner fear through their belief that once the earth had been inhabited by many monster snakes that persist today unseen.[62]

Among the Northern Saulteaux the assumption of male dominance is clearly expressed in the expectation that a man's potential sexual rights over the woman he chooses must be respected. A woman who turns a man down too abruptly insults him and invites aggression. There is a Northern Saulteaux tale about a girl who was considered too proud because she refused to marry. Accordingly, a group of medicine men lured her out into the bush, where they each raped her in turn.[63] Such tales provide women with a fairly good idea of how they should behave toward men.

In sum, although these three groups are geographically scattered and culturally divergent, similar processes are at work. Like the Comanche and Cheyenne, the power and fertility symbols are defined in male terms, and males alone are granted the right to manipulate these symbols ritually. The exclusion of women from male ceremonies provides a basis for aggressive displays toward women and solidifies men in their struggle to overcome circumstances hostile to human life. One might surmise that any threat to the existence of the social group will result in the glorification of the male role at the expense of the female role. In the face of overwhelming odds and threats to the traditional way of life, it appears as if men unleash aggression toward women and exclude them from secret ceremonies held to bolster power that is in short supply.

The relationship between colonialism, a marginal food base, and female power

Prolonged contact with Europeans in many cases transformed both the symbols and actuality of female power. The expansion of the Europeans also resulted in waves of migration in which many peoples were pushed into marginal territories, disrupting their traditional equilibrium between natural resources and social needs. Where European technology enabled people to exploit a new and richer ecological niche, the time of plenty usually did not last long. The heyday of the Plains Indians, for example, quickly came to an ignominious end, and tribal identity and personal honor were shattered.

Tribal identity and personal honor were interconnected for Plains Indian men. The former was upheld by fighting for the latter and vice versa. Plains Indian women depended on men and horses for dietary mainstays and for the safety of themselves and their children. As long as buffalo were plentiful and safety not a factor, the sexes were probably more integrated in the daily routine. Sexual integration is certainly suggested by Iron Teeth's description of her life as a Cheyenne girl, woman, wife, and mother. However, as the military conflicts on the Plains intensified, women came to play a more segregated and subordinated role.

The decline of Iroquoian female power was an adaptive response to progressive anomie. Contact with the French and English eventually resulted in Iroquoian men being unable to excel at the activities that had once afforded them honor and social identity. Encouraged by missionaries and colonial officials, Iroquoian men redefined male and female roles. The redefinition of roles turned women into homemakers and men into cultivators of the soil. The old women who resisted the new way were threatened with execution for witchcraft. Thus, the Iroquoian women's world diminished in scope and power.

Igbo and Iroquoian women had a new sex-role plan forced upon them. One might ask why these women did not resist as fiercely as the Plains Indian warriors resisted white encroachment. Unknown thousands of tribal men died to protect their traditional way, but only a handful of women died in defense of the women's world. The reason for this can be found in the distinction between women as givers of life and men as the expendable sex. Women do not continue to fight because they are not expendable for the survival of the group. Tribal men prolong the fight because their manhood and tribal honor are expressed by their willingness to die defending both.

The impact of Westernization on female political power was discussed in the last chapter in connection with the effect of technological complexity. Though in some cases Westernization

157

Table 7.1. *Relationship between female economic and political power or authority (Stata) and time of description (A14)*

Time of description	Females have no economic or political power or authority (scale score 1–4)		Females have economic power or authority (scale score 5)		Females have economic and political power or authority (scale score 6–7)		Row totals (N)
	N	%	N	%	N	%	
1520–1880 (1)	6	16	4	17	20	28	30
1881–1905 (2)	6	16	5	22	12	17	23
1906–25 (3)	3	8	4	17	13	18	20
1926–58 (4)	23	60	10	44	27	37	60
Column totals	38	100	23	100	72	100	133[a]

Data are given for number (N) and percentage of societies. Pearson's $R = -0.17$, $p = 0.03$. See Appendix A for discussion of A14.
[a]No information for 23 societies.

opened opportunities for women, in most instances contact with the male-dominated European society had a deleterious effect. It is no accident that most (63%) of the societies of this study in which females enjoy political power are societies that were described before 1925, whereas most (60%) of the societies in which there is no female economic or political power are societies that were described later (see Table 7.1). Time of description is not a wholly reliable measure of Westernization, but one can expect that, by and large, societies described in the mid-twentieth century have been the most affected by contact with Europeans.

Migration and food shortage also inhibit the expression of female political power (see Tables 6.3. and 7.2).[64] It would appear from the case studies presented in this chapter that men react to stress caused by food shortage or by the circumstances of migration by banding together, excluding women from male-oriented power ceremonies, and by turning aggression against women. These case studies are by no means unique. Many examples of similar behavior can be cited.

Table 7.2. *Relationship between female economic and political power or authority (Stata) and nature of the food supply (Sub 13)*

Nature of the food supply	Females have no economic or political power or authority (scale score 1–4)		Females have economic power or authority (scale score 5)		Females have political and economic power or authority (scale score 6–7)		Row totals (N)
	N	%	N	%	N	%	
Food supply is constant (1)	5	14	4	17	22	32	31
Food supply fluctuates with storage techniques to insure against periods of famine (2)	20	57	11	48	36	53	67
Food supply fluctuates with no storage techniques to insure against periods of famine (3)	10	29	8	35	10	15	28
Column totals	35	100	23	100	68	100	126[a]

Data are given for number (N) and percentage of societies. Pearson's $R = -0.22$, $p = 0.007$.
[a] No information for 30 societies.

Thus, in addition to inhibiting the female political voice, migration and food stress encourage the development of male dominance. The exceptions to this general rule are instructive on the bases for male oppression of females. These exceptions are examined in subsequent chapters as we move to consider the bases for male dominance and sexual inequality.

PART IV

The dynamics of male dominance and sexual inequality

Men stand superior to women in that God hath preferred the one over the other . . . Those whose perverseness ye fear, admonish them and remove them into bed-chambers and beat them; but if they submit to you then do not seek a way against them.

Sūra 4:34, The Quran

Every attitude, emotion, thought, has its opposite held in balance out of sight but there all the time. Push any one of them to an extreme, and . . . over you go into its opposite.

Doris Lessing, *The Four-gated City*, p. 601

8 · The bases for male dominance

Sex-role plans are part of the system of meanings by which a people explain their success, come to terms with their fears, enshrine their past, and stamp themselves with a sense of "peoplehood." The unique identity people weave for themselves, the cup they mold from which to drink of life, mediates sexual identities. Hence, sex roles must be viewed as an interdependent part of the logico-meaningful system that defines and gives direction to a people's life. If this system of meanings develops in the absence of forces threatening social survival, women wield economic and political power or authority and the power relationship between the sexes is balanced.

If the system of meanings that defines sexual identities is threatened by internal or external forces, meanings may be recombined, with the result that sexual identities are revised or new ones fabricated. If the whole complex of traditional roles is undermined, people will fight as if they were struggling to hold on to life itself. As the Igbo women said in the aftermath of the women's war, "we are all dying."

When the cup of life that defines the male world is broken, men organize to protect their traditional rights, as the Igbo women organized to protect theirs. Sometimes the struggle against hostile forces includes controlling and manipulating women as if they were objects in a game played only by men. The circumstances under which men attempt to make women pawns in their struggle are discussed in this chapter. As will be seen, however, women do not always accept subordination by men.

Male dominance: mythical and real

Anthropologists have proposed various, partially overlapping definitions of male dominance. Ernestine Friedl defines male dominance as "a situation in which men have highly preferential access, although not always exclusive rights, to those activities to which the society accords the greatest value, and the exercise of which permits a measure of control over others."[1] Friedl's definition is more specific than the one employed by William Divale and Marvin Harris in their discussion of the "male supremacist complex." These authors define male dominance in terms of an "institutionalized complex" consisting of "asymmetrical frequencies of sex-linked practices and beliefs," such as postmarital residence, descent ideology, form of marriage, bride price, the sexual division of labor, and sex roles in leadership.[2] Thus, Divale and Harris assume that any social institution or practice that is oriented to the male principle implies domination by men.

The definition of male dominance used here is more narrow. Male dominance is restricted in this study to the two general types of behaviors that have been described in previous chapters. First, there is the exclusion of women from political and economic decision making. Second, there is male aggression against women, which is measured here by the following five traits: the expectation that males should be tough, brave, and aggressive; the presence of men's houses or specific places where only men may congregate; frequent quarreling, fighting, or wife beating; the institutionalization or regular occurrence of rape; and raiding other groups for wives. The presence of all five traits in a society indicates a high degree of male aggression; the absence of all five indicates that male aggression is weakly developed.[3]

The extent to which traits measuring male aggression and female power overlap in some societies is shown in Table 8.1. Twenty-eight percent of the societies in which females wield political and economic power or authority are characterized by the extremes of male aggression. Looking at the societies in which females have economic control but no political power, it can be seen that over half (53%) are prone to male aggression. The Mundurucu fit into the latter category: Women enjoy economic autonomy and males display aggression against women. Despite efforts by men to control them by force, Mundurucu women neither accept nor agree with the male assessment of their inferior status. The relation between the Mundurucu sexes, Murphy and Murphy say, is "not, then, one of simple domination and submissiveness, but one of ideological dissonance and real opposition."[4]

The Mundurucu case illustrates that male aggression against women is not necessarily joined with female passivity. In some societies it is expected that women will fight back. In others, it is assumed that women will adopt the submissive role. The following quote from the Quran, for example, codifies real male dominance and female subordination: "Men stand superior to women in that God hath preferred the one over the other . . . Those whose perverseness ye fear, admonish them and remove them into bed-chambers and beat them; but if they submit to you then do not seek a way against them."[5]

The frequency (see Table 8.1) with which female economic or political power coexists with male aggression against women shows that the Mundurucu sex-role plan is not unusual. In discussing the bases for male dominance, it is essential to distinguish male aggression against women from the exercise by women of political and economic power. Where the former exists in the presence of the latter, the term *mythical* male dominance will be employed to describe the relationship between the sexes. Where males turn aggression against women and/or women are excluded from economic and political decision making, the relationship between the sexes will be defined as *unequal*. Finally, where males do not display aggression against women and women exercise political and economic authority or power, the relationship between the sexes will be defined as *equal*. Employing these criteria as guidelines, the relationship between the sexes is classified as equal in 32% of the societies of this study and unequal in 28% (see Table 8.2). The remaining 40% of the societies either fit the criteria expressive of "mythical" male dominance or represent cases in which women exercise economic but no political power.[6]

The notion of "mythical" male dominance was adopted from Susan Carol Rogers's discussion of the "myth of male dominance" in peasant societies. Rogers gives examples of peasant societies in which there is a balance between formal male authority and informal female power. She argues that a nonhierarchical power relationship between the categories "male" and "female" is maintained by "the acting out of a 'myth' of male dominance." The myth of male dominance, she says, is expressed "in patterns of public deference toward men, as well as their monopolization of positions of authority and prestige." She shows, however, that males do not actually dominate, nor do males or females literally

Table 8.1. *Relationship between male aggression (Msupa) and female political and economic power or authority (Stata)*

Male aggression[a]	Females have no economic or political power or authority (scale score 1–4)		Females have economic power or authority (scale score 5)		Females have political and economic power or authority (scale score 6–7)		Row totals (N)
	N	%	N	%	N	%	
No indicators of male aggression (scale score 1)	2	7	1	7	12	24	15
Men's houses are present and/or men are expected to be tough (scale score 2–3) and	6	21	3	20	12	24	21
Interpersonal violence is present (scale score 4) and	3	11	1	7	6	12	10

Rape is institutionalized or reported as frequent (scale score 5)	6	21	2	13	6	12	14
and							
Wives are taken from hostile groups (scale score 6)	11	39	8	53	14	28	33
Column totals	28	99	15	100	50	100	93[b]

Data are given for number (N) and percentage of societies.

[a] For discussion of male aggression measure, see Appendix F. This measure forms a Guttman scale.

[b] No information for 63 societies.

Table 8.2. *Male dominance (MD) and sexual equality*

Male dominance[a]	Women exercise economic and political power or authority	Men raid other groups for wives and/or rape is institutionalized or frequent	Societies	
			N	%
Sexes are equal	Yes	No	45	32
Some or mythical male dominance[b]	Yes	Yes	55	40
Sexes are unequal, real male dominance	No	Possibly	39	28
Column totals			139[c]	100

[a]For construction of this measure, see Appendix F.
[b]Includes some cases where women have *economic power only* and there is no male aggression.
[c]No information for 17 societies.

believe males to be dominant. The perpetuation of the myth, she says, "is in the interests of both peasant women and men, because it gives the latter the *appearance* of power and control over all sectors of village life, while at the same time giving to the former *actual* power over those sectors of life in the community which may be controlled by villagers."[7]

A claim for nearly universal sexual asymmetry could be made *if* mythical male dominance is defined as a form of sexual asymmetry. However, if mythical male dominance is understood as representing a form of balanced sexual opposition, as Rogers argues and as I have argued for societies like that of the Mundurucu, such a claim is unwarranted.

The criteria for classifying societies as sexually equal deserves comment in light of the universal sexual asymmetry argument. Louise Lamphere, who articulates the latter position, defines sexual equality as a situation "in which all men and women (regardless of social group or strata) could and actually did make decisions over the *same* range of activities and people, that is, exercise the *same* kinds of control" (emphasis mine). Sexual inequality, she says, would be a situation "where there were some decisions which women could not and did not make, some activities from

168

which they were excluded, and some resources which they did not control."[8] By this definition, in all human societies men are unequal in some respects and women are unequal in others. There is no society I know of in which the sexes give equal energy to exactly the same activities and decisions. Nor are there many societies in which both sexes have the same access to the same resources.

My position regarding the definition of sexual equality falls in what Lamphere defines as the "complementary but equal" argument, which she attributes to Alice Schlegel, Jean Briggs, Carolyn Matthiasson, and others.[9] Given Lamphere's definition of equality, it is not surprising that she disagrees with these authors. For example, referring to Schlegel's description of Hopi sexual balance, dualism, and interdependence, Lamphere interprets the exclusion of women from the Kachina cult and from participation in facets of male ceremonialism as evidence for sexual asymmetry, whereas Schlegel interprets the Hopi ceremonial cycle as bringing together the different functions equated with masculinity and femininity into an expression of unity.

Schlegel's description of the function of the Hopi ceremonial cycle suggests sexual symmetry. Hopi male ceremonialism is more exclusive and more prevalent because of the double nature of men, as conceived by the Hopi, as opposed to the single nature of women. The duality of masculinity is represented in ceremonial symbolism expressing the male role as germinator, activator, and guardian of life, on the one hand, and the predatory nature of males needed in their roles as warriors on the other. These antithetical roles, she shows, are expressed in different ceremonies and associated with different men's fraternities.

Hopi women have only one function: to give life. As Schlegel says, "Women, however, do not partake of this dual role of life givers and life destroyers; their single nature is to give and keep life."[10] The Hopi ceremonial cycle contrasts the double nature of men with the single nature of women, and in so doing ceremonies appear to be more male than female oriented. However, women play a vital role in these ceremonies. They grind the sacred cornmeal, the symbol of natural and spiritual life and a necessary ingredient in almost all ceremonies. Women can and will refuse to play their appointed role in male ceremonies as a way of exercising veto power over male political decisions.[11]

Table 8.3. *Relationship between type of subsistence economy (Econ)
and male dominance (MD)*

Subsistence mode	Societies where sexes are equal		Societies with some or mythical male dominance		Societies where sexes are unequal		Row totals	
	N	%	N	%	N	%	N	%
Animal economies								
Hunting	3	25	6	50	3	25	12	100
Animal husbandry	3	21	5	36	6	43	14	100
Fishing	7	54	4	31	2	15	13	100
Plant economies								
Gathering	7	54	3	23	3	23	13	100
Semi-intensive agriculture (fruit trees and/or vegetable gardens)	2	15	7	54	4	31	13	100
Shifting cultivation of fields	13	35	12	32	12	32	37	99
Advanced agriculture	10	27	18	49	9	24	37	100
Column totals	45 (32%)		55 (40%)		39 (28%)		139[a]	

[a]No information for 17 societies.

Thus, Hopi sexes do not participate in the same way in Hopi
ceremonial life, nor do they participate in the same way in Hopi
social life. However, the interdependence between the sexes
shows that both are required for the functioning of the whole in a
way not found in sexually unequal societies, where males may
independently conduct public social and ceremonial affairs. It is
clear that Lamphere and Schlegel employ different definitions of
equality. One uses equality in the sense of *sameness,* the other uses
equality in the sense of *interdependence* and *balance.* Since equality
can mean both, perhaps the solution would be to employ an altogether different label, such as *sexual symmetry.*

Table 8.4. *Relationship between traits indicative of the "outer" cultural configuration and male dominance (MD)*

Origin symbolism (A05)	Societies where sexes are equal (1)		Societies with some or mythical male dominance (2)		Societies where sexes are unequal (3)		Row totals (N)
	N	%	N	%	N	%	
Feminine	11	32	2	5	3	12	16
Couple	12	35	14	35	6	24	32
Masculine	11	32	24	60	16	64	51
Column totals	34	99	40	100	25	100	99[a]

$\chi^2 = 13.32$ ($df = 4$), $p = 0.01$.
Correlation between male dominance scale and: (1) percentage of strictly female work activities (AH 84) – Pearson's $R = 0.15$ ($N = 139$), $p = 0.04$; (2) percentage of integrated work activities (AH 85) – Pearson's $R = -0.12$ ($N = 139$), $p = 0.08$.
[a]No information for 57 societies.

The correlates of male dominance and sexual inequality

Male dominance is associated with increasing technological complexity, an animal economy, sexual segregation in work, a symbolic orientation to the male creative principle, and stress. Table 8.3 shows that the sexes are most likely to be equal in gathering, fishing, and shifting cultivation economies. The sexes tend to be unequal in animal husbandry societies. The intermediate category of male dominance (which includes mythical male dominance) is prevalent among advanced agriculturalists, hunters, and horticulturalists. Table 8.4 shows that feminine or couple origin symbolism is more frequently found in sexually equal than in sexually unequal societies. This table also shows that sexual segregation is positively associated with male dominance and sexual integration is negatively associated with male dominance.

Male dominance is significantly associated with environmental and historical conditions, suggesting that the dominance of women is a response to stress. The results displayed in Table 8.5 show that in favorable environments and in autochthonous cultural conditions, sexual equality (or symmetry) flourishes, whereas in unfavorable environments or in the face of cultural disruption (measured by the experience of recent migration), mythical male dominance or sexual inequality prevails. For nearly three-fourths of the sexually equal societies (71%), migration is reported as occurring "very early," "long ago," or it is said that the people are "aboriginal to the area." Approximately the same proportion of sexually unequal societies (70%) are reported as being recent arrivals in their area within the last 100–150 years or the people are said to be expansionist oriented. In support of the importance of a favorable environment (as measured by the nature of the food supply), Table 8.5 shows also that sexually equal societies are less likely to be faced with periods of famine than sexually unequal societies. Other sources of stress related to male dominance are endemic warfare and chronic hunger (see Table 8.6).

Anthropological explanations for male dominance

In recent years anthropologists have paid considerable attention to the etiology of male dominance. Several explanations that have been offered are supported by the results discussed in the preceding section. These explanations and others are reviewed here before addressing what seems to me one of the most important questions of this study: Why does the human solution to stress elevate males to a position of dominance and not females?

Marvin Harris presents one answer to this question when he argues that male supremacism is caused by an imbalance between protein sources and population density. Female infanticide, he says, occurs with greater frequency in regions of protein deficiency because of the need to produce hunters and warriors to compete for the available protein supplies. This slows population growth. The resulting shortage of marriageable women, however, requires men to take them from hostile groups. Polygyny, the mark of a successful and powerful hunter and warrior, exacerbates the shortage of women and, hence, the competition for women. A cycle of violence is established which, Harris argues, supplies the key for understanding the etiology of male suprema-

Table 8.5. *Relationship between male dominance (MD), experience of migration (Mig), and nature of the food supply (Sub 13)*

	Societies where sexes are equal		Societies with some or mythical male dominance		Societies where sexes are unequal		Row totals (N)
	N	%	N	%	N	%	
Experience of migration[a]							
Migration is reported as occurring "very early," "long ago," or people are said to be "aboriginal to the area"	22	71	14	34	7	30	43
Migration is reported as being "recent" within the last 100–150 years or people are said to be migrating conquerors	9	29	27	66	16	70	52
Column totals	31	100	41	100	23	100	95[b]
Nature of the food supply[c]							
Food supply is constant	18	43	9	17	5	14	32
Food supply fluctuates with storage techniques to insure against periods of famine	21	50	28	53	21	58	70
Food supply fluctuates with no storage techniques to insure against periods of famine	3	7	16	30	10	28	29
Column totals	42	100	53	100	36	100	131[d]

[a]$\chi^2 = 12.35$ ($df = 2$), $p = 0.002$.
[b]No information for 61 societies.
[c]$\chi^2 = 15.27$ ($df = 4$), $p = 0.004$.
[d]No information for 25 societies.

Table 8.6. *Relationship between male dominance (MD), chronic warfare (War), and food stress (Sub 14A)*

	Societies where sexes are equal		Societies with some or mythical male dominance		Societies where sexes are unequal		Row totals (N)
	N	%	N	%	N	%	
Chronice warfare							
War is absent, periodic, or occasional	18	50	11	22	6	18	35
War is endemic or chronic	18	50	38	78	28	82	84
Column totals	36	100	49	100	34	100	119[a]
Food stress							
Food is constant	25	64	8	16	7	20	40
Occasional hunger or famine	10	26	28	56	19	54	57
Periodic or chronic hunger or evidence of protein deficiency	4	10	14	28	9	26	27
Column totals	39	100	50	100	35	100	124[b]

War: $\chi^2 = 10.76$ (df $= 2$), $p = 0.005$. Sub 14A: $\chi^2 = 26.63$ (df $= 4$), $p = 0.000$.
Appendix B gives reference for Sub 14A.
[a]No information for 37 societies.
[b]No information for 32 societies.

cism. According to Harris, male supremacist institutions arise as a "by-product of warfare, of the male monopoly over weapons, and of the use of sex for the nurturance of aggressive male personalities." Warfare "is not the expression of human nature, but a response to reproductive and ecological pressures. Therefore, male supremacy is no more natural than warfare."[12]

Harris argues that male supremacism is a result of the male monopoly over weapons, but Ernestine Friedl emphasizes the greater control men have over strategic resources because men are the hunters and the expendable sex in activities endangering lives. Friedl argues that among foragers men have greater control than women over the extradomestic distribution and exchange of valued goods and services because of the male monopoly on hunting large game. Among shifting agriculturalists, she says, men have this control because of the male monopoly on the clearing of land and its allocation. Women do not hunt large game because of the difficulties of carrying burdens, food, or children while searching for the game. Men rather than women clear land because new lands often border territories of other peoples with whom warfare poses a potential threat. Warfare, she argues, is primarily the responsibility of males because "a population can survive the loss of men more easily than that of women." Thus, men, by virtue of their control of warfare and land allocation, "are more deeply involved than women in economic and political alliances which are extradomestic and which require for their maintenance the distribution and exchange of goods and services."[13] Friedl concludes that a degree of male dominance exists in all known societies if male dominance is defined as the measure of control over others accorded men because of their preferential access to valued activities.[14]

Nothing in the results displayed in this chapter contradicts either Harris or Friedl. Male dominance is associated with warlikeness and ecological stress, as Harris suggests. Friedl's argument that male dominance is characteristic of foragers is correct for those foragers who rely mainly on hunting. Her argument does not apply to foragers relying mainly on gathering (see Table 8.3). What she has to say about the greater expendability of men is consistent with the discussion presented in Chapter 4. Her definition of male dominance excludes consideration of the interdependence of the male and female worlds. Although she recognizes the ways in which men control people and resources, Friedl does not recognize the ways in which women exercise power and control.

Sherry Ortner argues for universal male dominance on ideational rather than materialist grounds. Women are associated with nature, she says, because a woman's body and its functions are more involved more often with "species life" in contrast to "man's physiology which frees him more completely to take up the projects of culture." Following Simone de Beauvoir, Ortner contends that although a "woman's body seems to doom her to mere reproduction of life; the male, in contrast, lacking natural creative functions, must . . . assert his creativity externally, 'artificially,' through the medium of technology and symbols." In addition, male activities involving the destruction of life are given more prestige than the female's ability to create life. In the words of de Beauvoir, "It is not in giving life but in risking life that man is raised above the animal; that is why superiority has been accorded in humanity not to the sex that brings forth but to that which kills."[15]

Ortner's analysis strikes a responsive chord in those who have no knowledge of the superior and supernatural importance attached to the creation of life in societies like those of the Iroquois, Hopi, Dahomeans, and Ashanti, to mention but a few. In Western society, or in any society dominated by the outer/animal configuration, Ortner's analysis appears particularly applicable. However, with more thought one begins to wonder. Do all societies make a distinction between nature and culture? What about the instances in which men are associated with animals and women with "a civilizing influence"? For example, the Dahomeans are said to have been concerned about their animal-oriented cults because humans were giving birth to animals; thus they adopted the nature and dual-sex-oriented cult of Mawu-Lisa because it enabled them to give birth to humans (see discussion in Chapter 3). "Even in American culture," as Susan Carol Rogers points out in a critical analysis of Ortner's position, "women are by no means always associated with nature!" American sexual imagery portrays men as lustful and animalistic, subdued by the more responsible and civilized woman. The idea of rowdy, antisocial males who would revert to animality in the absence of the "gentler sex" can be traced far back in Western thought.[16]

Harris, Friedl, and Ortner assume universal sexual asymmetry for different reasons. Other anthropologists begin their discussion of male dominance by pointing out that prior sexual egalitarianism was displaced by male dominance. In addition to the work of Eleanor Leacock, who has argued this point longer than any other modern anthropologist, the research of Kay Martin and Barbara Voorhies is relevant.

Martin and Voorhies's argument for the conditions associated with feminine and masculine forms of social structure is remarkably similar to the viewpoint advanced here for the bases of male dominance and female power. These authors contend that descent and residence rules oriented to the maternal line are adaptive in favorable environments where conquest has not subjugated peoples, whereas descent and residence rules oriented to the paternal line are adaptive where resources are scarce or where populations have been subjugated by "patrilineal invaders."[17]

"While matrilineal structures are accommodating and integrative," Martin and Voorhies say, "patrilineal ones are acquisitive and internally divisive." The accommodating nature of matrilineal forms results from the dispersion of related men due to the practice of matrilocality, a practice that promotes widespread cooperation and coordination of groups. The latter form of organization, I would add, encourages integrative political structures, such as the Ashanti and Iroquois confederacies. Because patrilineality and patrilocality consolidate related men, this form of social organization promotes stable political systems in circumstances where competition for scarce resources is the basis for sociocultural survival or expansion.[18]

Martin and Voorhies imply that patrilineality is more likely to be associated with sexual inequality and matrilineality with sexual equality. Based on the societies of this study, these authors are correct. Fifty-two percent of the matrilineal societies as compared to 19% of the patrilineal societies are sexually equal (see Table 8.7). Similarly, 50% of the matrilocal societies as compared with 21% of the strictly patrilocal societies are sexually equal (see Table 8.7).

Table 8.7 shows that there are many fewer matrilineal and matrilocal societies, which has been amply documented by previous cross-cultural studies.[19] Martin and Voorhies attribute the low frequency of matrilineal systems in the ethnographic present to their replacement by more expansive, exploitative patrilineal systems. They note the change from matrilineal to patrilineal forms over wide regions of Africa documented by George P. Murdock. They refer to the example of the Tumbuka, who before 1780 "resembled most of the neighboring tribes in adhering to matrilineal descent, inheritance, and succession, in requiring matrilocal bride-service rather than a bride-price, and in permitting an ultimate shift to avunculocal residence," according to Murdock. Between 1780 and 1800 the Tumbuka came under the influence of "patrilineal invaders." Around 1855, the Tumbuka were subjugated by new rulers "with even stronger patrilineal institutions." "In consequence of their influence," Murdock says,

Table 8.7. *Relationship between descent (H10), residence (H09), and male dominance (MD)*

	Societies where sexes are equal		Societies with some or mytical male dominance		Societies where sexes are unequal		Totals	
	N	%	N	%	N	%	(N)	%
Descent rule								
Patrilineal	12	19	27	42	25	39	64	100
Matrilineal	11	52	3	14	7	33	21	99
Bilateral	22	41	25	46	7	13	54	100
Column totals	45		55		39		139[a]	
Residence rule								
Patrilocal	12	21	24	42	21	37	57	100
Matrilocal or avunculocal	17	50	7	21	10	29	34	100
Patrilocal with matrilocal as alternative	9	28	16	50	7	22	32	100
Ambilocal or neolocal	7	44	8	50	1	6	16	100
Column totals	45		55		39		139[a]	

H10: $\chi^2 = 18.91$ ($df = 4$), $p = 0.0008$. H09: $\chi^2 = 15.58$ ($df = 6$), $p = 0.02$. Appendix B gives reference for H10 and H09.
[a]No information for 17 societies.

"the Tumbuka abandoned even nominal bride-service, adopted the full-fledged South African bridepiece, or *lobola,* substituted the eldest son for the younger brother as the preferred heir and successor, and transformed what had originally been matrisibs into indubitable exogamous patrisibs."[20]

From this and other examples, Martin and Voorhies conclude that the replacement of matrilineal systems "by more expansive exploitative ones, has occurred widely in the primitive world." Matrilineal systems are underrepresented in the ethnographic present because "the ecological adaptations and niches that this type of organization fosters and sustains have all but disappeared in the modern world."[21]

If there has been a widespread transition from female-centered or sexually equal social systems to male-centered or sexually unequal systems, as Martin and Voorhies and Leacock suggest, one wonders how the transition may have come about in everyday behavior. Some of the ways by which male dominance supersedes female power have been discussed in previous chapters, and other ways will be discussed in the next chapter. The myth of male dominance is one way in which the sexes deal with changing circumstances. According to Rogers, the myth of male dominance enables women to retain control of their own sphere, which in the case of the peasant societies she describes is the central unit of the community and the only sphere over which villagers have much control.[22]

Mythical male dominance represents a waystation where opposing and conflicting sexual power principles may coexist. Rogers describes the kinds of conditions that would, logically, cause a shift favoring the male or female end of the power spectrum. She says that if the bases for female power are retained and the activities by which men express authority are lost, women's power will increase and the myth of male dominance will no longer be expressed. If, however, the reverse occurs, male dominance can become a reality, as happens when the center of female power vanishes, women become more dependent on men, and males retain their access to formal rights and duties. The system can collapse completely, with neither sex achieving dominance over the other, if neither sex no longer depends on the other or if either sex is forced to recognize publicly that men are not actually dominant.[23]

From the native's point of view

In light of the variety of anthropological views regarding the development of male dominance, it is interesting to discover that in many societies explanations for "rule by men" exist. These explanations are found in stories recorded by anthropologists in many parts of the world that tell about the time when females ruled and men were forced to seize power from women. Usually the reasoning behind the male rebellion against women is female tyranny or gross incompetence. Women are depicted as the source of unbearable stress and men as being forced to dominate women in order to combat oppression, which is perceived in gigantic proportions.

For example, there is a South American tale about the time "before the Giants wandered through the woods with their heads above the treetops," when "all the forest was evergreen . . . the Sun and Moon walked the earth as man and wife, and many of the great sleepy mountains were human beings." Women were powerful and men "lived in abject fear and subjection," because even though men had "bows and arrows with which to supply the camp with meat," only women had the power "to bring sickness and even death to all those who displeased them." Later, in the mythical sequence of events, the men decide to end the tyranny by killing all women; "there ensued a great massacre, from which not one woman escaped in human form." When the young girl children, untouched by the killing frolic, matured, they replaced the wives who had been killed. In order to maintain the upper hand, men instituted a secret male society and "banished forever the women's lodge." Women were not allowed to participate in the activities of the male society under penalty of death.[24]

This myth can be interpreted as a fantasized explanation for the disorder following Europeanization. The Giants who walk with their heads above the treetops symbolize something that is out of order – a powerful force that stalks the land. Before they came, life was more easily meshed with nature and women were more powerful. The coming of the Europeans to the part of South America where this myth was recorded could easily be perceived in these terms. The Europeans introduced the horse and musketry, causing drastic changes in the way Indians lived. Slaughter and massacre were not limited to conflict between Europeans and Indians. Indians raided other groups for horses, captives, and wives. In this tale, it is women who become the symbols of oppression, not Europeans or warring Indians. In the tale, men win the struggle against the oppressive force by subjugating women. Perhaps the struggle between men and women is a metaphor for the struggle between Indians and Europeans.

In other tales of former female power, the source of oppression is conceived differently but the response is the same: Men seize power from incompetent or power-hungry females. The Kikuyu of Africa have a tale that explains that men were forced to seize power because women became too domineering and ruthless in their capacity as rulers. The Mundurucu tale (see Chapter 2) explains male dominance as resulting from women's inability to hunt meat to feed the trumpet (i.e., fertility) spirits. Male dominance in a tale recorded from the Bambara of Africa is said to have been established in order to bring sanity into a world torn by the actions of a jealous female spirit and the power-hungry exploits of her male counterpart. In this tale order is introduced into the world through the establishment of a supreme being who controls sex antagonism. What can happen if the tension between male and female is not resolved is shown by a tale recorded from the Jivaro of South America. In this tale the origin of just about everything is based on the antagonism between male and female spirits. When the tension between the sexes becomes intolerable, the embodiment of war is introduced, whose purpose is to ensure that the various factions generated from the antagonism between male and female remain in perpetual conflict.[25]

Generally, myths of former female power are found in societies in which there is both male dominance and female power. This is true for the Mundurucu, Bambara, Kikuyu, and Fore. In all of these societies women have considerable autonomy. Naomi Quinn points out that male status among the Mundurucu is insecure and thus their ideology of dominance is defensive and uneasy.[26] Myths of former female power provide men with a rationale for segregating themselves from women and a reason for dominating "tyrannical" women. Wherever men perceive women in such terms, it is likely that women have considerable informal power. Thus, myths of former female power mirror the paradoxical relationship between the sexes that actually exists.

Male dominance: part of a cultural configuration or a solution to stress

In this chapter a distinction has been drawn between mythical and real male dominance. Real male dominance is likely to be found where survival rests more on male than on female actions. It is easy to imagine dependence on the male world evolving when expansion, migration, or social stress puts men in the position of fighting literally and figuratively to maintain an old or to forge a new sociocultural identity in the face of pressures threatening to destroy this identity. In such circumstances, both men and women work to protect the larger identity and supporting world view that mediates sexual identities. For the sake of social and cultural survival, women accept real male domination. Their lives and those of their children may rest on their willingness to do so. The Cheyenne, and probably the Hebrews, represent examples of male dominance in the face of real threats to sociocultural survival.[27] These are the kinds of societies where the greater access of men to valued resources gives men a measure of control over others. Male dominance as conceived by Friedl applies in these instances. Women willingly accept domination in exchange for protection and food.

Mythical male dominance is less easy to comprehend. First, the bases for mythical male dominance are not self-evident. Why do men perceive women as tyrannical and needing to be subjugated in the face of their own felt lack of power? "Why," I have been asked, "do women become the metaphorical lightning rod during times of stress and colonial disruption?" Why not men also?

Answers to such questions are found in Marvin Harris's explanation for male supremacism. Another kind of answer is provided by the work of John and Beatrice Whiting, who argue that male aggression is motivated by the need to break a primary identity with powerful women. A boy who grows up in a household in which his mother and other adult women control the resources will envy the female status, covertly practice the female role, and develop what they call a "feminine optative identity." If, upon reaching adulthood, the boy discovers that his childhood view of the relative power of males and females was distorted, that the balance of power between the sexes favors men beyond the domestic sphere, the boy will develop "a strong need to reject his underlying female identity." This need will lead to "an overdetermined attempt to prove his masculinity, manifested by a preoccupation with physical strength and athletic prowess, or attempts to demonstrate daring and valor, or behavior that is violent and aggressive."[28] Thus, the Whitings contend that male dominance displays are a reaction to a perception of female power.

Which answer one chooses to the question is ultimately a matter of individual taste. Harris has uncovered the external conditions that lead to male violence and the Whitings provide a framework for viewing the psychodynamics that may be involved. For reasons to be advanced in the next chapter, though I have no quarrel with these solutions to the puzzle of male aggression, I prefer a different approach.

9 · Why women?

In the last chapter several theoretical frameworks were outlined that could be employed to explain why women become the symbols of tyranny and men the terrorizers in times of stress and cultural disruption. The Whitings' psychoanalytic framework and the "techno-environmental" explanation proposed by Marvin Harris are particularly appealing because they confront male aggression and male supremacism. Unfortunately, however, these approaches are presented at a level of generalization that treats male aggression as a homogeneous phenomenon and obscures the full texture and patterning of interacting lives in difficult circumstances.

I do not wish to discount the reality of aggression born from adversity stressed by Harris nor the potential importance for men of separating themselves from women emphasized by the Whitings. However, it seems to me that because male supremacist behavior is played out with differing degrees of intensity and inclusion or exclusion of women – a fact amply demonstrated in this chapter – an explanation is required that preserves the variety in the cultural phrasing of male aggression.

The framework I have adopted for answering the question I have posed draws from the work of Margaret Mead and Mary Douglas. Although these women did not write explicity on male dominance, their way of viewing human behavior has influenced my thinking. More than most anthropologists, they have managed to employ a comparative approach without sacrificing the particularity of behavior. Their ideas and concepts will be evident in the general framework suggested in this chapter for understanding a people's reaction to stress.

The aggressive subjugation of women must be understood as part of a people's response to stress. However, adaptation to stress does not always include the subjugation of women. In this chapter descriptions of how men and women respond to depletion of the food supply, disease, and migration are presented. Each case study is matched with another in which the cultural configuration is slightly different but the sources of stress are similar. This approach of matching case studies helps to illuminate the importance of the configuration of culture in shaping a people's reaction to stress.

Defining the oppressor

When people sense that their universe is out of order, that they are victims of circumstances beyond their control, they look among themselves for the oppressor, or they examine their behavior for wrongdoing, or they do both. As Mary Douglas says, "Each tribe is found to inhabit a universe of its own, with its own laws and its own distinctive set of dangers which can be triggered off by incautious humans."[1] People regard their universe as a *whole* that is composed of different parts. A major disorder in one part is presumed to disturb the relations that exist among all the parts. People respond to the disorder by fixing blame and establishing punishments in order to restore balance. Who or what is blamed, and how and why, affects the relationship between the sexes.

Human beings do not separate themselves from nature; rather, they immerse themselves in the world around them, investing the physical world they know, as Mary Douglas says, "with a powerful backlash on moral disorder."[2] Epidemics may be blamed on incest or sorcery; the disappearance of game animals from the forest may be blamed on human quarreling or too much sex. To understand who or what is blamed when disorder strikes, it is useful to ask how males and females are equated with the vital processes of the physical world. For example, where women are equated with fertility and growth and men with aggression and destruction, people react to an imbalance between the food supply and population needs by controlling female fertility, repressing male sexual energy, and in some cases migrating to new territories. Such reactions usually result in an overdependence on male destructive capacities, with the result that the male role is accorded greater prestige and females are perceived as ob-

185

jects to be controlled as a means for limiting population growth.

Margaret Mead says that every human society is faced with two population problems: "how to beget and rear enough children and how not to beget and rear too many." In a growing economy there cannot be too many healthy children, and the emphasis is on reproduction. On the other hand, she notes, "When fecundity threatens vigour, social pressures against childbearing may become apparent." Peoples with a limited amount of land, Mead says, "struggle incessantly with the question of balance: how to get the right number of boys and girls, how many children to save and rear, when the life of one child should be sacrificed to the life of a sibling . . ." The problem of balance may be resolved in many ways. People let their young emigrate, or they develop some form of industry, or in some cases they develop such a negative attitude toward reproduction that sexual activity is viewed with disgust.[3]

A concern for balance is also found in the notion that there is a fixed amount of energy in the universe and that the expenditure of energy in one vital activity implies a loss in some other vital sphere. The most frequent example of this concern is the idea that the investment of energy in sexual activity is antithetical to success in some other endeavor. Another example is the Ashanti belief that a birth in this world means a death in the world of the ancestors. The way people perceive energy and the importance they place on conserving the amount that exists will become apparent in the case studies that follow.

During times of stress people become concerned about whether the energy vital to human life is being drained by energy inimical to life. During these times ancient metaphors for sexual identities become particularly salient. These metaphors determine which sex, if either, is blamed and which is held responsible for restoring order. If life and social continuity are attributed to the actions of men or animals, men will take charge of restoring order and acquire a measure of control. If life and social continuity are attributed to the fertility capacities of women and women have control of fertility ritual, women will take charge.

Whether male dominance is part of the solution to stress depends on the previously prevailing configuration of culture. If a people's sex-role plan is part of a cultural configuration emphasizing cooperation, immersion of the group in nature, and the feminine principle, male dominance is unlikely to result unless the

186

source of stress makes the fertility of women inimical to life itself. On the other hand, if a people's sex-role plan contains male and female principles, cooperation, and competition, as is the case with the dual-sex cultural configuration, the stage is set for mythical male dominance. If both sexes have been traditionally associated with the sources of power, both will respond to stress by attempting to maintain their traditional power while striving to leave room for the other to maneuver. Finally, if the traditional sex-role plan is part of the "outer" configuration, women will become objects to be controlled in a game played by men for the purposes of men. Thus, in the arena of gender power relations, as in so many other human affairs, prior cultural configurations do much to shape human responses to stressful change.

The case studies that follow elaborate these ideas in particular cultural circumstances. We begin by returning to the Mbuti *molimo* ceremony, one of the few times, if not the only time, in Mbuti life when male dominance is expressed. This ceremony is interesting because it shows how Mbuti men and women respond to the sense that things are out of kilter and need to be readjusted so that relations between them and their environment are once again in balance. How a sexually integrated and basically cooperative people respond to periodic stress is instructive. The other examples are drawn from societies where the stress creates a more oppressive atmosphere. In most of the cases examined, the solution involves male dominance behavior. In one case the solution involves women as the central actors. This case is included in order to show that the solution to stress does not always elevate males at the expense of females.

Men, animals, and women: the Mbuti and the Desana

The Mbuti pygmies described in Chapter 1 are a sexually integrated, cooperative people who depend upon a maternal, predominantly nurturant supernatural figure. The way in which the cultural configuration of the pygmies shapes their response to stress can be compared with that of the Desana, a sexually segregated, competitive people who depend on a sexually charged, decidedly masculine force for all energy vital to life. During times of stress similar processes can be observed at work in these societies. However, the Mbuti do not experience the severity of stress that confronts the Desana. The Mbuti solution to stress reaffirms the balance and interdependence between the sexes, whereas the Desana solution encourages male aggression and hostility against women.

Explaining to Colin Turnbull the reason for the *molimo* ceremonies, held when the Mbuti feel that all is not well between themselves and the forest, upon which they depend for everything, an old Mbuti man said: "The forest is a father and mother to us and like a father or mother it gives us everything we need – food, clothing, shelter, warmth . . . and affection. Normally everything goes well because the forest is good to its children, but when things go wrong there must be a reason."[4] Things go wrong, the old man said, at night when the people are asleep, when no one is awake to protect humans from harm. At night army ants may invade the camp or leopards may come in and steal a hunting dog or even a child. The old man said that such things would not happen when people are awake. Thus, he reasoned, "When something big goes wrong, like illness or bad hunting or death, it must be because the forest is sleeping and not looking after its children."[5]

Because things go wrong when the forest is "asleep," the forest must be "awakened" so that it looks after the interests of the people. The old man said: "We wake it up by singing to it, and we do this because we want it to awaken happy. Then everything will be well and good again. So when our world is going well then also we sing to the forest because we want to share our happiness."[6]

One way the Mbuti "awaken" the forest is to sound the *molimo* trumpets. These trumpets are referred to as "the animal of the forest" and are kept from the sight of women, who are supposed to believe that the sound of the trumpet is made by an animal and that to see the trumpet would bring death. It is also believed that the women used to possess the *molimo* trumpets and that they were stolen from them by the men. This is the main reason why the women must be barred from viewing the trumpets. Were they to have access to the trumpets, it is thought, the women might try to seize them from the men.[7]

A ceremony called the "lesser" *molimo* is held when hunting is bad. This ceremony involves men alone. After supper the women and children are bundled away safely in the huts and the men prepare for a night of eating and singing to the forest. When the men sing in the camp, the sound of the trumpets echoes the men's song from the depths of the forest. Sometimes the sound of the trumpet is that of an angry animal who will endanger the lives of women and children. Other times the trumpet's sound is mournful and pleads with the forest and men for food. The trumpets are fed food and water and passed through the flames of the *molimo* fire in an act that signifies the male role in copulation.[8] These acts suggest that men are responsible for the well-being and fertility of animals.

The "lesser" *molimo* ceremony is one of the few times when men and women are separated and men imitate a dominant role. This ceremony signifies the responsibility of men in connection with animals and the hunt. Women and children are bundled off into the huts in order to protect them from the dangerous forces emanating from the forest world during the night. The animal nature of men is expressed in the association of the trumpets with masculinity and animality. The manipulation of the trumpets during the ceremony, however, indicates also that with the aid of their forest, men are meant to control animal nature for the good of the community.

The idea that the trumpets were stolen from women suggests that it was from women men believe they found the means to control the destructive forces that stalk the forest at night and that it was from women they received their animal nature. Stealing the trumpets implies also that masculinity must be aggressively separated from femininity, that men in order to be powerful and to have control must take these rights from women by force.

The whole community participates in the "greater" *molimo,* a ceremony held when hunting is bad, someone has died, there is widespread sickness, and death seems to rule life. In this ceremony the Mbuti conception of male and female is thrown into sharp relief. While the "lesser" *molimo* is spoken of as "waking" the forest, the "greater" *molimo* ideally is a festival of joy. The purpose of this ceremony, Turnbull says, is to symbolically establish the triumph of life over death.[9]

The focal role in this ceremony is played by an old woman (see Chapter 1 for a description of this woman's actions during the ceremony). This woman, together with the nubile girl with whom she dances, symbolizes the forces of life and of death. The old woman is referred to as "mother," the same term used to address the forest in its capacity as giver of life and death. In her ceremonial acts the old woman symbolizes these two forces. When she stamps out the fire, the symbol of life, she enacts the meaning of death. When she scatters the embers and allows the fire to be revitalized and rebuilt by the men, she enacts the transference to men of the role they are to play in connection with life.

The men revitalize and rebuild the fire with a dance that simulates copulation. Turnbull says that fire is primarily connected with women; the hearth is often referred to as the vagina.[10] When the men rebuild the fire and sing to the forest, they are serving as agents for restoring order. Women, on the other hand, appear to be placed in the role of either giving or taking life. They do not, at least within the framework of the *molimo* ceremonies, act as mediators between positive and negative forces.

The symbolism of the old woman tying the men with a roll of twine suggests that in their role as life takers women have ultimate control but that this control is inimical to the survival of the group. When the old woman ties the men, they stop singing, which means that the male capacity to rejuvenate the forest has been bound. The men say: "This woman has tied us up. She has bound the men, bound the hunt, and bound the molimo. We can do nothing." By untying the men the old woman gives them control once again. But in order to be freed the men must admit that they have been bound and they must give the woman something as a token of their defeat. Once she has been given an agreed-upon quantity of food and cigarettes, the old woman unties each man. As each is untied, each begins to sing again, which signifies that once more the *molimo* is free.[11]

Turnbull says that the *molimo* festival serves as an integrating factor in Mbuti life. It also expresses the latent antagonisms that exist between the sexes while uniting the band in a common expression of their dependence upon the forest. The *molimo* forces "an acknowledgement of the most basic dependency of all, that of life and death."[12] The *molimo* is also an enactment of the interdependence between male and female. The latent antagonism between the sexes to which Turnbull refers could be viewed as an expression of the basic antithesis between forces meant to give as well as take life (associated with females) and forces meant to regenerate the forces of life from those of death (associated with males).

In contrast to the Hopi ceremonies described by Schlegel, the *molimo* expresses the double nature of women as well as of men. Men and women stand for life and death in different ways, women more directly than men. Men regenerate life in the "greater" *molimo* and enact the role of destructive animality in the "lesser" *molimo*. Though the old woman's superior position is assured by the deferential behavior of the men, it is the ceremonial give-and-take between male and female and between men and the forest that controls and harmonizes opposing forces in the Mbuti forest world.

The Desana are a small subgroup of some thousand Tukano Indians who live in the equatorial rain forests in the Colombian Northwest Amazon. The Desana imagine that there is a fixed quantity of energy that flows in a closed circuit "between man and animal, between society and nature."[13] They live by a set of strict rules formulated to maintain a biotic equilibrium, which they believe is necessary because of the natural tendency of men to consume without restraint and to exploit the environment.[14] The concept of a fixed quantity of energy flowing in a closed circuit means that every particle of energy that is removed must be converted into a form that can be reincorporated into the circuit. For example, when an animal is killed, the energy of the local fauna is displaced into the field of society, because the consumers of the food acquire energy that previously belonged to the animal.[15] The energy taken from the animal, however, must eventually be replaced by masculine energy.

"The cultural focus of the Desana is the hunt," Gerardo Reichel-Dolmatoff says, "and as hunters they live in close contact with their natural environment." Their home is the forest, the same forest that is the home of the game animals they pursue. Both animals and man draw from the same single source of reproductive energy. Because the hunter needs animals for food and procreative energy, the hunter must foster the fertility of animals. Thus the game animals are thought to depend on the actions of the hunters for the increase of their species. Being dependent on men, the game animals "fear that human sexuality, which always diminishes the total potential, may set a limit to their own powers of procreation." The sexual act must be selectively controlled by men, Reichel-Dolmatoff says, in order to establish a balance and guarantee survival.[16]

The Desana have a concept for masculine energy, which is called *tulári*. The feminine equivalent is called *bogá*, which means transformation and creation. *Tulári* makes *bogá* function. The two together "are fertilization and fecundity; they are the great current that circulates."[17] These concepts are not applied to humans alone. Anything perceived as having force, power, and impulse is *tulári*. Anything that attracts or is a recipient is *bogá*.[18]

In the activity of the hunt, hunters represent *tulári* and animals *bogá*. It is believed that animals are "a voluntary succubus, fertilized by man, that multiplies its own animal species."[19] Hunting is described as being "practically a courtship and a sexual act, an event that must be prepared for with great care in accordance with the strictest norms."[20] The verb *to hunt* translated means "to make love to the animals." It is said that "to kill is to cohabit." The hunter must make himself sexually attractive to the animals. One of the principle conditions in preparing for the hunt is sexual abstinence because, in the words of a Desana male, "The animals are jealous." Sexual contact before the hunt "would be like a theft for them . . . Only those who have had no sexual contacts can count on the sympathy of the animals." The hunter must also purify himself internally by taking emetics and externally by taking a bath in the river. After an animal is killed, the hunter speaks to it, especially if it is a female, observes its genitals, and comments on their size or form.[21]

Over the years (it is not known for how long) there has been a growing scarcity of game and an increase in the female sphere of horticulture (due to the demand from neighboring Indians and rubber collectors for horticultural produce). Because the fertility and fecundity of humans and animals draw from the same source, consisting of male (*tulári*) and female (*bogá*) energy, and since this energy source is "a restricted capital," evidence that game animals are less abundant means to men that male energy is being depleted. This causes men to become anxious about their sexual and procreative powers. Sexual repression is one means by which men seek to restore these powers to original levels.[22] Another way in which men seek to restore their procreative powers in connection with animals is to exclude women from male ritual equipment and certain ritual activities. By so doing, men ensure that human female energy (*bogá*) will not contaminate male energy (*tulári*) needed for success in hunting.

The measures taken by men to restore animal energy result in male dominance behavior, at least to the eye of the outside observer. Men order women around, occasionally subject them to sexual assaults, and exclude them from the ritual activities meant to fertilize nature. The structure of thought among the Desana is largely determined by the activity of the rain forest hunter and reflects deep preoccupation with the relationship between males and animals. Sexual repression in order to retain and accumulate animal energy serves both as a conscious control of the birthrate and, equally important, conserves the imagined quantity of sexual energy. According to Reichel-Dolmatoff, sexual repression to maintain the biotic equilibrium causes serious psychological problems, which are expressed "in the high incidence of homosexuality, acts of aggression, and other manifestations." All of this, he suggests, can be traced to the problems created by the Desana being a sedentary group that tenaciously insists on the hunt as a cultural focus. "The biotic equilibrium," he says, "is thus easily upset." Not surprisingly, the Desana male is described as neither contented, nor balanced, nor well adjusted.[23]

As might be expected from their ideological and actual preoccupation with animals, the Desana creation myth is masculine in tone. The creator of the universe is the sun, whom the Desana call Sun Father. Perhaps at one time the female principle, which is associated with earth and water in Desana creation cosmology, played a greater or equal role. Though male dominance does not exist among the Desana to the degree described for the Mundurucu (see Chapter 2), similar cultural mechanisms are at work. In both cases female procreative energy is feared, men take steps to conserve and control it, and animals play an important part in fantasized sexual intercourse. The interesting difference is that among the Mundurucu, women are thought to have intercourse with animals; among the Desana, men fertilize animals. The Mundurucu have a Mother of the Game, the Desana have a Master of the Game.

These two lowland South American groups are part of a widespread tropical forest cultural complex that includes sexual separation, inequality, and antagonism. These are "hunting" cultures, but meat furnishes only a small proportion of the total daily food supply. Although the tropical forest in which they live is not prime hunting territory, these peoples cling to the hunting way of life. They illustrate "the cultural and demographic effects of a dependence on hunting in an area where hunting is neither profitable nor easy.''[24] Their continued emphasis on hunting in an unfavorable environment where the produce of horticulture and fishing supplies most of the daily food supply is testimony to the persistence of the outward orientation. It also suggests that they once relied predominantly on hunting and, perhaps, gathering. The Desana insist that they are hunters and say that many of the plants grown by them were introduced in recent times. They fish, but this activity also seems to be an introduction from other groups. In spite of a fluctuating food supply, the food surplus from horticulture is traded rather than used to compensate for the scarcity of meat. The Desana provide an interesting illustration of how an animal orientation in the face of ecological stress and masculine origin beliefs may encourage the development of male dominance.

External and internal threats to social survival: mythical versus real male dominance in the New Guinea highlands

The Enga of the western highlands of New Guinea conserve male energy by controlling female fertility. Enga men believe that copulation is detrimental to male well-being. A vital fluid is believed to reside in a man's skin that makes it sound and handsome, a condition that determines and reflects male mental vigor and self-confidence. This fluid is also manifested in a man's semen. Every ejaculation thus depletes a man's vitality, and overindulgence is thought to dull a man's mind and leave his body permanently exhausted and withered. A man does not enter his gardens the day he copulates because female secretions still adhering to him may blight his crops. He also does not try to cook meat lest it spoil. The result is that the ordinary husband copulates with his wife only as often as he thinks necessary to beget children.

Most Enga bachelors believe that sexual abstinence is the best safeguard against pollution, enervation, and deterioration of appearance. Some fear the dangers of sexual intercourse so much that they try to postpone marriage. In addition to their fear of sexual intercourse, menstrual blood is thought to destroy the plants men use for wealth, pig, and war magic.[25]

Shirley Lindenbaum argues that these beliefs represent men's attempt to balance the ratio between population and resources in an area where land is scarce and neighboring groups constantly fight each other for the few resources.[26] Meggitt suggests that the

Enga equate femininity with sexuality and peril because wives are acquired from neighboring groups who are in competition for the same resources. The Enga have a saying, "We marry the people we fight."[27] The hostility between the Enga sexes may act as an effective population control mechanism, as Lindenbaum suggests, and may reflect the hostile relationship between the groups that the husband and wife represent, as Meggitt implies. The maintenance of such intersexual hostility and, incidently, of male dominance over women, is a way of curbing female fertility. The fear of excess fertility is very evident in this region of New Guinea, where infanticide and the killing of widows within 24 hours after the death of their husbands is common.[28]

The relationship between the Enga sexes is one of domination–subordination. Enga women are denied participation in public affairs, treated as minors, and denied any title to valuable property.[29] For the most part Enga women are the less mobile sex and maintain a narrower range of social relationships. Enga origin mythology centers on "sky dwellers," who appeared at a particular locality where they met women (whose presence there is unexplained) whom they married; they eventually founded the patrilineal descent groups. Some founders originated first in animal or insect form, then married ordinary women and raised human sons. Other sky men arrived carrying "eggs of the sun": stones from which their wives or children sprang. These stones, for most Enga clans, represent sacred symbols that are the foci of rituals designed to propitiate clan ghosts in times of adversity.[30] Thus, the Enga sacred tribal symbols are predominantly male in tone.

In contrast to the Enga, the Fore of the eastern highlands exhibit a fundamental cleavage between the sexes in myth, ritual, and social action. Cooperation between the sexes is important, both in ritual and in everyday life.[31] During important peace-making ceremonies, women may be present to listen and will take part in the discussion.[32] The origin mythology of the Fore focuses on the creative exploits of a female and her male consort, both of whom first emerged from a swamp in Fore territory. This female is identified with the earth, and in the story of creation, her husband receives less emphasis. This couple peopled the countryside, established gardens, and introduced creatures, plants, and trees useful to man, along with various behavior patterns, rituals, and ceremonies. All people are considered children of the female creator.

According to R. M. Berndt, the two Fore creators represent the forces of nature upon which people are directly dependent. However, the greatest dependence is on the fertility powers of the female creator.[33]

The female creator symbolizes fertility and is identified with the earth. Male strength and animal, human, and garden fertility depend on offerings of salt and blood to this woman.[34] The major ceremonies are fertility ceremonies. Because the creators copulated in a garden before the creation of people, gardens are a popular place for intercourse. The breaking of the ground with digging sticks in gardening is likened to the impregnation of the earth mother.[35] Although Fore men may talk about female pollution, they lack the Enga sense of horror. Premarital and extramarital affairs abound, and Fore are cavalier in their approach to incest.[36]

Thus, Fore ritual and sexual behavior are devoted to promoting fertility and growth, whereas Enga ritual and sexual behavior are devoted to repressing sexuality. Contrary to the Enga, the Fore have ample land for a small population. The Fore readily admit newcomers and provide them with fertile land. The main problem confronting the Fore is to maintain group strength in the face of aggressive neighbors and a lowered reproductive capacity due to the presence of *kuru*, a fatal neurological disorder that attacks childbearing women more than men.[37] This threat to Fore social survival increases the Fore emphasis on fertility. *Kuru* also encourages male dominance because of the Fore belief that all wrongs must be "balanced" by some form of retaliation.

In the past when wrongs involved members of different Fore districts, warfare resulted. Until recently, when fighting was suppressed by the colonial administration, warfare was the main form of intercourse between the districts of the region. Warfare was justified as a means of exacting compensation or revenge from another district for a real or imagined injury.

Warfare was brought to a halt in the late 1950s by government and mission edicts. Soon after, a *kuru* epidemic struck the South Fore. The cause of the epidemic was traced to sorcery by political rivals, and the males of several hard-hit social groups began to police their borders as if they were preparing to defend against an attack. Having no other means to seek compensation, men sought to retaliate with sorcery. The high mortality rate among childbearing women from *kuru* reached such proportions that the

South Fore began to fear extinction. For several months in late 1962 and early 1963, members of hostile South Fore groups gathered to discuss the emergency created by the sexual imbalance. Reputed sorcerers confessed their past activities and everyone reaffirmed the Fore belief that *kuru* results from sorcery. It was agreed that the *kuru* epidemic would end if unity replaced factionalism, and sorcery, considered to be a pernicious form of concealed warfare, came to an end. Women participated in these meetings, just as they had in peace-making ceremonies of the past.[38]

The *kuru* problem did not end, however, and sorcery accusations continued. In 1970, when Shirley Lindenbaum returned to the South Fore area, she found that close alliances had dissolved and political affiliations had shifted because of sorcery accusations. One group had emigrated to settle with kin and friends in the southeast frontier. Those who remained said they had rid themselves of a pack of bad sorcerers. Traditional expressions of outrage continued to flow back and forth between individuals and groups as aggrieved parties, out to settle debts, were thought to seek restitution in the form of *kuru* sorcery. Only men were involved in this process. "For a man to lose his wife," Lindenbaum says, meant the loss of "the very foundation of his existence." Since the primary victims of *kuru* were childbearing women, it was assumed that the sorcerers were exacting revenge on other men's wives to compensate for the death of their own.[39]

The *kuru* epidemic increased status competition among men. Since women were the victims of the disease, they increasingly became defined as weak and inferior. Traditionally, however, men had been defined as the weaker, but not necessarily the inferior, sex. A man's physical strength was believed to be contained in his "flute," which men once stole from women. The flutes symbolize male dominance over women, but males are thought to have acquired dominance and strength from women. In the myth of the origin of the sacred flutes, women are said to have had them first and to have lost them through the duplicity (or because of the physical violence) of men. In other myths it is said that female pubic hair turned the male from an effeminate creature into a man with warlike qualities.

Maleness is assured by performing sacred rites with the flutes, from which women are excluded on pain of death.[40] Should a woman see a man's flute, his strength fails; playing the flute en-

197

hances a man's strength. Only at death, when a man's flute is broken and buried with him, does his physical strength disappear.[41] The main reason men give for segregating themselves from women while performing rites involving the flutes is their prior ownership by women: "They must not see us because we are doing something associated with them."[42]

Thus, traditionally at least, men feared, respected, and depended on female "natural" powers. Women maintained the image of male dominance by playing the flute game. Women are reported as acting frightened when the flutes were played, huddling in their dwellings out of sight. Though they supposedly cannot see the flutes, on pain of death, women know what the flutes look like. They "play the game" because they want their menfolk to be strong, as they themselves must be strong. Women do not feel it is unjust for men to segregate them from the flutes.[43]

Fore male dominance is uneasy because of male dependence on female natural powers. As Shirley Lindenbaum points out, "Fore men have carved out a political domain by taking public responsibility for certain important aspects of reproduction and human survival." Although the flute myths are myths about the subjugation of women, "they are also embryonic statements in the history of the battle of men to control women's bodies." As one Fore man put it, "Women's menstruation has always been present; men's bleeding, that came later."[44]

To conclude, Fore men fear for their powers of reproduction, whereas Enga men fear women and the dangers of excess fertility. The Fore exhibit behavior suggestive of mythical male dominance, but male dominance among the Enga seems very real. As Meggitt says regarding the Enga, "The men have won their battle and have relegated women to an inferior position."[45] Meggitt's discussion of male–female relationships in the New Guinea highlands also recognizes the need for discriminating between types of male dominance behavior. On the basis of comparison between two highland societies, the Enga and the Kuma (who are much like the Fore), he says: "We must discriminate between at least two kinds of inter-sexual conflict or opposition – the Mae (Enga) type and the Kuma type. The one reflects the anxiety of prudes to protect themselves from contamination by women, the other the aggressive determination of lechers to assert their control over recalcitrant women."[46]

198

Why women?

From this discussion, one can conclude that real male dominance evolves when the primary dependence for social continuity during times of severe stress is found in the male world, and mythical male dominance evolves when the primary dependence for social continuity involves both males and females.

The experience of migration: the Azande versus the Bemba

In the face of oppression, cultural disruption, or ecological stress, whole populations, small groups, or individuals may leave their territory and migrate to seek relief. The nature of the migration experience and the type of environment that is colonized can have a significant impact on traditional sex-role interaction. Several pertinent questions come to mind. What is the sex ratio of the migrating population? Does the colonized environment offer the same adaptive possibilities, ensuring the maintenance of tradition, or does the new environment impose the need for new choices? Depending on the circumstances presented by the newly colonized environment, and depending on the ideological assumptions people bring with them, traditional sex roles will be maintained, or transformed, or new ones fabricated.

The exodus from Egypt into Canaan is a classic and familiar example of one pattern of migration. The cultural heritage of the Hebrews represented a decided "outward" orientation. Before the Hebrews of the family of Jacob settled in Egypt under the rule of Joseph, they were, like other Hebrew tribes, wanderers and adventurers who obeyed the call of a masculine god. They migrated peacefully into Egypt to escape famine, and they eventually left Egypt because of political oppression. During their subjugation in Egypt, Moses emerged as their culture hero. He led his people out of bondage by setting forth Yahweh, then only a minor tribal god, as the major symbol of order and power. The convenant established in the Sinai desert proclaimed Yahweh the only and all-powerful God who must be obeyed at all costs, if the Hebrews were to succeed in their attempt to establish their supremacy in a new land.

The male culture hero who is the focus of migration stories and who instructs his people in proper conduct is commonly found in tribal legend and lore. An example, discussed in Chapter 7, is Sweet Medicine, the Cheyenne culture hero who is described as "a

199

great holy man" whom the Cheyenne met in their wanderings and who instructed them in the proper usage of the four Sacred Medicine Arrows given to Sweet Medicine by the Great Spirit to protect the Cheyenne against death and famine. The Arrows shared the supreme power of the Great Spirit and identified the Cheyenne as the "particular, singled out people."[47] Like the Hebrew Ark of the Covenant, the Arrows represented a body of rules by which life was to be lived and adversity could be conquered. The dependence of the Cheyenne on the arrows represented a primary dependence on the male world for social continuity.

Migration has clearly been an important factor in the history of sex-role plans. Migration disrupts old ways and forces people to adopt new ones in order to maintain their integrity as a group in their new land. The battle for supremacy in a new land may include the subjugation of women. To illustrate the importance and complexity of the migration experience, the sex-role plans of two African societies are described. These two groups have experienced migration with different forms of cultural disruption and with different consequences for the relationship between the sexes.

The Azande of central Africa migrated as a group of hunters, without agriculture, and expanded into their present territory by conquering peoples possessing agriculture, from whom they took wives. Though they do not live in a marginal territory, the Azande have never developed adequate food preservation and storage techniques to insure against periods of food shortage. Thus, in addition to living as conquerors of hostile groups, they fear hunger. Sexual inequality and male dominance among the Azande are extreme.

The Bemba of south central Africa also migrated into their present territory but, the evidence suggests, with little cultural disruption. They migrated with women and, more important perhaps, with domesticated plants. Although they experience periods of hunger in the absence of food storage techniques, sexual equality among them is evident.

The culture history of the Azande begins with the movement of the Ambomu peoples who, from a large game-hunting base and a mobile economy, migrated into the area now referred to as Zandeland, where they grew and prospered at the expense of the peoples they either dispossessed or absorbed.

Why women?

The amalgam of peoples today referred to as the Azande owes
its origins to a large body of the Ambomu people who, consolidated under the leadership of the Avongara clan, moved from
their homeland in what is now the Central African Republic into
what is now Zaire, and then eastward, southward, and also north-
ward into Sudan. Evans-Pritchard, who studied the Azande and
lived among them, places the time about the middle of the eighteenth century, and says that in the course of their movements
"they conquered vast territories, driving before them or bringing
into subjection a number of foreign peoples whose descendants
were in varying degrees assimilated to their Mbomu conquerors,
the resultant amalgam forming the Zande people as we know
them today."[48]

During the migrations, wars, and conquests, the Avongara
grew in power. Today they rule the Azande as an aristocratic
class. In piecing together the origin of the Avongara ruling clan
(from myths, verbal traditions, and early accounts), Evans-Pritchard concludes that a man called Basenginonga established some
sort of preeminence over the Ambomu people, "which his descendants developed into the complete domination of the Avongara in
historic times."[49] Thus, at least according to present-day beliefs,
the hegemony of a vast territory by one clan is traced to a single
male figure and his descendants.

A single male figure also initiates the main events in the Zande
creation story. A man called Bapaizegino put mankind with the
rest of creation into a round canoe and closed it, except for a small
hidden entrance by which it could be opened. He sent a messenger
to his sons (Sun, Moon, Night, Cold, and Stars), saying that he
was dying and they were to come immediately. Only the Sun
treated the messenger in the way that the son of a king was supposed to treat his father's messenger. Here in the story appear
Zande notions of royal obligations. When an Avongara king dies,
his sons must vie for hegemony over their father's territory. In the
creation myth, since the Sun behaved properly, he was given the
secret of the hidden opening. Hence it was the Sun who eventually
opened the canoe, out of which poured "men and beasts and trees
and grasses and rivers and hills." The Sun thus became king of all
things.[50]

Bapaizegino is equated with the supreme being called Mbori.
They are believed to be one and the same person. There is some

201

evidence that Mbori is a product of European and missionary influence. The Zande creation myth sounds less Christian and more a mythical account of the Ambomu exodus and final ascendancy of one son. The canoe that is so central to the story is out of place because the Azande have probably only seen canoes among foreigners living on the banks of the big rivers that they may have crossed during their migrations. There is another story that equates the Ambomu exodus with the flight of the Hebrews. This story tells of "a great witch doctor of the past who cut a river in twain to allow the Azande to pass over to the other side and who eventually ascended into the heavens, reminding us in these two feats of Moses and Elijah."[51]

Azande folklore is almost entirely concerned with a man called Ture who is the hero of numerous tales. He belongs to folklore rather than to sacred mythology; he embodies the average Zande and appears in a cycle of tales in which animals talk. He is sometimes vaguely associated with Mbori and is said to have walked about with him. Mbori and Ture belong to the "hazy supra-sensible world."[52] Neither exercises much power over everyday life, although Mbori is believed to have given men magic and oracles and is the cause of everything.[53] Mbori is not given a personal gender but what is sometimes called an animal gender. Persons are given the personal pronouns *ko* (masculine) and *li* (feminine). The animal pronoun *u* is given to animals, ghosts, the supreme being, certain heavenly bodies, and a number of vegetables and tools that have an especially intimate relationship with human beings.[54]

Associated with each Azande clan is the notion of common descent from some animal, reptile, or insect. The totems of aristocratic clans like the Avongara are the larger, more ferocious beasts. It is believed that the physical strength and energy of the dead pass into the totem animal in a manner reminiscent of the Desana belief that energy flows in a closed circuit. An observer of Zande belief writes:

I am under the strong impression that the Zande does not believe that the dead man is simply and entirely transformed into a (clan) beast, or that his *soul* enters into a beast, but rather that his store of energy or vital spark goes back into the common fund of vital energy which enables man and beast (of the clan) to persist and thrive.[55]

Why women?

The centrality of animals in Zande folklore and notions about clan origins was, perhaps, due to the importance of hunting. Commenting on the importance of agriculture compared to hunting, a nineteenth-century traveler noted that agriculture was definitely secondary and assigned completely to females (as it still is). When the Ambomu conquest was still in process, this traveler said, "Men most studiously devote themselves to their hunting, and leave the culture of the soil to be carried on exclusively by the women."[56] He noted, in evidence, that the entire costume of those in a certain king's court was "composed of skins . . . as became a hunting people." The women, he said, "wore an apron of hides."[57] Today the Azande are primarily agriculturalists, with most of the work being assigned to women. However, Evans-Pritchard believes that the Ambomu were "in past times primarily a hunting people,"[58] who adopted agriculture in the course of their migration. This change, he thinks, is important for understanding their political success. The mobile economy facilitated movement, but the increase in the power of the Avongara and the assimilation of foreign peoples were facilitated by the "greater stability a growing dependence on cultivated crops might have brought about."[59]

Most food is still grown by women. In the Zande royal economy "women are the real wealth – their labor and child-bearing, their productive and reproductive functions." The more wives a man has, the greater is the hospitality he can offer, thus attracting to himself followers who provide him with yet more labor and other services. The more children he has, the more solid is his dynastic line. In the early twentieth century, before British conquest and the collapse of the Avongara political system, Zandeland was composed of a number of kingdoms all related to the Avongara line. In each the political structure was similar. There was a king who offered hospitality and was responsible for public order, the upkeep of communications, and defense of the territory. For those who lived in his territory he was the "father–ruler to his people and they his children–subjects."[60] A king planted his sons out in the provinces, where they were almost independent monarchs ruling autonomous states. When the king died, his sons vied with one another for his territory. During the expansion, elder princes would enlarge their domain at the expense of foreign peoples. Once the momentum of expansion had slowed down, the domain of a prince could grow only by fighting against brothers or other kinsmen.[61] Later in Zande history, dynastic rivalries frequently led to wars and assassinations. The violence was added to by Arabs and Europeans. Evans-Pritchard says that

Zande history is very largely a chronicle of patricides, fratricides, and the slaughter of sons and cousins on a Visigothic scale . . . The slaughter was appalling. Very few of the kings died a natural death, and those who, in our way of thinking, did so are thought by Azande, who regard all deaths as brought about by human action, to have perished by curses or sorcery on the part of their kinsmen.[62]

The position of Azande women is best understood by examining their exclusion from any dealing with the "poison oracle." The most important regulator of everyday life among the Azande is a practice known as consulting the poison oracle. No venture is undertaken without authorization of the poison oracle. It is consulted in all collective undertakings, in all life crises, in all serious legal disputes, and in all matters strongly affecting individual welfare. "In short, on all occasions regarded by Azande as dangerous or socially important, the activity is preceded by consultation of the poison oracle."[63]

The poison oracle is a male prerogative and "one of the principal mechanisms of male control and expression of sex antagonism." Considering the degree to which social life is regulated by the poison oracle, Evans-Pritchard says:

We shall at once appreciate how great an advantage men have over women in their ability to use it, and how being cut off from the main means of establishing contact with the mystical forces that so deeply affect human welfare degrades woman's position in Zande society. I have little hesitation in affirming that the customary exclusion of women from any dealings with the poison oracle is the most evident symptom of their inferior social position and means of maintaining it.[64]

Women do, however, have some recourse. They are not entirely powerless: It is said that although women hate and fear the oracle, if they find some of the poison in the bush they "will destroy its power by urinating on it."[65] Thus, again, internal secretions from women are viewed as having the capacity to nullify male power.

Why women?

Sexual separation and antagonism are pronounced. Zande noblemen and commoners of good social position are constantly spying on their wives; as far as possible, such men will never let them out of their sight. Wives are treated as if they were enemies. One wonders if women were not in the past taken from the groups conquered by the Ambomu. If the Ambomu borrowed plants from these groups, as Evans-Pritchard says they did, they may have acquired the plants and horticultural practices through the women they married. This would explain why horticulture is primarily assigned to women. The system of marriage exchange is also interesting in this respect. Spears pass in one direction and wives in the other. Group A gives spears to group B in return for a wife. Group B passes these spears to Group C to obtain a wife.[66] Spears in exchange for wives inspires the image of warfare for women. This could account for both the power and the subjugation of women; like enemies, they are to be feared and controlled.

Evans-Pritchard remarks that "it was the ancient custom of the nobles (Avongara) to take their kinswomen to wife, including their sisters on the spearside and their daughters."[67] However, elsewhere he describes customs in which large numbers of women from captured groups were given as wives, servants, or citizens to noblemen.[68] Adding to the sexual opposition bred by the capture of women is the custom of late marriage for men, which results either in sexual repression or adultery. Before the ages of 30 to 35, males were deprived of access to females, because women were monopolized by older men who would marry girls young enough to be their granddaughters.[69] The shortage of women created by polygyny undoubtedly led to a higher incidence of rape and encouraged the seizure of women in warfare.[70]

Sexual repression, polygyny, and warfare for women supply a major key for understanding sexual inequality and male dominance among the Azande. Furthermore, Azande culture history shows neither the time depth nor the cultural continuity found in African kingdoms, where female power is legendary. The Zande culture is not one culture but an amalgamation of many; it is a grand melting pot ruled by a noble class, the Avongara. The Ambomu began their migrations as a hunter/gatherer group with, at the most, simple agriculture. Since then, the growth of their culture has been a product of conquest and assimilation. There is, in short, not much about their culture that can be described as autochthonous.

Like the Azande, the Bemba (south central Africa) are shifting horticulturalists, with hunting a secondary but important activity. Horticultural activities among the Bemba are interconnected with elaborate rituals, which include a concern with the fertility of women and of the soil. Hunting rites and magic also exist but do not dominate the feminine province. What dominates is duality, in which the male and female principles are joined in a complementary relationship. Strong mystic links are thought to exist between Bemba husband and wife.[71] Women play a prominent role in the Bemba account for their origin, which describes their beginnings in another land and why they left that land. Bemba rituals display more balance between the male and the female spheres, neither of which has been elaborated on at the expense of the other. Instead, the two are frequently joined in the same ritual setting.

The Bemba cultivate indigenous African crops. There is evidence that they have had these crops for a long time. Although the Bemba left their homeland and migrated to another land, theirs is not a patchwork culture. According to oral tradition, they brought with them the crops that figure most importantly in their ritual cycle. The Bemba declare that their first ancestor, Citi Muluba, "travelled from the Luba country carrying in his hair the seeds of Kaffir corn, finger millet, Kaffir beans, cow peas, pumpkins, and the small wrinkled cucumbers known as *amankolobwe.*" Their most important economic rites center on the cultivation of these crops, particularly Kaffir corn and their staple food, finger millet. Kaffir corn, beans, and finger millet are African cultigens; pumpkins and cucumbers are of New World origin, probably introduced by the Portuguese in the seventeenth century. In their oral tradition, the Bemba take care to distinguish how and when they got certain crops. They say, for example, that they have grown maize and ground nuts "for a long time," that sweet potatoes were introduced by Swahili traders at the end of the nineteenth century, and that they learned to grow cassava from a neighboring tribe.[72]

The largest and most highly organized tribe in northeastern Rhodesia, the Bemba are of Congo origin and apparently invaded their present territory at the end of the seventeenth or the beginning of the eighteenth century. They moved into a territory inhabited by other recently arrived groups, who originated from the same general cultural tradition. The Bemba pushed these groups out and established their paramount chief as the ruler of the area. They have much in common with their neighbors; all have a tradition of Congo origin, speak similar languages, and are predominantly agricultural (as they were before migrating). Descent, clan affiliation, and succession to office pass through the female line, and residence after marriage is with the woman's family. At puberty there is an elaborate initiation ceremony for girls but no corresponding ritual for boys. It is in this ritual that we see the association of maternity with fertility of the soil.[73]

The Bemba have a centralized form of government with the paramount chief, the Citimukulu, at the apex. He is a hereditary ruler with a fixed title drawn from the royal clan known as the crocodile people. He traces his descent in the female line for more than 25 holders of the office. He rules over his own district, the center of the Bemba country, and acts as overlord to a number of territorial chiefs, who achieve office in the same way and are members of the same clan. Sisters and maternal nieces of the chiefs are given the title of chieftainess, Banamfumu. They succeed to titles and rule over villages. The chief's mother, the Candamukulu, rules over a small territory of her own and plays an important part in tribal councils. The power of the chief rests on the people's belief in his supernatural powers over the prosperity of the land. He has the power to approach the tribal deities and must carry out the rites that affect the food supply.[74]

In Bemba tribal life, women, unlike men, are admired for their industry and resource in finding food in the bush. They are honored for bearing children and for courage in childbirth. Women play an important part in everyday life. Royal women can have districts of their own, and junior princesses often act as heads of villages. When women wield political authority, they are regarded as having more gentleness and hospitality to the needy than men have. In addition to political functions, senior women have important ritual duties. Like their brothers, they are in charge of ancestral shrines. The senior wives of chiefs are highly honored, because they have charge of the royal fire. They have in their hands the capability to destroy or maintain the supernatural powers of the chief. Ordinary women can plead their own cases in courts of law. Though not free to contract their first marriage, they are able to break a marriage contract fairly easily and contract a second. Men of other tribes consider Bemba women to be quite unmanageable. They say, "These Bemba women! My word! They are fierceness itself."[75]

The Bemba are convinced that food is eaten to give them physical energy, and they talk about "the giddiness of a man who is hungry." The food supply fluctuates seasonally, and when they are hungry they will not work, saying, "We are waiting till the millet is ripe and we have begun to eat again – until our arms have grown strong."[76] There are several types of ritual associated with plants and the agricultural cycle. They pray or offer sacrifices at all the chief events of the agricultural year, such as tree cutting, sowing, and harvest. Owing to discouragement from local missionaries, these rites do not have the same richness and complexity as before; however, the beliefs associated with the rites continue to dominate people's thoughts and affect their agricultural efforts, even though the ceremonies might be abandoned. When food is scarce, these ceremonies are resumed.[77]

Other rituals reflect the importance that the Bemba attach to fertility and the food supply. There is an elaborate and lengthy girls' initiation ceremony, the Chisungu, which prepares a girl to be a mother and a woman. The ceremony signals that a girl is ready to marry. It is literally a marriage training school: The girl is taught all the sacred, magical, and practical aspects of marriage, womanhood, childbearing, and childrearing. She is taught how to purify herself after intercourse, what to do about menstrual blood, and proper practices in connection with fire. All of these activities she must perform correctly in order to conserve the health of children and the productivity of the land.

This elaborate treatment of fertility occurs in a society in which there are high infant and maternal mortality and periods of hunger. Just as the Desana recognize the growing scarcity of game and take certain precautions, the Bemba recognize food shortages and the dangers of childbirth. Because food is necessary to supply vital energy and children to continue the mother's line, the Bemba turn to ritual to conserve the food supply and the descent group. In response to a question challenging the protective rites performed for children, they said: "Well, just look what a lot of our children die." Audrey Richards says this concern cannot explain their emphasis on fertility because high infant mortality is "too common in

Bantu society for this to be more than a contributory cause to the desire for fertility."[78] She hypothesizes that the emphasis on fertility is a product of a matrilineal descent system and of the belief that the child is formed from the physical contribution of the mother alone, not the father. In patrilineal societies it is common for the man to "buy" a wife, that is, to give something in exchange for a wife. If she turns out to be barren, whatever is given may be returned or another wife provided. In a matrilineal society, the children belong legally to the mother's family, and it is to their gain if she produces children. If a girl is barren, they have no recourse but to try to prevent such an occurrence by resorting to ritual. It is not thought that husbands could be sterile, only that they might be impotent. For this reason, symbols of virility are also stressed in the Chisungu. In the marriage ceremony that follows the Chisungu, the bridegroom gives a sign of his potency by throwing a burning brand out of the house.[79]

In central Africa there is a high correlation between girls' puberty rites and matrilineal organization. The ceremonies are considered to be a preface to marriage. There is general fear that a girl who has not received the magic protection of the rite will either be barren or will face difficulty in childbirth. Frequently these rites begin with puberty and end with the celebration of pregnancy and marriage. The role of the nubile girl is glorified, and the man from another clan who will give her fertility is praised. The distribution of ceremonies is related to matriliny, agriculture, and, often, to the absence of livestock. Richards notes that in this area the introduction of stock is usually followed by the giving of cattle as a marriage payment. When high marriage payments are made, she says, the Bemba matrilineal pattern, which she associates with girls' fertility ceremonies, tends to disappear.[80]

To conclude, the Bemba left their original homeland and traveled to a new land carrying "seeds in their hair." They did not dispossess alien tribes but incorporated or pushed out groups having a similar cultural tradition. They grew and expanded but maintained ancient cultural traditions from which women were not excluded, if for no other reason than that descent was traced through the female line. The Chisungu, the girls' puberty rite, focuses on the maternity and fertility that are so important for the continuity of the group and on the continuation of an abundant food supply.

Azande history begins with the exodus of the Ambomu, who must have been so organized that conquest and incorporation were possible. The evidence suggests that the Ambomu moved more as a group of warriors than as related families; they migrated with the male and not the female part of their aboriginal culture. Azande women are more like slaves and enemies than partners in a similar cultural tradition. This is understandable if the Ambomu migrated as a group of hunters who were forced to learn agriculture and to take wives from the peoples they conquered. Such a practice would have had the additional function of facilitating the incorporation of alien populations.

Conclusion

Generally, male dominance evolves as resources diminish and as group survival depends increasingly on the aggressive acts of men. Male oppression of women, however, is neither an automatic nor an immediate response to stress. Other solutions to stress are possible. All solutions depend on such factors as a people's traditional concept of power, the manner in which they define adversity, and the degree to which their group identity is endangered.

The evidence suggests that men and women respond differently to stress. Men almost always respond to stress with aggression, though not necessarily with dominance. Men seek to preserve a threatened identity by retaliating by force and engaging in competition for status with other men. In this struggle, men are frequently faced with the existence of traditional female power. Mythical male dominance arises when women seek to maintain their power base while leaving men room to maneuver. For example, women may react to the male attempt to seize control by "playing the game" of balancing formal male power against informal female power. Females seem to respond to stress in these instances by striking a conciliatory note.

In other instances women fight for their rights. They succeed unless men kill a few token women to show that the battle for male domination is real. In these cases women acquiesce. They do not believe that "the trees that bear the fruit" or "the mothers of men" should die. If there is a basic difference between sexes, other than the differences associated with human reproductivity, it is that women as a group have not willingly faced death in violent conflict. This fact, perhaps more than any other, explains why men have sometimes become the dominating sex.

PART V

Conquerors of the land flowing with milk and honey

A wandering Aramean was my father (Jacob); and he went down into Egypt and sojourned there, few in number; and there he became a nation, great, mighty, and populous. And the Egyptians treated us harshly, and afflicted us, and laid upon us hard bondage. Then we cried to the LORD the God of our fathers, and the LORD heard our voice, and saw our affliction, our toil, and our oppression; and the LORD brought us out of Egypt with a mighty hand and an outstretched arm, with great terror, with signs and wonders; and he brought us into this place and gave us this land, a land flowing with milk and honey.

Deuteronomy 26:5–9

Epilogue

My goal in these last few pages is to dwell briefly on the genesis of two of the guiding symbols of Western male dominance – the patriarchal, decidedly masculine God and the sexual, inferior female who tempts the male from the path of righteousness. The story that I reconstructed includes a familiar theme: Collective sentiments centering on maleness and masculine symbols acquire coercive power by defining females as the "other" and feminine symbols as evil.

No doubt, many believe that the secularized society in which we live has liberated us from the directive power of such symbols. I disagree. Feminist theologian Carol P. Christ states the argument clearly. Symbols associated with the religious rituals of birth, marriage, and death – rituals we all attend – "cannot fail to affect the deep or unconscious structures of the mind of even a person who has rejected these symbolisms on a conscious level – especially if the person is under stress." She continues: "Religions centered on the worship of a male God create 'moods' and 'motivations' that keep women in a state of psychological dependence on men and male authority." A woman can never have her full sexual identity affirmed as being in the image and likeness of God, an experience freely available to every man and boy of her culture.[1]

We have little information on how boys and girls are affected by prevailing religious symbols. My experience in observing my son and daughter has been instructive. Upon reading the Biblical passage "So God created man in his own image, in the image of God he created him; male and female he created them" (Genesis 1:27),[2] my son exclaimed: "How could God have created a female in his own image if God was male?" His solution to this puzzle is not unlike that of the Gnostic Christians, discussed in the last section of this chapter. "Obviously, God must have been part female in

215

order to have created male and female in his own image," my son declared. So far, my daughter has shown no interest in the question of who God is. Her personal identity is tied up with symbols of her own making: teddy bears, sunshine, and flowers. Having abandoned public symbols of femininity, she seems quite free to inform teachers who do not know better that fourth-grade girls should be treated no differently than fourth-grade boys.

To some extent all of us look to symbol systems to discover how to behave. Personal identities are inextricably linked with social form. Religious symbols and social form are part of the same underlying blueprint. Though we may reject the messages implied by the former, we cannot escape being guided by the latter.

Today, feminists seek to change the blueprint. Feminist theologians hope to change the guiding sacred symbols, other feminists work for change in the secular domain. Both seek to change the script that directs our behavior. In these last few pages, I want to look at the historic origins of the sacred part of this script. The story I have pieced together focuses on a narrow historical issue: the fate of goddess worship in Biblical popular culture and early Christianity.

The goddess and Yahweh cults in Canaan

When the semi-nomadic Hebrew tribes entered Canaan *ca.* 1300 B.C., they brought Yahweh, originally a tribal god who symbolized the collective identity of the Judeans. In Canaan, the Hebrews worshipped Yahweh as well as Canaanite gods and goddesses. The priests of the Yahweh cult argued that "awhoring after foreign gods" brought Yahweh's wrath upon the people and caused the destruction of Hebrew cities in Canaan.[3] For example, Jeremiah claimed that the "God of Israel" had said to him:

You have seen all the evil that I brought upon Jerusalem and upon all the cities of Judah. Behold, this day they are a desolation, and no one dwells in them, because of the wickedness which they committed, provoking me to anger, in that they went to burn incense and serve other gods that they knew not, neither they, nor you, nor your fathers (Jeremiah 44:1–3).

One of the "gods" worshipped by the Hebrew people was a goddess called the "Queen of Heaven." When Jeremiah brought the message of the Lord's wrath to Judean refugees in Egypt, they answered that it was the Queen of Heaven, not Yahweh, upon whom they depended for prosperity and to whom they offered worship. In response to Jeremiah's message from the Lord, they countered:

As for the word which you have spoken to us in the name of the Lord, we will not listen to you. But we will do everything that we have vowed, burn incense to the queen of heaven and pour out libations to her, as we did, both we and our fathers, our kings and our princes, in the cities of Judah and in the streets of Jerusalem; for then we had plenty of food and prospered, and saw no evil. But since we left off burning incense to the queen of heaven and pouring our libations to her, we have lacked everything and have been consumed by the sword and by famine (Jeremiah 44:16–18).

That "Queen of Heaven" was modeled after one of the most famous and powerful of the ancient Near Eastern goddesses, Inanna, the tutelary deity of a Sumerian city–state. The Sumerians flourished in southern Babylonia from the beginning of the fourth to the end of the third millenium B.C.[4] They were a migrating people who came from another land and settled on the Tigris–Euphrates plain in an area inhabited by an indigenous agricultural people and by warlike Semitic nomads who posed a constant threat to Sumerian political stability. The Tigris–Euphrates plain was a hot, arid, barren land with "the hand of God against it." The Sumerians almost literally built their civilization out of dust and clay, because there was nothing else there except the waters of the Tigris–Euphrates, which were channeled into the arid fields, turning Sumer into "a veritable Garden of Eden."[5]

Little is known about the secular power of women in Sumerian culture. In religion, however, female deities were venerated and worshipped from the beginning to the end of Sumer's existence. The Sumerian Inanna, whose exploits and deeds were recorded in many of the Sumerian epic tales and whose image is left in Sumerian art, provided the prototype for the goddess who was to play a central role in the religious ritual and popular consciousness of all ancient Near Eastern peoples.[6] She is variously described as "the queen of heaven, the goddess of light and love"; "the ambitious, aggressive, demanding goddess of love . . . and war"; and "the tutelary deity of Erech . . . a goddess who throughout Sumerian history was deemed to be the deity primarily responsible for sexual love, fertility, and procreation . . ."[7]

Progress, rivalry, and superiority are native to the philosophy and psychology of the Near East.[8] All of these attributes are reflected in Inanna's personality. In many ways she is the symbol of the Sumerian personality "writ large." The intense rivalry between the Sumerian city–states is found in the relationship between Inanna and her spouse as well as between numerous Sumerian male and female deities. In the epic tales Inanna is depicted as struggling to maintain superiority over a competitive husband or a jealous sister. The contrast between the natural aridity of the Sumerian desert and the lushness created by irrigation is repeated in the duality of Inanna's personality. She is variously represented as a union of opposites: of good and evil, of life giving and life taking, of boundless rage and all-embracing love.

Inanna did not disappear with the fall of Sumerian civilization. Though her name was changed, her character remained in the form of Ishtar of Akkad and Anath of Canaan.[9] Following their penetration of Canaan, the Hebrew tribes worshipped Anath and Asherah, believed to be Anath's mother. Asherah was the chief goddess of the Canaanite pantheon. She figured prominently as the wife of El, the chief god. Her full name was Asherah of the Sea, suggesting that her domain was the sea. Her husband's domain was heaven. She was referred to also as "Goddess" and "Progenitress of the Gods." Her children included Baal as well as Anath.[10]

Anath exhibits many features in common with Inanna. She is described as the goddess of "love and war, virginal and yet wanton, amorous and yet given to uncontrollable outbursts of rage and appalling acts of cruelty."[11] Anath is not mentioned by name in the Bible. However, the "Queen of Heaven" referred to in Jeremiah (44:15–19) is believed to be Anath. Anath may also be the same as the goddess Astarte who is mentioned by name in the Bible.[12]

Archeological evidence leaves no doubt of the importance of goddess worship among the Canaanite Hebrews. The Canaanite fertility cults attracted the infiltrating Israelite tribes for centuries. Even in Jerusalem, the center of the worship of Yahweh, a sanctuary of one of the Canaanite cults was found containing hundreds of the mother goddess figurines.[13]

Epilogue

The Hebrews entered into Canaan, *ca.* 1350 B.C., as animal pastoralists and changed from a life of semi-nomadism to sedentary farming. Their adoption of agriculture meant that they had to establish a relationship with the soil. They became dependent upon rainfall and on the rotation of the seasons for crops and concerned about fertility – a concern basic to the Canaanite religion of Baal and his consort Anath.

The purpose of the eroticized Canaanite religion was to preserve and enhance the fertility upon which people were dependent for their existence in the precarious environment of the Fertile Crescent. This religion catered to the human desire for security by seeking to control the gods in the interest of human well-being. As such, this religion was diametrically opposed to the cult of Yahweh, which the Judean tribes brought from Egypt.

The development of the Yahweh cult among the Hebrews was closely connected with the political ascendency of Moses and the migration of the Hebrews from Egypt. Before the Exodus from Egypt, Yahweh was the tribal god of the Judeans, one of the Hebrew tribes. The cult of Yahweh was extended in Egypt to include other Hebraic tribes absorbed by Judah.

One of the members of the absorbed tribes was Moses, who became an ardent protagonist of Yahweh.[14] Moses was both a religious and political leader. He revealed Yahweh to his people as a redeeming power who makes exclusive, ethical demands on man's will. At the same time, through the mechanism of the covenant, Moses united Yahweh and the Judean tribes into a single ethical community.

When the Israelites entered Canaan, only Judah, the confederacy that settled in the south, had adopted Yahweh. Judah came to dominate all the Hebrew tribes in Canaan during the time of David in response to the threat of the Philistines, who invaded Canaan after the coming of the Israelite tribes. Yahweh then became the god of all Israel. Until then the Hebraic tribes who had settled in the northern region of Canaan thought of Yahwism as a southern cult – specifically, a Judean cult – rather recently come to Israel, and intimately associated with Moses.[15]

The expansion of Yahwism did not bring about the end of goddess worship among the Hebrews. Goddesses fulfilled different needs than did Yahweh and, hence, could be strictly separated. Those who believed in the goddesses saw no incompatibility be-

219

tween the control exercised by the goddesses over certain areas of human life and nature and the rule Yahweh exercised over others.[16]

This is another example of an outer-oriented people embracing an inner orientation. Like the Dahomeans, the Hebrews entered a new land as an animal-oriented people and conquered a group of indigenous agriculturalists. Agriculture made the Hebrews dependent on their environment in a new way. If, as so often is the case, women were the main cultivators, one can imagine Hebrew women being attracted to the fertility cults both because they accorded women a special place and because they guaranteed agricultural success. Like the Dahomeans, the Hebrews probably saw no reason for assimilating different cult figures.

Eventually, however, the inherent conflict between the Yahwist and the fertility cults proved too great for both to survive. The people of Israel were forced to resolve a basic question: Was the meaning of human life in Canaan to be disclosed in relation to divine powers within nature or in relation to the Lord of history?[17] This question was not resolved in practice for centuries. In theory, however, it was resolved very early by the Hebrew prophets who, like Moses, sought to form the Hebrew tribes into one social body, united by one set of laws, and led by one religious figure – the Lord God.

Adam and Eve: migrating men and foreign goddesses

Many biblical stories repeat the theme of a vengeful, jealous god who violently punishes his people for "awhoring after foreign gods." The most widely known of the Hebrew creation stories, the story of Adam and Eve in the Garden of Eden, does not, at least on the surface, depict the wrath of God as violent. Rather, this story appears to tell of man's vulnerability and subordination to a superior being. A close reading, however, suggests that it contains themes that resolve the conflict between Yahwism and goddess worship.

The Garden of Eden story offers a prologue to what is known as the Yahwist epic, the earliest of the four major documents that make up the Pentateuch, or the "Five Books of Moses."[18] The Yahwist is the name given to a Judean prophet who lived during the reign of Solomon (*ca.* 961–922 B.C.).[19] This was a crucial period in Israel's history, a time when the disparate Hebrew tribes had achieved unification. Solomon, the son of David, had built a great colonial empire. He is also said to have had 700 wives and 300 concubines. He used these unions to establish close political and cultural ties with surrounding peoples. Solomon allowed his wives to practice their native religion, going so far as to build special shrines for them in Jerusalem, his capital city. Although Solomon probably regarded himself as a loyal worshipper of Yahweh, his broad-minded hospitality led him to incorporate elements of the Baalist religion in his Mosaic heritage.

The age of Solomon was simply another chapter in a long-standing conflict between Mosaic faith and surrounding religions. It was not Yahweh's intention that Israel should become a great nation in the sense of a vast colonial empire. Rather, Israel was to remain separated from other nations by the covenant calling. But it was difficult to maintain faithfulness to the Mosaic tradition when the gods of the Fertile Crescent made irresistible claims upon men's lives. Incited by expansion and success, the tendency during Solomon's reign was toward tolerance and compromise. To draw Israel back to her distinctive faith, to keep this faith from falling into oblivion among the religions of the Fertile Crescent, Yahweh's uncompromising, jealous demand for absolute allegiance was essential.[20]

In addition to the threats from without, ancient antagonisms between the northern and southern tribes threatened to weaken if not destroy the Mosaic tradition. Although united by David, the northern and southern kingdoms split apart immediately after Solomon's death in 925 B.C.[21] In this climate of great promise and great threat, the prophet who scholars call the Yahwist, or J, emerged as the champion of the Mosaic faith. The Yahwist saw his mission as one of promulgating the unity of the Hebrew people by recording their history in a manner that would give literary expression to the Mosaic tradition. As a Judean, the Yahwist must have been a loyal follower of Yahweh. His purpose "was to confess Israel's faith in Yahweh, whose saving deeds had been manifested in Israel's history."[22] The Yahwist was mainly interested in the events of the Exodus and the struggles of Israel to become a nation in Canaan.

Drawing on traditions appropriated by Israel from Canaanite cult legends, some of which are traceable to Sumerian prototypes, the Yahwist recast Canaanite traditions in Mosaic terms. Stories that were originally Canaanitish were simply made Israelitish. Religious tales originally connected with the Canaanite god Baal, the goddess Anath, or the Babylonia god Marduk and the goddess Tiamat were told of Yahweh.[23] In the Yahwist epic Yahweh appears throughout as the one great God, the Creator, the only God for Israel. He controls the forces of nature and the forces of history. He is a moral God who, in the words of one Biblical scholar, "demands righteousness, rewards faith and kindness, innocence and unselfishness, but punishes wickedness and oppression." In return for making Israel "a great and prosperous nation," Yahweh demands complete loyalty.[24]

The Garden of Eden story captures the Mosaic meaning of the Exodus from Egypt and the entrance into Canaan. Within the context of paradise, the Yahwist spells out the consequences for those who refuse to acknowledge the sovereignty of their creator and savior in their new land. The motifs of the story, though they are drawn from a wide range of ancient Near Eastern oral and literary traditions, are woven by the Yahwist so as to impress on men's minds the debt they owe to their creator.

The events of the Garden of Eden story begin in a desert environment in which there was no man to till the ground:

In the day that the LORD God made the earth and the heavens, when no plant of the field was yet in the earth and no herb of the field had yet sprung up – for the LORD God had not caused it to rain upon the earth, and there was no man to till the ground (Genesis 2:5).

This description is consonant with the Hebrew's sojourn in the Sinai desert, where water was scarce, there was no food, and existence was precarious. Because they were not agriculturalists but pastoral nomads at the time, there literally was no man to till the ground.

Next in the story there is a shift to an oasis environment, in which man is formed from the ground and becomes a living being: "But a mist went up from the earth and watered the whole face of the ground – then the LORD God formed man of dust from the ground, and breathed into his nostrils the breath of life; and man became a living being" (Genesis 2:6–7). After their sojourn in the Sinai Desert, Moses leads his people to the oasis of Sinai, which would be like a place where water would come from the ground as "a mist went up from the earth." It is at the oasis of Sinai where Moses establishes a covenant with Yahweh, thereby forming Israel as a nation. Thus, the theme of forming man from the dust can have two meanings. It may imply the formation of Israel as a nation and it may signify the new bond the Hebrews were soon to forge between man and earth as agriculturalists in Canaan.

The following is a description of the land where the Lord God puts the man he has formed:

And the Lord God planted a garden in Eden, in the east; and there he put the man whom he had formed. And out of the ground the LORD God made to grow every tree that is pleasant to the sight and good for food, the tree of life also in the midst of the garden, and the tree of the knowledge of good and evil (Genesis 2:8–9).

The garden "in the east" is reminiscent of the "land flowing with milk and honey," which the Lord gave to his chosen people after he had delivered them from bondage and bound them to follow his laws. The "tree of the knowledge of good and evil" symbolizes the Canaanite goddess Asherah, whose places of worship were marked by trees and whose image was frequently carved from a trunklike form.[25] The union of good and evil in the goddess symbol is like the union of these qualities in the Sumerian Inanna and the Canaanite Anath.

Upon putting Adam in the Garden, the Lord God commanded him, "You may freely eat of every tree in the garden; but of the tree of knowledge of good and evil you shall not eat, for in the day that you eat of it you shall die" (Genesis 2:16–17). The Hebrew tribes were called upon to be God's servants in exchange for the land of Canaan; so when Adam is transferred to the Garden of Eden, his is called to a state of service to God. He is forbidden to partake of the goddess symbol – the tree of knowledge of good and evil. The act of eating in this passage has been frequently equated with sexuality. In fact, ritual sex was common in sacred Canaanite shrines marked by the tree symbol of the goddess. Thus, eating of the fruit suggests engaging in sexual intercourse at a sacred shrine.

Because the man is alone in this new realm, the Lord God makes a "helper fit for him" (Genesis 2:18). She is called "Woman, because she was taken out of Man" (Genesis 2:23). Making Eve out of Adam's rib is tantamount to declaring that a proper mate is to be taken from within the man's culture. This is consonant with the Old Testament assertion that the land of Palestine was a gift to the pure-blood descendants of Israel. The people of Israel were not supposed to marry foreign women; they were to be a people of pure religion, living in isolation in their Promised Land.[26] Neither in fantasy nor in reality, however, did the Jews follow these prescriptions.

The identity of Eve presents something of an enigma. She may represent Canaanite women married to Hebrew men, who introduced their husbands to the worship of foreign gods and goddesses. Another possibility is that Hebrew women and not men were attracted to the foreign religion because women held an inferior role in the Yahweh cult.[27] Both possibilities place women in the position of enticing men away from the cult of Yahweh.

The fall from grace involves Eve and two ancient Canaanite sacred symbols, the serpent and the tree. When the serpent entices Eve to eat of the forbidden fruit, it says: "For God knows that when you eat of it your eyes will be opened, and you will be like God, knowing good and evil" (Genesis 3:5). Participation in the Canaanite religion meant being like God. Ritual sex was practiced as a form of worship. Male and female sacred prostitutes were present at the shrines and the gods were worshipped in sexual rites. Divine powers were disclosed in the mystery of fertility. The purpose of religion was to preserve and enhance the fertility upon which people depended for their existence. Sacred rites were performed to control the gods in the interest of human well-being.[28]

The tension between being "like" God and serving God is dramatically resolved in the Garden of Eden. God's anger, his jealousy, and his power are mightily expressed, first toward the serpent, then toward Eve, and finally toward Adam. The serpent is reduced to biting the dust and, curiously, God puts enmity between the serpent and Eve – between his seed and her seed (Genesis 3:15) – suggesting that the serpent also represents Canaanite men. Both Adam and Eve are made servants to the will of God. Both are forced out of the Garden (and consequently out of Canaanite sacred sanctuaries) to a life of pain, sorrow, and toil. Lest they be drawn back to their old ways, God installs at the east of the Garden of Eden "the cherubim, and a flaming sword which turned every way, to guard the way to the tree of life" (Genesis 4:24).

And so at the level of allegory and the piling up of metaphors, the competing pulls of two powerful religions, both serving the needs of the Hebrews in Canaan, are resolved. These two religions maintained a relative balance as long as the Hebrews did not face destruction from foreign oppressors. The threat from their borders reminded them that they had turned from their leader. To recoup their forces, they admitted their fall from the covenant pact and rationalized it by shifting the blame onto the practice of Canaanite fertility rites by Hebrews. To control their tendencies in non-Yahwistic directions, the Hebrew prophets attempted to submerge all reference to fertility and to other deities in the books that became their law.

In God's image

The sex-role plan codified in the Garden of Eden story is one with which we are all familiar. Less well known is the egalitarian relationship between the sexes implicit in the first chapter of Genesis. Having created all else:

Then God said, "Let us make man in our image, after our likeness; and let them have dominion over the fish of the sea, and over the birds of the air, and over the cattle, and over all the earth, and over every creeping thing that creeps upon the earth. So God created man in his own image, in the image of God he created him; male and female he created them (Genesis 1:26–7).

Chapter 1 of Genesis is attributed to the Priestly Writer (P), whose document (referred to as the Priestly Code) was written during and after the Jewish exile in Babylonia (*ca.* 597–538 B.C.) and adopted later in Jerusalem. The Priestly Writer, like the Yahwist, was concerned with writing a history of God's dealings with his people, beginning – as had the Yahwist – with creation. P incorporated the Yahwist epic (as well as the Epic of the Northern Kingdom attributed to E) into his comprehensive presentation, which explains why the Yahwist version of creation follows P's version.[29]

Scholars have commented on the resemblance between P's version of creation and the Babylonian creation myth. The Babylonian "Genesis" begins when nothing except the divine parents, Apsu and Tiamat, and their son Mammu existed. Apsu was the primeval sweetwater ocean, Tiamat was the saltwater ocean, and Mammu probably represented the mist rising from the two bodies of water. P's version of creation begins when "the earth was without form and void, and darkness was upon the face of the deep" (Genesis 1:2). The word for deep in the Hebrew text is t^{e}hôm, which scholars say is the Hebrew translation of ti'āmat, which also means watery deep. The theme of "the Spirit of God . . . moving over the face of the waters" (Genesis 1:2) could refer to Apsu, who mingles his waters with those of Tiamat to beget heaven and earth in the Babylonian tale.[30] P's exclusion of the Babylonian divine figures as such from his version of creation is explained by the Hebrew emphasis on monotheism.

Whereas the Babylonian "Genesis" describes warfare and conflict between the divine parents and their offspring, a sense of peace and order prevails in the Priestly account. In Genesis, male and female are created "in our image" (suggesting divine parents) and both sexes are given dominion "over every living thing" (Genesis 1:27–8). Humans and animals alike are given only vegetable food to eat, suggesting that bloodshed and slaughter are not part of the divine plan.[31] Completing this sense of peace and order is the last verse, which ends with the formula: "And God saw everything that he had made, and behold, it was very good" (Genesis 1:31).

Life for the Judean exiles in Babylon was prosperous. Even after the Jews were able to return to Judah, many preferred to stay on in Babylonia. In Babylonia the Jews became active in agriculture as well as in a variety of lucrative trades. Since Babylonia was a much richer country than Judea, the economic position of the Babylonian Jews was considerably better than that of their Judean counterparts.[32]

Within this climate, the sense of belonging to the covenant community flourished rather than weakened. The exiles, many of whom were priests, preserved the sacred writings they had brought with them from Jerusalem. The people continued to look to the priests for exposition of Israel's faith.

The exile was a time for consolidating Israel's history. The Priestly Writer fused together old traditions, including the Yahwist epic, and added his own material. In this manner, the story of Israel was presented in full as a comprehensive unity.

The early Christians

The early Christians recognized both the utopia described in the Priestly version of creation and the divinely ordained chain of authority described in the Yahwist version. Christians known as the "Gnostics" preferred the Priestly version; those called "orthodox" emphasized the Yahwist version.[33] Gnostic texts "abound in feminine symbolism" applied to God. This symbolism is derived from Biblical texts in some instances and is reminiscent of ancient Near Eastern goddess symbols in others. For example, several Gnostic theologians concluded from their interpretation of Genesis 1:26–7 that God is dyadic ("Let *us* make humanity") and that "humanity, which was formed according to the image and likeness of God (Father and Mother) was masculo-feminine."[34]

Another Gnostic text (1 of the 52 found in 1945 in the Upper Egyptian desert near the town of Nag Hammadi) is written in the words of a feminine divine whose dualistic nature recalls the Sumerian Inanna and the Canaanite Anath. She says:

I am the first and the last. I am the honored one and the scorned one. I am the whore, and the holy one. I am the wife and the virgin. I am (the mother) and the daughter . . . I am she whose wedding is great, and I have not taken a husband . . . I am knowledge, and ignorance . . . I am shameless; I am ashamed. I am strength, and I am fear . . . I am foolish, and I am wise . . . I am godless, and I am one whose God is great (Thunder, Perfect Mind 13.16–16.25).[35]

Like Hebrew prophets, the orthodox Christians described God in monistic, masculine, and authoritarian terms. These Christians rejected Gnostic writings for their select list of 26 that comprise the New Testament collection. By the time their selection process was concluded (*ca.* A.D. 200), "virtually all the feminine imagery for God (along with any suggestion of an androgynous human creation) had disappeared from 'orthodox' Christian tradition."[36] Orthodox Christians looked to Genesis 2 for their endorsement of the domination of women. For example, in the pseudo-Pauline letter to Timothy, we read:

Let a woman learn in silence with full submissiveness. I do not allow any woman to teach or to exercise authority over a man; she is to remain silent, *for* Adam was formed first, then Eve and furthermore, Adam was not deceived, but the woman was utterly seduced and came into sin . . ." (2 Timothy 2:11–14).[37]

The orthodox version of the life of Christ also places women in a subordinate role. In sharp contrast, women play a central role in Gnostic accounts. For example, *The Gospel of Philip* (one of the Nag Hammadi texts) tells of the rivalry between the male disciples and Mary Magdalene because she is first among the Savior's companions. Christ, it is said:

(loved) her more than (all) the disciples and used to kiss her (often) on her (mouth). The rest of (the disciples were offended) by it . . . They said to him, "Why do you love her more than all of us?" The Savior answered and said to them, "Why do I not love you as much as (I love) her?" (63.32–64.5).[38]

Another text, *The Dialogue of the Savior*, identifies Mary Magdalene as one of three disciples chosen to receive special teaching. This text singles Mary out for praise because "she spoke as a woman who knew the All" (139:12–13).[39]

Jealousy and misogyny are traits that Gnostic writers ascribe to the Jewish God and to the disciple Peter. One Gnostic author says that the masculine God of Israel is a jealous God who, after his Mother had departed, declared: "I am a jealous God, and besides me there is no one." The author of *The Apocryphon of John* interprets this statement to mean that there is more than one God. "For," this author explains, "if there were no other one, of whom would he be jealous" (13.8–14).[40]

The author of *The Gospel of Mary* alludes to Peter's jealous feelings toward Mary because of her position among the disciples. For example, in response to the disciples' eagerness to listen to what Mary could tell them about the Lord after the Crucifixion, the infuriated Peter asks: "Did he really speak privately with a woman, (and) not openly to us? Are we to turn about and all listen to her? Did he prefer her to us?" (17.18–18.15). In another text, Mary says to Jesus that she dares not speak freely because "Peter makes me hesitate; I am afraid of him, because he hates the female race" (Pistis Sophia 36.71).[41]

Many Gnostic communities were egalitarian in structure. According to Irenaeus, the Bishop of Lyon (*ca.* 180), who wrote polemics denouncing them as heretics, the Gnostics – male and female together – decided by lot who would take the role of priest, offer the sacrament, act as bishop, read the Scriptures for worship, and address the group as a prophet. Such practices prompted the North African theologian Tertullian (*ca.* 190) to say: "Those women among the heretics . . . teach, they engage in discussion; they exorcise; they cure," they may even baptize and act as bishops![42]

Orthodox Christians organized themselves into a strict order of ranks – bishops, priests, deacons, laity. The bishop acted as a "monarch," disciplinarian, and judge over the laity. This dominance–subordination relationship also extended to the relationship between the sexes. By the late second century, Elaine Pagels says, "Orthodox Christians came to accept the domination of men over women as the proper, God-given order – not only for the human race, but also for the Christian churches."[43] In his letter to the disorderly Corinthian community, the apostle Paul reminds the people of the divinely ordained chain of authority. He says: "But I want you to understand that the head of every man is Christ, the head of woman is her husband, and the head of Christ is God" (1 Corinthians 11:3).

The Gnostics criticized the authoritarian structure of the orthodox church. Thinking of themselves as "children of the Father" who joined together as equals, "enjoying mutual love, spontaneously helping one another," Gnostics referred to "ordinary Christians" as offspring of the "demiurge" who "wanted to command one another, out-rivaling one another in their empty ambition."[44] Throughout the early Christian period, orthodox Christian leaders (all of whom were male) worked to suppress Gnostic teaching. Gnostics were referred to as "agents of Satan," "heretics," "worldly," "without authority," and "without discipline."[45]

The bishops mounted a prolonged campaign against heresy. The climate of the times was one in which might determined right. By the fourth century, when Christianity became an officially approved religion, the orthodox bishops, who had previously been persecuted by the police, took command of them. They burned copies of books denounced as heretical and treated

229

possession of such books as a criminal offense. Fortunately, someone in Upper Egypt, possibly a monk from a nearby monastery,
hid the banned books to protect them from destruction. The
books remained buried for some 1,600 years until discovered in
1945 by an Arab peasant.[46]

The forces that favored the ascendancy of the orthodox pattern
and the suppression of the Gnostic pattern repeat a familiar theme
– male dominance is endorsed in a climate of social stress and competition by populations that have adopted male religious symbolism. As the Israelites sought to preserve the integrity of their masculine God and, hence, themselves in the face of adversity in
Canaan, the orthodox Christians fought to establish their church
in the face of religious persecution. Stories about the martyrs were
circulated widely among the orthodox communities to warn all
Christians of their common danger and to strengthen the communities internally and in relation to one another.[47]

The orthodox Christian church gained strength from the death
of its members. Tertullian boasted to the Roman prosecutor that
"the oftener we are mown down by you, the more we grow in
numbers: the blood of the Christians is seed!"[48] When Ignatius,
Bishop of Antioch and a great opponent of heresy, was con-
demned, he embraced the death sentence with joyful exultation.
He saw in it an opportunity to "imitate the passion of my God."
Writing to the Christians in Rome, Ignatius said: "Allow me to be
eaten by the beasts, through whom I can attain to God." Ignatius
was outraged at the Gnostic belief that since Christ was a spiritual
being, he only appeared to suffer and die. If Christ's "suffering
was only an appearance," Ignatius said, "then why am I a pris-
oner, and why do I long to fight with the wild beasts? In that case,
I am dying in vain."[49]

Clearly, Ignatius did not die in vain. The question before us
now is: Did the Gnostic Christians live in vain?

Gnostic theology and Hebrew goddess worship treat female
power as part of the God-given order. The religious symbols
found in these traditions create "moods" and "motivations" en-
couraging psychological independence and reciprocity between
the sexes. These symbols have an obvious appeal for those who
are unable to accept a dominance–subordination relationship between the sexes. Today, after some 2,000 years of relative obscurity, female supernatural symbols are resurfacing as women seek

new guideposts. Beaten down by men, women who have had "enuf" cry out in a contemporary play, "I found God in myself and I loved her fiercely."[50] A new theology is emerging that focuses on birth, maternity, and union with nature as religious experiences. The resurrection of goddess symbols by contemporary feminists shows, once again, that people seek to align sacred and secular sex-role plans.

The seeds of sexual equality and male dominance existed from the beginning of written history in the Near East. Populations jostling each other for power strengthened domination by males and weakened sexual equality. The cultural configuration underlying male dominance provides the core values by which most of us live and think. However, the idea of sexual equality and female power was not completely obliterated from the Western consciousness. Throughout the centuries these ideas have remained, clothed in the imagery of art and literature, to remind us of other possibilities.

The inclusion of other possibilities, no matter how buried these may be, is one of the reasons that Judaism and Christianity have survived as great traditions. If a people can find alternatives within their cultural tradition enabling them to meet current exigencies, they are strengthened and so is their culture. Today's exigencies suggest that we may have taken the domination of nature too far. As a young feminist said to me, we are experiencing a backlash from nature. Pollution and the depletion of natural resources, together with the knowledge that the technology of male dominance has given us the wherewithal to destroy all life on earth, have created a different kind of stress. The ethic that sanctions control and dominion is now the problem, not the solution. Our hopes for social survival no longer rest on domination but on harmonizing competing forces.

Appendix A · Sample

The Standard Cross-Cultural Sample published by Murdock and White (1969) formed the basis for this research. It offers to scholars a representative sample of the world's known and well-described societies. The complete sample consists of 186 societies, each "pinpointed" to an identifiable subgroup of the society in question at a specific point in time. The time period for the sample societies ranges from 1750 B.C. (Babylonians) to the late 1960s. The societies included in the standard sample are distributed relatively equally among the six major regions of the world. Table A.1 presents the geographical distribution of the Standard Cross-Cultural Sample.

Sources for the majority of the standard sample (64%) are represented by the Human Relations Area Files. In these cases, library research was necessary only to acquire information not covered by sources lodged in the files. Sources for the remainder of the standard sample were acquired from the library at the University of Pennsylvania or read at other libraries. When all the sources had been read and coded for variables in the study, it was discovered that, due to the degree of missing information, 30 societies had to be dropped from the sample. Thus, the results of this study rest on a sample size of 156. The geographical distribution of this subsample is also presented in Table A.1. It can be seen from this table that by and large the same geographical distribution represented by the full standard sample is maintained in the subsample (with the exception that the Circum-Mediterranean is underrepresented by a few percentage points and North America is overrepresented by a few percentage points).

Other characteristics of the sample are presented in Tables A.2, A.3, and A.4. Table A.2 lists the societies by major type of subsistence economy. Most of the societies consist of either advanced

Sample

Table A.1. *Geographical distribution of Standard Cross-Cultural Sample and subsample used in this study*

Geographical area	Standard Cross-Cultural Sample		Sample for which adequate information was available[a]	
	N	%	N	%
Sub-Saharan Africa	28	15	24	15
Circum-Mediterranean	28	15	19	12
East Eurasia	34	18	30	19
Insular Pacific	31	17	27	17
North America	33	18	31	20
South and Central America	32	17	25	16
Column totals	186	100	156	99

Data are given for number (N) and percentage of societies.
[a]This sample is a subsample of the Standard Cross-Cultural Sample and represents those societies for which there was adequate information on most of the variables employed in this study.

Table A.2. *Major types of subsistence economy (Econ) represented in sample*

Subsistence mode	No. of societies	%
Advanced agriculture	43	27
Horticulture (semi-intensive agriculture)	15	10
Simple or shifting cultivation	43	27
Domestic animals	14	9
Fishing	15	10
Gathering	14	9
Hunting	12	8
Column totals	156	100

Code for subsistence mode taken from Murdock and White (1969:353).

233

Table A.3. *Number and percentage of foraging and nonforaging societies (For)*

	No. of societies	%
Foraging societies (hunting, gathering, or fishing more important than agriculture or domestic animals)	38	24
Nonforaging societies (agriculture or domestic animals supply the bulk of the food)	118	76
Column totals	156	100

Table A.4. *Range of pinpointed dates (A14) for sample societies*

Time of description	No. of societies	%
Before 1881	38	24
1881–1905	27	17
1906–25	22	14
1926–65	69	44
Column totals	156	99

agriculturalists or shifting cultivators. Advanced agriculture refers to the use of irrigation, fertilization, crop rotation, or other techniques that largely eliminate fallowing. Simple or shifting cultivation applies to subsistence economies where new fields are cleared annually, cultivated for a year or two, and then allowed to revert to forest or brush for a long fallow period.

Table A.3 presents the proportion of the sample societies that can be classified as foragers (i.e., subsisting mainly on some combination of hunting, gathering, or fishing) or as nonforagers (i.e., subsisting mainly on plant or animal domestication). Table A.4 presents the range of pinpointed dates for the sample societies. Though over half (58%) of the sample societies were described after 1906, a sizable proportion (24%) were described before 1881.

Sample

Thus, the sample of societies on which this study is based is representative not only of societies in different parts of the world but of societies varying in complexity, relying on a variety of subsistence technologies, and described for different time periods.

Appendix B · Variables

The variables used in this study are listed in Table B.1. The data were drawn from three sources: 1) the journal *Ethnology*, 2) library materials, or 3) the Human Relations Area Files. The data obtained from the cross-cultural codes published in *Ethnology* were supplied in card form by the Cross-Cultural Cumulative Coding Center housed at the Department of Anthropology of the University of Pittsburgh. The data obtained from library materials and the Human Relations Area Files were part of a much larger study supported by the National Institute of Mental Health. These data were coded by graduate students in anthropology at the University of Pennsylvania using codes developed by me on one-third of the Standard Cross-Cultural Sample.

The final coding was carried out using the full Standard Cross-Cultural Sample of 186 societies and involved collecting information for 31 types of variables. When the coding was completed, a random sample of societies was selected for checking. The percentage of items on which coders and checkers agreed averaged 88% of the 21 variables checked for each society. Disagreements were resolved by still another coder, who rechecked the material. In many cases I made the final decision. After this process was completed, the decision was made to drop 30 societies from the full sample because of a high degree of missing information. Even so, as can be determined by examining the tables in this book, there are many variables for which information was lacking in as much as 40% of the reduced sample of 156.

The variables used in this study are listed in Table B.1 with a listing of the tables in which each appears and a short note on whether the information used to code the variable was acquired especially for this study or obtained from *Ethnology*.

Variables

Table B.1. *List of variables*

Variable name and source	Tables in which variable appears
Origin symbolism (A05). See discussion in Chapter 3 and Appendix C. Coded for this study.	3.1, 3.2, 3.3, 3.5, 4.3, 6.2, 8.4, C.5, C.6, D.1
Proximity of fathers to infants (Inf 23). (When values lumped, labeled Inf 23A.) Taken from Barry and Paxson (1971:472).	3.2, 3.4, C.5, C.6, D.1
Type of animals hunted (Sub 05D). Taken from Murdock and Morrow (1970: 304–5).	3.3, 3.4, C.5, C.6, D.1
Type of subsistence economy (Econ). Taken from Murdock and White (1969:353).	3.5, 4.2, 6.1, 8.3, A.2
Percentage of sexually segregated technological activities, that is, activities performed predominantly or exclusively by females (AH 84). Computed from data provided by University of Pittsburgh (Cross-Cultural Cumulative Coding Center) based on codes published by Murdock and Provost (1973:203–4).	4.1, 4.2, 4.3, 4.4, 8.4, D.1
Percentage of sexually integrated technological activities, that is, activities performed by both sexes with "approximately equal participation or with a roughly equivalent division of subtasks" (AH 85). See explanation for previous variable (AH 84).	4.1, 4.2, 4.3, 4.4, 8.4, D.1
Training young boys for competition (Com). (When values lumped, labeled Coma.) Taken from Barry et al. (1976).	4.4, D.1
Number of menstrual taboos (H16). Discussed in Chapter 5. Types of taboos taken from Young and Bacdayan (1965). Information coded for this study.	5.1, 5.2, 5.3, 5.4
Number of taboos reflecting male avoidance of female sexuality (A11). Discussed in Chapter 5. Coded for this study.	5.5
At least some wives taken from hostile groups (Wie). Coded for this study.	5.3, 8.2, F.1, F.2, F.3
Prevalence of warfare (War). Coded for this study.	5.3, 8.6

237

Table B.1 (*cont.*)

Variable name and source	Tables in which variable appears
Prevalence of scalp taking (Scal). Coded for this study.	5.4
Nature of food supply (fluctuation and storage) (Sub 13). Adapted from Murdock and Morrow (1970:306–8) code entitled Preservation and Storage of Food.	5.5, 7.2, 8.5
Female economic and political power or authority (Stat). Consists of six measures, which form a Guttman scale. Scale properties discussed in Appendix E. Coded for this study and based on scale published by Sanday (1973, 1974). When values lumped, labeled Stata or Statb.	6.1, 6.2, 6.3, 71, 7.2, 8.1, 8.2, E.1, E.2, F.3
Evidence of migraton (Mig). Coded for this study.	6.3, 8.5
Time of description (A14). Pinpointed time for sample societies. See discussion in Appendix A. From Murdock and White (1969).	7.1, A.4
Male aggression scale (Msup1). Consists of five measures, which form a Guttman scale. Scale properties discussed in Appendix F. Coded for this study. (When values lumped, labeled Msupa.)	8.1, F.1, F.2, F.3
Male dominance (MD). Combination of female power (Stat) and male aggression (Msup1) scales. See discussion in Chapter 8 and Appendix F. Coded for this study.	5.2, 8.2, 8.3, 8.4, 8.5, 8.6, 8.7, F.3
Food stress: prevalence of hunger (Sub 14A). Coded for this study.	8.6
Prevailing descent rule (H10). Taken from Murdock and Wilson (1972:261–2).	8.7
Prevailing practice of residence after marriage (H09). Taken from Murdock and Wilson (1972:261).	8.7
Additional variables are cited in appendixes but not employed in text.	See appendixes

Appendix C · Analysis of the relationship between environment, fathers' proximity to infants, and origin symbolism

The discussion of the classification of origin stories in Chapter 3 was based on a careful examination of the themes in the origin stories of one-third of the Standard Cross-Cultural Sample. The details regarding the development of this classification are presented in this appendix. Sixty-one societies were selected from the Standard Cross-Cultural Sample by selecting every third society from the list presented by Murdock and White (1969). One-third of the sample was employed in order to determine whether there was a pattern in origin stories that warranted classifying them for use in statistical analysis.

Of the 61 societies, descriptions or verbatim accounts of creation stories were available for 43. This means either that creation stories do not exist in some societies or that the observer has not always collected or published these stories. The 43 stories vary greatly in degree of elaboration. Some peoples are compelled to describe the origin of everything in the world, visible and invisible, animate and inanimate, in great detail. For example, Geoffrey Gorer (1938:223) says that the Lepcha of South Asia have a creation story that takes 7 whole days in its telling by heart. For other peoples, the necessity to explain the world around them is greatly simplified. Henri A. Junod (1927, Vol. II:302), who describes the Thonga of Africa, says that these people give little thought to the problem of creation. Their answer to the question of the origin of the world is contained in the riddle: "What is it that created Heaven and Earth? – Nature!"

Four of the 43 societies had to be excluded (reducing the final number to 39 stories) because there were contradictory versions of creation. For example, the Trukese, an Insular Pacific society, have several stories from which it was impossible to derive consistent themes. One story states that a female god made human beings, another that a male god was responsible for creation. Still another states that the first man and woman derived their existence from the earth, and another, with pronounced Genesis overtones, says that woman was made from a rib on the man's left side. This does not complete the Trukese notions of the origins of things, because other tales tell about people who are supposed to have descended from animals and plants or state that the mother is the bearer of the clan (Bollig 1967:87–8).

The 39 stories selected for the analysis presented in this appendix may not be the only versions of creation that existed in the sample society. However, examination of these other versions showed that they echoed similar gender-related themes and, hence, the one version selected for analysis was more or less representative of the others that existed.

The first step involved listing for each story: 1) the type of creative agent, 2) the place from which the creative agent is said to originate, and 3) the method used to create the first people. Six types of creative agents characterized most of the stories. These types and the names of the societies, with tales falling in each, are listed in Table C.1.

The types of places from which each of the six kinds of creative agents are said to originate are listed in Table C.2. It is clear from this table that, as argued in Chapter 3, female creators originate from within something; supreme being and animal creators originate from without or from a void; couple creators originate from both within and from without; and culture-hero creators are divided between those originating from within something and those originating from without.

The method by which each of the six types of creative agents makes the first people is categorized in Table C.3. There are two primary modes of creation – from the creator's body, as in sexual union, birth, and self-propagation, or from other than the body, as in making people magically out of clay, transforming people from plants or animals, and chiseling people from wood. With a few exceptions, female and couple agents create from the body. Male, animal, and supreme being creators create from other than the body.

Table C.1. *Types of creative agents in 39 creation stories*

Creator	Africa	Circum-Mediter-ranean	South Asia	East Eurasia	Insular Pacific	North America	South America	Row Totals
Sexless creator					Iban Aranda			2
Female creator or ancestress	Shilluk Tuareg		Semang Lepcha			Copper Eskimo	Nambicuara	6
Couple creators or ancestors	Ashanti				Samoa Tikopia Alorese	Omaha	Jivaro	6
Male culture-hero or ancestor	Kikuyu Thonga		Andaman Islanders Toda				Bribri (Central America) Aymara Tupinamba Mundurucu Shavante	9
Animal creator or ancestor						Yokuts Creek Papago		3
Supreme being or force	Hausa Bambara Hottentot Tiv Azande Amhara	Rwala Egyptians		Gilyak		Bellacoola Gros Ventre Comanche	Tehuelche	13
Column totals	11	2	4	1	5	8	8	39

Table C.2. *Origin of first creator or ancestor*

Creator	From within (water, earth, etc.)	From within and from without	From without (sky, up, out, etc.)	Void	No information
Sexless creator	Iban		Aranda		
Female creator or ancestress	Nambicuara Shilluk Semang Lepcha				Copper Eskimo Tuareg
Couple creators or ancestors	Tikopia	Alorese Ashanti Omaha	Samoa Jivaro		
Male culture-hero or ancestor	Thonga Andaman Islanders Aymara Toda Shavante		Kikuyu Tupinamba Mundurucu Bribri		
Animal creator or ancestor			Yokuts Creek	Papago	
Supreme being or force			Hottentot Gilyak Bellacoola Hausa Amhara Tiv Azande Rwala Egyptians Comanche Tehuelche	Bambara	Gros Ventre

Table C.3. *Mode of first-mentioned creation*

Creator	From the body			Cannot be determined
	Union and/or birth	Self-propagation	From other than the body	
Sexless creator	Iban		Aranda	
Female creator or ancestress	Shilluk Copper Eskimo Lepcha Tuareg	Nambicuara	Semang	
Couple creators or ancestors	Samoa Tikopia Ashanti Omaha Jivaro Alorese			
Male culture-hero or ancestor	Kikuyu Bribri		Mundurucu Thonga Andaman Islanders Aymara Toda Shavante Bribri	Tupinamba
Animal creator or ancestor	Papago		Yokuts Creek	
Supreme being or force	Bambara	Tiv	Azande Hottentot Gilyak Bellacoola Rwala Egyptians Comanche Tehuelche Gros Ventre	Hausa Amhara

The trends displayed in Tables C.2 and C.3 associate the female with nature and natural processes, the male with the sky and magical processes. These trends led to categorizing the 39 creation stories by whether they are predominantly masculine or feminine in tone, or whether they display symbolism relating to both. Where at least two of the three attributes discussed (i.e., sex of the creative agent, place of origin, mode of creation) are feminine or allude to containing symbolism, the story was classified in the feminine category. Where at least two are masculine or allude to outer symbolism, the story was classified in the masculine category. Where the three attributes are mixed in a story (suggesting masculine–feminine and inner–outer), the story was classified in the masculine–feminine category. The stories from the 39 societies are listed in Table C.4. The proportion of masculine, feminine, and mixed stories is nearly identical to that presented in Chapter 3 (Table 3.1) for 112 stories – nearly half (49%) of the stories are masculine, 31% are mixed, and 21% are feminine.

The analysis presented in Chapter 3 of the interconnection among environment, childbearing, and sexual symbolism in origin stories is consistent with the causal chain presented by Beatrice and John Whiting in their psychocultural model of the relationship between personality and culture. The causal chain they postulate is predicated on the assumption that human behavior is constrained by particular environmental adaptations and accidents of history, which form what the Whitings call the "maintenance system." Among other things, the maintenance systems of a society include "the basic customs surrounding nourishment, sheltering, and the protection of its members" (Whiting and Child 1953:310). These maintenance systems pattern the child's learning environment and socialization processes. Adult personality and magico-religious beliefs are considered by the Whitings to be a consequence of the interaction among environment, maintenance system factors, and socialization (Whiting and Whiting 1975:4; see also Whiting 1964).

The psychocultural model postulated by the Whitings suggests that fathers' proximity to their infants may mediate between environmental variables and beliefs about origins. Correlational and regression analyses provide evidence to support this linkage. As can be seen in Table C.5, fathers' proximity to infants is more clearly correlated with subsistence variables than is origin symbol-

Table C.4. *Classification of gender symbolism in creation stories*

Stories with Feminine accent	Stories with Masculine and Feminine equally prevalent	Stories with Masculine accent
Iban	Samoa	Bribri[a]
Nambicuara	Alorese	Aymara[a]
Shilluk	Ashanti	Toda
Copper Eskimo	Omaha	Tupinamba
Semang	Jivaro	Mundurucu
Lepcha	Kukuyu[a]	Yokuts
Tuareg	Thonga[a]	Creek
Tikopia	Andaman	Hottentot
	Islanders[a]	Gilyak
	Shavante[a]	Hausa
	Papago[a]	Amhara
	Bambara[a]	Bellacoola
	Tiv[a]	Azande
		Rwala
		Egyptians
		Tehuelche
		Gros Ventre
		Comanche
		Aranda

[a]There is ambiguity in the criteria for classification. In these cases the final decision was based on the prevalence of the masculine and feminine principles as creation unfolds.

ism. The pattern of correlations in this table indicates that an orientation to animals is associated with distant fathers. Fathers are more distant from infants when animal husbandry contributes greatly to the food supply and when large game are hunted. Fathers are in closer proximity to infants when gathering or fishing contribute substantially to food needs. These latter associations support the contention that an inward or plant orientation is also a reflection of childcare customs and a people's food source.

Origin symbolism is more significantly related to fathers' proximity to infants than it is to any of the subsistence variables. The magnitude of the correlation between the role of the father and origin symbolism supports the Whitings' contention that child-

Appendix C

Table C.5. *Correlation of subsistence variables with proximity of father to infants and gender origin symbolism*

Subsistence variable	Proximity of father to infants (Inf 23)[a]	Origin symbolism (A05)[a]
Importance of agriculture (Sub 02)	NS	−0.22 ($N = 112$) ($p = 0.01$)
Importance of animal husbandry (Sub 03)	−0.27 ($N = 133$) ($p = 0.001$)[b]	NS
Importance of fishing (Sub 04)	0.14 ($N = 132$) ($p = 0.06$)	NS
Importance of hunting (Sub 05)	NS	NS
Large game hunted mainly (Sub 05D) (1 = No, 2 = Yes)	− 0.28 ($N = 113$) ($p = 0.001$)	0.19 ($N = 99$) ($p = 0.03$)
Importance of gathering (Sub 06)	0.25 ($N = 130$) ($p = 0.002$)	NS
Proximity of father to infants (Inf 23)	—	−0.34 ($N = 95$) ($p = 0.000$)

Subsistence variables refer to contribution to overall food supply. A low value means no contribution, a high value means subsistence activity contributes more than any other activity. Codes and data taken from Murdock and Morrow (1970). N, number of societies; p, probability value; NS, not significant.
[a]For Inf 23 code see Table 3.2. High value (5) indicates close proximity, low value (1) indicates no close proximity. A05 code: 1 = Feminine, 2 = Couple, 3 = Masculine.
[b]Correlation coefficient = Pearson's R.

care customs mediate between a people's environment and their religious beliefs.

These conclusions are confirmed by the regression equations presented in Table C.6. Fathers' proximity to infants is entered as the dependent variable and the subsistence variables are entered as the independent variables in the first equation. Hunting large game, the importance of animal husbandry, and the importance of gathering account for most of the variance explained in the dependent variable. It should be noted that the subsistence variables explain only 20% of the variance in the dependent variable, which means that other variables not considered here are also important

Table C.6. *Regression equations*

Regression I. Dependent variable = father's proximity to infants (Inf 23)[a]

Variables in the equation	R^2 Change	β	F
Hunting large game (Sub 05D)	0.08	−0.33	Sig
Importance of agriculture (Sub 02)	0.02	−0.02	NS
Importance of animal husbandry (Sub 03)	0.07	−0.24	Sig
Importance of fishing (Sub 04)	0.01	−0.03	NS
Importance of gathering (Sub 06)	0.02	0.19	Sig
Total	0.20		

Regression II. Dependent variable = origin symbolism (A05)[b]

Variables in the equation	R^2 Change	β	F
Hunting large game (Sub 05D)	0.04	0.01	NS
Importance of agriculture (Sub 02)	0.03	−0.31	Sig
Importance of animal husbandry (Sub 03)	0.00	−0.16	NS
Importance of fishing (Sub 04)	0.00	−0.12	NS
Importance of gathering (Sub 06)	0.04	−0.16	NS
Proximity of father to infants (Inf 23)	0.10	−0.35	Sig
Total	0.21		

[a]Multiple $R = 0.45$; $R^2 = 0.20$; $df = 5,107$; $F = 5.38$ (sig).
[b]Multiple $R = 0.45$; $R^2 = 0.21$; $df = 6,88$; $F = 3.7$ (sig).

[see Whiting (1964) for a discussion of the effect of additional environmental variables on the role of the father in the care of children].

In the second regression equation reported in Table C.6, origin symbolism is entered as the dependent variable, and the subsistence variables and fathers' proximity to infants are entered as the independent variables. The subsistence variables explain 11% of the variance in the dependent variable and fathers' proximity alone explains an additional 10%. Thus, although it is clear that environmental variables are not unrelated to a people's cosmological concepts, the proximity of fathers to their infants is very significant.

Appendix D · Configurations for the division of labor

In Chapter 4 it is argued that a high percentage of sexually segregated technological activities is part of a cultural configuration in which men hunt and pursue large game, fathers are uninvolved with the care of infants, there is an emphasis on competition in the rearing of children, and masculine origin symbolism dominates creation stories. Sexual integration, on the other hand, is associated with less emphasis on competition in childrearing and feminine origin symbolism in creation stories. Table D.1 presents the correlation between these variables.

The dual-sex configuration is also described in Chapter 4. This configuration represents the separation of the sexes and a balanced division of labor where both sexes contribute differently but in equal proportion to everyday concerns. The data of this study do not allow me to demonstrate statistically the probable origins of the dual-sex configuration. The descriptive materials presented in Chapters 3, 4, and 6 suggest that the dual-sex orientation grows out of a ritual concern with both plant gathering or incipient cultivation *and* the predatory activities of men.

Table D.1. Correlation between environmental, behavioral, and symbolic factors listed in Figure 4.1

Variable	Predominantly female technological activities (%) (AH 84)[a]	Sexually integrated technological activities (%) (AH 85)[a]	Competition (Com)[a]
Importance of hunting (Sub 05)	0.28 (N = 153) (p = 0.000)	−0.20 (N = 153) (p = 0.000)	0.14 (N = 115) (p = 0.07)
Large game hunted mainly (Sub 05D)	0.24 (N = 136) (p = 0.002)	NS	0.19 (N = 102) (p = 0.03)
Proximity of fathers to infants (Inf 23)	−0.18 (N = 133) (p = 0.02)	NS	−0.27 (N = 100) (p = 0.003)
Emphasis on competition (Com)	0.25 (N = 116) (p = 0.003)	−0.17 (N = 116) (p = 0.03)	—
Origin symbolism (A05)	0.18 (N = 112) (p = 0.03)	−0.30 (N = 112) (p = 0.001)	0.16 (N = 82) (p = 0.07)

N, number of societies; p, probability value; NS, not significant.
[a]See Table 4.1 and Appendix B for AH 84, AH 85 coding. See Table 4.4 and Appendix B for Com coding. High values (6–8) mean emphasis on competition, low values (0–1) mean little emphasis on competition.

Appendix E · Construction of the measure for female economic and political power or authority

The measure for female economic and political power and/or authority is adapted from the operational definition of female status in the public domain I employed in two previous articles (see Sanday 1973, 1974). This measure refers to the ability or right of women to control economic goods or participate in decision making beyond the domestic domain. The measure does not include the *degree* to which women participate in economic and political activities. The measure is only concerned with *whether* women have power (defined as the ability to act effectively on persons or things) or authority (defined as the right to make a particular decision and to command obedience) in economic or political matters (see Sanday 1974:190–2, for discussion of these distinctions).

The dimensions I have used for coding female economic and political power are listed below. Four of these measures are similar to the indicators I used in my previous articles. Two are new and refer to female autonomy. The indicators are as follows:

1. *Flexible marriage mores (H01)*. Divorce is permitted to men and women *or* punishment for adultery is mild or absent.
2. *Females produce nondomestic goods (H02)*. In addition to items for domestic use, females produce for wider distribution.
3. *Demand for female produce (H03)*. There is moderate or great demand for produce or products of female labor beyond individual household subsistence-level items, from within or outside of the area.
4. *Female economic control (H04)*. Females control allocation of disposal of products of their own labor beyond the domestic sphere.
5. *Female political participation (H05)*. Females have *at least* an important indirect influence in public decision making *or*

Table E.1. *Female economic and political power
or authority scale (Stat)*

| | Scale score | | | | | | | |
| | High | | | | | Low | | |
Scale indicators	7	6	5	4	3	2	1	Totals
6. Female solidarity groups	p	—	—	—	—	—	—	
5. Female political participation	p	p	—	—	—	—	—	
4. Female conomic control	p	p	p	—	—	—	—	
3. Demand for female produce	p	p	p	p	—	—	—	
2. Females produce non-domestic goods	p	p	p	p	p	—	—	
1. Flexible marriage mores	p	p	p	p	p	p	—	
Number of societies	17	22	20	15	6	9	7	96[a]
Percentage of societies	18	23	21	16	6	9	7	100
Number of errors	10	11	5	11	4	13	0	54[b]

Indicator present is signified by p. Dash (—) means indicator is absent.
[a]No information on at least one indicator for 60 societies.
[b]Coefficient of reproducibility = 0.91.

there are at least a few political roles allocated to women.

6. *Female solidarity groups (H06)*. Female solidarity groups are present that: 1) are unofficial groups formed by females to help one another and to discuss matters of extra-domestic importance or 2) are official groups recognized in society whose function is to consolidate female economic, social, or political power.

These indicators form a Guttman scale (see Table E.1). This means that as one advances to the next step on the scale, the previous indicators are also present. The scale begins with a residual category in which women have none of the rights just listed, which implies no female political or economic power or authority. The last item on the scale, female solidarity groups, represents the

251

Table E.2. *Female economic and political power or authority scale (Stat) (with missing information)*

	Societies	
Scale score	N	%
1. No indicator present	11	8
2. Flexible marriage mores and	9	7
3. Females produce nondomestic goods and	5	4
4. Demand for female produce and	13	10
5. Female economic control and	23	17
6. Female political participation and	41	31
7. Female solidarity groups	31	23
Column totals	133[a]	100

[a]Because of missing information on too many indicators, 23 societies were not included.

most advanced form of female political and economic power or authority and implies that all of the other items are present.

That these indicators form a Guttman scale is suggestive of the antecedents of female political and economic power or authority. It seems reasonable to suggest that female economic and political control is based on flexible marriage mores, female production for nondomestic distribution, demand for female produce, and control by females of this produce. Thus, the scale presented in Table E.1 provides further insight to the bases for female power or authority.

The scale properties are presented in Table E.1. This table is based only on those societies for which information on all indicators was available ($N = 96$). In constructing the measure used in statistical associations with other variables, societies with missing information on one or two indicators were included ($N = 133$). The final scale score was determined by assigning a score on the basis of the indicators present. Thus, if female political participation is present and female solidarity groups are absent, a scale score of 6 is assigned. Table E.2 presents the frequency distribution for the final measure.

Appendix F · Male aggression scale and male dominance measure

The male aggression measure introduced and discussed in Chapter 8 was constructed from five indicators, which form a Guttman scale. The indicators are listed below, beginning with those reflecting minimal aggression:
1. Males are expected to be tough and brave (Macho).
2. There are one or more places where males congregate alone, or males occupy a separate part of the household, or there is sharp ceremonial segregation of the sexes (Mho).
3. The degree of interpersonal violence is moderate or frequent (Viol 1).
4. Incidents of rape are reported (suggesting that rape is not uncommon) or rape is thought of as a means for punishing women, or rape is part of a ceremony (RA5).
5. At least some wives are taken from hostile groups (Wie).

Table F.1 presents the cumulative property of these indicators. The information presented in this table is based only on the sample of societies for which information on every indicator was present ($N = 50$).

The final male aggression measure was constructed using cases for which there was no information for some indicators. Scale scores were assigned on the basis of the highest indicator present. Thus, if taking wives from hostile groups was present and at least some of the other indicators were also present, the case was assigned a scale score of 6. If rape was present along with interpersonal violence and/or the presence of men's houses, the case was assigned a score of 5. If, on the other hand, either rape or taking wives from hostile groups was present and the other indicators were absent, the presence of either one of these indicators (in the absence of the others) was treated as an error. Using this procedure it was possible to increase the sample size from 50 to 107. In

Table F.1. *Male aggression scale (Msup1)*

Scale indicators	High					Low	Totals
	6	5	4	3	2	1	
5. Wives taken from hostile groups (Wie)	p	—	—	—	—	—	
4. Rape institutionalized or reported as more than occasional (RA5)	p	p	—	—	—	—	
3. Interpersonal violence moderate or frequent (Viol 1)	p	p	p	—	—	—	
2. Separate places for men (Mho)	p	p	p	p	—	—	
1. Ideology of male toughness (Macho)	p	p	p	p	p	—	
Number of societies	15	8	9	6	5	7	50[a]
Percentage of societies	30	16	18	12	10	14	100
Number of errors	5	6	5	4	4	0	24

Indicator present is signified by p. Dash (—) means indicator is absent.
[a]No information on at least one indicator for 106 societies.
[b]Coefficient of reproducibility = 0.90.

49 cases there was too much missing information to warrant assigning a score. The frequency distribution for the final scale is presented in Table F.2.

The male dominance measure was constructed from the score for the female economic and political power scale and the male aggression scale for each society. Table 8.2 presents the guidelines used in the construction of the male dominance measure. These guidelines are summarized as follows:

1. The sexes are considered equal when women have political and economic power and/or authority and male aggression in the form of rape or raiding other groups for wives is absent.

Table F.2. *Male aggression scale (Msup1)*
(with missing information)

	Societies	
Scale score	N	%
1. No indicator present	15	14
2. Ideology of male toughness and	5	5
3. Separate places for men and	18	17
4. Interpersonal violence moderate or frequent and	12	11
5. Rape institutionalized or reported as more than occasional and	19	18
6. Taking wives from hostile groups	38	35
Column totals	107[a]	100

[a]Because of missing information on too many indicators, 49 societies were not included.

2. Mythical male dominance is considered present when women exercise economic and/or political power or authority and male aggression against women is also present. Cases where women have economic power or authority but no political power or authority, and male aggression is absent, are also placed in this category (referred to as "some" male dominance in tables).

3. The sexes are considered unequal when women have no economic and/or political power or authority. Defined in these terms, sexually unequal societies do not necessarily include male aggression against women. However, as Table F.3 shows, in most (60%) of the sexually unequal societies, rape or wife raiding is also present.

Using these guidelines for the construction of the male dominance measure means that male dominance is measured by both female economic and political rights *and* male aggression against women. Table F.3 presents the relationships between male dominance and these two scales.

Table F.3. *Relationship between male dominance measure, female political and economic power scale, and male aggression scale*

	Sexes are equal		Some or mythical male dominance		Sexes are unequal		Row totals (N)
	N	%	N	%	N	%	
Female economic and political power scale							
Women have no economic or political power or authority (scale score 1–4)	0	0	0	0	37	100	37
Women have economic and political power or authority (scale score 5)	0	0	22	45	0	0	22
Women have economic and political power and authority (scale score 6–7)	42	100	27	55	0	0	69
Column totals	42	100	49	100	37	100	128[a]
Male aggression scale							
Aggression against women in form of rape or raiding for wives is absent (scale score 1–4)	31	100	6	15	12	40	49
Raiding for wives and/or rape is present (scale score 5–6)	0	0	35	85	18	60	53
Column totals	31	100	41	100	30	100	102[b]

Data are given for number (N) and percentage of societies.
[a]No information for 28 societies.
[b]No information for 54 societies.

Notes

Preface

1 See Sanday (1973, 1974). The female status scale presented in these articles is utilized here as the measure for secular female power (see Chapter 6 and Appendix E).
2 This research was supported by Grants No. R01 MH28978 and R01 MH25936 awarded by the National Institute of Mental Health. I am grateful to Gloria Levin, former Deputy Chief of the National Center for the Prevention and Control of Rape, and Joyce Lazar, Chief of the Social Sciences Research Branch, who administered these grants.
3 For the articles by Bacdayan and Schlegel, see Schlegel (1977). For the articles by Briggs and Richards, see Matthiasson (1974). For the other articles, see Okonjo (1976), Rogers (1975), Tanner (1974).
4 See Jordan (1968).

1. Introduction

1 The societies used in this study form part of the Standard Cross-Cultural Sample published by George P. Murdock and Douglas R. White (1969). Though their sample includes 186 societies, on only 156 of these was I able to find adequate information for the purposes of this study. The source material on which I relied was drawn largely from the Human Relations Area Files (HRAF). My use of the files represents a significant departure from previous usage which, as a rule, has abstracted bits and pieces of information for correlation analysis. Although I look at how patterns covary, my main interest is in examining the cultural context of sex-role configurations. Thus, the evidence I present relies as much on particularistic patterns as on statistical regularities.
2 Benedict (1934:35).
3 Mead (1963:284)
4 Geertz (1973:92, 217–18, 250).
5 My previous work on the subject of female status falls within the materialist framework (see Sanday 1973, 1974).
6 Ortner (1974:69).
7 Ibid., pp. 83–4.

257

8 Ibid., p. 84.
9 Geertz (1973:99).
10 Langer (1960:287).
11 Ibid., pp. 259–68.

1. Scripts for female power

1 Geertz (1973:417 – 18). The one striking exception to the cultural rule of playing down sexual differentiation is the cockfight, an all-male activity from which women are "totally and expressly excluded." Geertz's analysis of the cockfight is intriguing because it suggests that underneath the smoothness of Balinese life, in which sex differences are muted, there exists a primordial equation of maleness with animality, destruction, and the like. According to Geertz (1973:420–1), "in the cockfight, man and beast, good and evil, ego and id, the creative power of aroused masculinity and the destructive power of loosened animality fuse in a bloody drama of hatred, cruelty, violence, and death." Normally, these temperamental proclivities are not acted out. Geertz notes, however, that they are there to be acted on, as happened in 1965 when between 40 and 80 thousand Balinese were killed, largely by one another, during the upheavals following an attempted coup in Djakarta (1973:452).
2 Belo (1949:34).
3 Geertz and Geertz (1975:30, 115–16).
4 Covarrubias (1938:121).
5 Ibid.
6 Belo (1949:58).
7 Ibid., pp. 57–8.
8 Ibid., p. 15.
9 Ibid., pp. 14–15.
10 Schebesta (1963b:Vol. 2.2, 154).
11 Schebesta (1963a:Vol. 2.1, 160).
12 Ibid., pp. 56–63.
13 Ibid., p. 45.
14 Schebesta (1963b:Vol. 2.2, 126–8).
15 Ibid., p. 18.
16 Ibid., pp. 123, 45.
17 Ibid., pp. 46–7.
18 Ibid., pp. 69–70.
19 Ibid., pp. 132–3.
20 Schebesta (1963a:Vol. 2.1, 206).
21 Evans (1937:30–1).
22 Turnbull (1965b:248). Turnbull (1965a:261) reports an origin legend that begins: "When the great Forest was young" and there were "two Pygmy men and one Pygmy woman." In this legend the two men cohabit with "another woman" and "this is how Pygmies began."

23 Ibid., p. 19.
24 Ibid., p. 149.
25 Ibid., p. 178.
26 Ibid., pp. 181–2.
27 Ibid., pp. 270–1.
28 Ibid., pp. 261–7.
29 Turnbull (1961:150–5).
30 Ibid., pp. 186–7.
31 Sanday (1974:204).
32 Quain (1937:245–8).
33 P.A.W. Wallace (1946:11).
34 A.F.C. Wallace (1958:246).
35 P.A.W. Wallace (1946:14).
36 For description of the Iroquois longhouse, see A. F. C. Wallace (1969:22–3); for the Legend of Deganawidah, see P. A. W. Wallace (1946:11–14); for information on the longhouse in Iroquoian prehistory and the influence of women, see Ritchie (1965:296).
37 For this quotation see Parker's (1916:42) translation of the Constitution. The Constitution was transmitted orally along with a collection of wampum belts and strings, each of which served to recall each law or regulation. Fearing destruction of their ancient archives, the Six Nations of New York Indians elected The University of the State of New York the official custodian of their wampums in 1893. The knowledge preserved in this manner was reduced to written form in several versions and published in the early 1900s by Parker.
38 This myth was obtained in 1896 and published by Hewitt (1899–1900:221–54). In other versions of this myth the male twins are associated with good and evil. The evil twin emerges from his mother's armpit and the good twin is born the normal way. The two remain in perpetual conflict and battle (A. F. C. Wallace, 1969:86–91).
39 A. F. C. Wallace (1969:29).
40 See Chapters 6 and 7 for more details of Iroquoian history.
41 Wilks (1967:206–10).
42 Ibid., p. 208.
43 Rattray (1923:289–90).
44 Rattray (1929:75–80).
45 Fortes (1950:254–7).
46 Rattray (1923:81–4).
47 This reference was supplied to me by an Ashanti, Mr. Kwabena Owusubanahene.
48 Ibid., pp. 77–9.
49 Ibid.
50 Ibid., pp. 294–5.
51 Ibid., pp. 48–9.
52 Rattray (1929:342–3).
53 Rattray (1923:215).
54 Von Rad (1961:59).

2. Scripts for male dominance

1 Faulkingham (1971:163).
2 Onwuejeogwu (1971:281—2).
3 Faulkingham (1971:104—5).
4 Onwuejeogwu (1971:288—9).
5 Ibid., pp. 285—92.
6 Murphy and Murphy (1974:104).
7 Ibid., pp. 129—30.
8 Tocantins (1959:12—14).
9 Murphy (1958:69—79).
10 Murphy and Murphy (1974:89—95).
11 In a slightly different interpretation, Murphy and Murphy (1974:95) say that the long tubular shape of the trumpets makes them "a phallic symbol in the classic sense of the term." Because whoever controls the trumpets is the dominant sex, they also state that the myth is "a parable of phallic dominance, of male superiority symbolized in, and based upon, the possession of the penis." They call the tale of the male seizure of the sacred trumpets "an allegory of man's birth from woman, his original dependence upon the woman as the supporting, nurturant, and controlling agent in his life, and of the necessity to break the shackles and assert his autonomy and manhood." According to them, the mother is an eternal threat to self-individuation, a frustrater of urges, and a swallower of emergent identity. Men assert their autonomy and maintain their role through owning the sacred trumpets and guarding them from the sight of women.
12 Murphy (1957:1021—5).
13 Murphy (1958:39—40).
14 I am indebted to Murphy and Murphy (1974:87—91), whose description of the Mundurucu sexes suggested these insights.
15 Underhill (1939:90—1).
16 Underhill (1946:8—12).
17 Ibid., p. 253.
18 Ibid., p. 21.
19 Ibid.
20 Ibid., pp. 197—8.
21 Underhill (1936:15).
22 Underhill (1946:210).
23 Harris (1974:87).
24 Chagnon (1968:1).
25 Harris (1974:101).
26 Chagnon (1968:33).
27 Ibid., pp. 74—6.
28 Ibid., p. 84.
29 Ibid., p. 9.
30 Ibid., pp. 82—3.
31 Ibid., pp. 119—23.

32 Harris (1974:87, 102—4). For an interesting discussion of the bases for Yanomamo male supremacy, see Harris (1977a:67—78).
33 This account of Yanomamo cosmology and theology was adapted from
Chagnon (1968:44—8).

3. The environmental context of metaphors for sexual identities

1 Mead (1963:261—3).
2 Geertz (1973:218).
3 Neumann (1955:25).
4 Ibid., pp. 3—25.
5 The codes and the data for proximity of the father in infancy come from
Barry and Paxson (1971:472).
6 Gorer (1938:253—4, 297—8).
7 Schebesta (1963a:Vol. 2.1, 56—8, 274).
8 Firth (1936:133—40, 171, 166).
9 Fortes (1950:268).
10 Dubois (1945:147—53).
11 Levine (1965:83); Messing (1957:422—3, 426, 432—3).
12 Hoebel (1940: 49—50, 130).
13 Evans-Pritchard (1929:199; 1937:16); Larken (1926:18).
14 Murphy and Murphy (1974:164—72).
15 Each link of the causal chain displayed in Figure 3.1 is tested by using multiple
regression analysis. The results of the statistical analyses are presented in Appendix C. The first link is tested by entering proximity of the father to infants
as the dependent variable and subsistence variables reflecting a plant or animal
orientation as the independent variables. The results (presented in Appendix
C) provide statistical support for the hypothesized causal link. Hunting large
game, the importance of animal husbandry, and gathering account for a significant part of the variance in the dependent variable.
   To test the second link, the subsistence variables and the proximity of the
father are entered in a second multiple regression equation (see Regression II
in Appendix C), with type of origin symbolism as the dependent variable.
This equation is also significant; however, proximity of the father explains
the largest proportion of the variance in the dependent variable. As the presentation in Appendix C shows, the subsistence variables have a more direct
effect on the proximity of fathers to infants than on origin symbolism. This
suggests that the role of the father in infancy intervenes between the mode of
subsistence and notions about origin. Such results confirm the causal links
presented in Figure 3.1.
16 Spencer (1947:127—8).
17 Argyle (1966:21, 175—8, 196—7).
18 Dundes (1962:1037).

19 Mead (1968:236).
20 Whiting and Whiting (1975:4).
21 Dinnerstein (1979:10–11) commenting on Goldenberg's (1979) book *Changing of the Gods*.
22 De Vos and Romanucci-Ross (1975:364–5; see also discussion on pp. 363–71).
23 Spencer (1947:118).
24 Ibid., pp. 117, 131.
25 Ibid., pp. 128, 131.
26 Barnouw (1963:309–24)
27 Hamamsy (1957).

4. Plans for the sexual division of labor

1 Murdock and Provost (1973:210–11).
2 Brown (1970), Friedl (1975:59–60), White, Burton, and Brudner (1977:3–4). For other anthropological analyses of the sexual division of labor that go beyond the assumption of physical strength differences and consider cultural and adaptional factors similar to those considered here, see Martin and Voorhies (1975), Nerlove (1974), and Zelman (1977).
3 White, Burton, and Brudner (1977:3).
4 Mead (1968:168).
5 Meigs (1976:394).
6 Murdock and Provost (1973:211–12).
7 Mead (1968:178–80).
8 'Ammār (1954:21).
9 Murphy and Murphy (1974:129–30).
10 Kenyatta (1953:54).
11 Paques (1954:83–91).
12 Gorer (1938:104).
13 Ibid., pp. 298–314.
14 Ibid., pp. 223–4.
15 Ibid., p. 225.
16 Ibid., p. 451.
17 Polanyi (1966:54–7).
18 Argyle (1966:63–5).
19 Polanyi (1966:54–7).
20 Argyle (1966:87).
21 Lombard (1967:87).
22 Ibid., pp. 86–8.
23 Herskovits (1938:Vol. II, 85).
24 Polanyi (1966:56).
25 Okonjo (1976:45–8). For other examples of the dual-sex ideology, see Chapter 6 and the discussion of the Hopi in Chapter 8.
26 Ibid., p. 48.

27 The relationship between mode of acquiring food and certain child-training practices established by Barry, Child, and Bacon (1959) is consistant with the results diagrammed in Figure 4.1. These authors show that there are greater pressures to make children into obedient and responsible adults in agricultural societies than in hunting societies, which stress shaping children into "venturesome, independent adults who can take initiative in wresting food daily from nature."

5. Blood, sex, and danger

1 Young and Bacdayan (1965:230).
2 Stephens (1961:391).
3 Douglas (1966:3,115).
4 Ibid., p. 4.
5 Ibid., pp. 94–5.
6 Douglas (1970:132–4).
7 Woodburn (1968:51–2).
8 Lévi-Strauss (1948) notes this in his ethnography of the Nambicuara, and so does Turnbull (1965a) in his description of those periods of the year when the Mbuti are living a sedentary life among village cultivators. Draper, in describing the difference in sexual egalitarianism between foraging and sedentary !Kung Bushmen, concludes that the foraging context encourages female autonomy and the sedentary context decreases it (Draper 1975:109).
9 Douglas (1970:132–3).
10 Rattray (1927:69–70).
11 Ibid., p. 74.
12 Ibid., p. 72.
13 Ibid., p. 75.
14 Ibid., pp. 58–9.
15 Douglas (1975:69–70).
16 Ibid., p. 55.
17 Ibid., pp. 234–9.
18 Radcliffe-Brown (1922:6).
19 Ibid., p. 307.
20 Ibid., pp. 270–5.
21 Ibid., pp. 316–18.
22 Ibid., p. 318.
23 Ibid., p. 319.
24 Ibid., pp. 93–4.
25 Ibid., p. 94.
26 Ibid., p. 98.
27 Ibid., pp. 122–6.
28 Ibid., p. 256.
29 Ibid., p. 295.
30 Ibid., pp. 92–4.

31 Ibid., p. 39.
32 Ibid., pp. 43–4.
33 Ibid., pp. 44–7.
34 Ibid., pp. 47–8.
35 Ibid., pp. 138, 141.
36 Ibid., pp. 192–6.
37 McIlwraith (1948:Vol. 2, 500).
38 Ibid., pp. 338–42.
39 McIlwraith (1948:Vol. 1, 3).
40 Ibid., p. 263.
41 Ibid., pp. 761–2.
42 Ibid., p. 370.
43 Ibid., p. 371.
44 Ibid., p. 372.
45 Ibid., pp. 372–3.
46 Ibid., p. 575.
47 McIlwraith (1948:Vol. 2, 340–2).
48 McIlwraith (1948:Vol. 1, 168, 141).
49 Ibid., p. 171.
50 Boas (1898:27).
51 Ibid., p. 28.
52 McIlwraith (1948:Vol. 1, 42).
53 Though the Bellacoola attitude regarding menstrual blood is woven into an elaborate fantasy construction, there is some evidence that keeping female body fluids from the smell of fish was realistic. Several anthropologists who have conducted field research in the same Pacific Island society have noted (personal communication) that fish are extraordinarily attracted to human urine produced after eating asparagus. In this same society, tribal men are careful to avoid sexual intercourse before a fishing expedition, saying that the smell of sex scares the fish from their nets. Thus, it seems clear that fish react to strong odor.
54 Douglas (1975:60–8).
55 The types of menstrual restrictions were adopted from Young and Bacdayan (1965:226). The restrictions, in the order that they are listed here, form a Guttman scale, as shown by Young and Bacdayan. For purposes of this study the menstrual restrictions were counted. The proposition regarding the occurrence of menstrual taboos and hunting is not referred to in the discussion of the statistical results. This is because there is no relationship between the number of taboos and the importance of hunting or the hunting of large game. In societies where small game are hunted, there are the same number of menstrual taboos on the average as there are in societies where large game are hunted. This finding does not mean that menstrual taboos are not related to male hunting. It simply means that when males do not hunt they do other things (such as engage in warfare) that are also associated with the imposition of menstrual taboos.
56 The correlation between the number of menstrual taboos (H16) and the percentage of integrated work tasks is -0.32 ($N = 110$; $p = 0.001$) using Pearson's R.

57 See Mary Douglas's (1975:68–70) discussion of the "womb envy" hypothesis.
58 Douglas (1975:41–4).
59 Lindenbaum (1972:248).

6. The bases for female political and economic power and authority

1 Rosaldo and Lamphere (1974:3).
2 Harris (1977b:46).
3 Rosaldo and Lamphere (1974:3).
4 Schlegel (1974:554).
5 Sacks (1976:568). See also the reviews by Naomi Quinn (1977) and Susan Carol Rogers (1978) of anthropological studies of women's status for cogent criticisms of the universal male dominance argument.
6 These definitions are taken from Smith (1960:18–19). They are the same definitions I employed elsewhere in developing an operational measure of female status (see Sanday 1974:190 and discussion in Appendix E).
7 For examples of similar statements expressing tribal women's evaluation of themselves relative to males, see Rogers (1978:143) and Schlegel (1977).
8 Okonjo (1976:50).
9 Tanner (1974:146).
10 Ibid., p. 142.
11 Ibid., p. 145–6.
12 A. F. C. Wallace (1969:28–9).
13 Iroquoian tradition states that the confederation of the Five Nations (later a sixth was added) took place about the length of one man's life before the white man appeared (Schoolcraft 1847:120–1). The archeological evidence suggests that before this there was a long period during which there was intensive warfare between the tribal units that formed the League. The Constitution of the League of Five Nations confirms this with its emphasis on the importance of maintaining peace among the member nations. Before the formation of tribal units, the primary sociopolitical unit appears to have been the unfortified village composed of several houses, some of which were of the longhouse type. For information on the stages of Iroquoian prehistory, see William Ritchie's (1965) description of the archeology of New York State. The text of the Constitution has been recorded by Parker (1916). John Witthoft discusses prehistoric Iroquoian settlement patterns and speculates on the greater importance of women during this period (see Witthoft 1961: 70–2).
14 Rattray (1923:77–9).
15 Ibid., p. 216.
16 Ibid., p. 121.
17 Ibid., pp. 121–4.
18 Wilks (1967:207).
19 Harlan (1971:470–1).

20 Hammond and Jablow (1976:73).
21 Lévi-Strauss (1966:110).
22 According to the list of technological activities recorded by Murdock and Provost for the societies of the Standard Cross-Cultural Sample, Abipon women performed 65% of all technological activities.
23 Métraux (1946:206).
24 Ibid., pp. 197–9.
25 Ibid., p. 202.
26 Ibid., pp. 265–6.
27 Ibid., pp. 279–80; Dobrizhoffer (1822:20–23).
28 Hoebel (1940:119).
29 Dobrizhoffer (1822:139).
30 Ibid., pp. 154–5.
31 Métraux (1946:319).
32 Dobrizhoffer (1822:108).
33 Ibid., pp. 64–5, 76–7.
34 Ibid., pp. 86–7.
35 Ibid., pp. 65–6.
36 Métraux (1946:202).
37 Ibid., p. 220.
38 Draper (1975:82–3).
39 Ibid., pp. 84–5. See also Begler (1978:573).
40 Flannery (1935:83).
41 Flannery (1932:29).
42 Landes (1938:135–7).
43 Spindler (1962:19).
44 Boserup (1970:91).
45 Ibid., p. 92.
46 Ottenberg (1959:215). For a note on the status of women among the Apikpo Igbo as compared to the Igbo of western and southern Nigeria, see Van Allen (1976:65–6).
47 Mintz (1971:256).
48 Métraux (1951:147).
49 Mintz (1971:257).
50 Ibid., p. 264.
51 Ibid., pp. 259–60.
52 Leacock (1978:255).
53 Boserup (1970:56), Martin and Voorhies (1975:298–9).
54 See Rogers (1978:157) for a discussion of some examples.

7. The decline of the women's world: the effect of colonialism

1 See Quinn (1977:184). The impact of modernization on traditional female power is discussed by Boserup (1970), Bossen (1975), Hamamsy (1957), Leacock (1978), McElroy (1975), Martin and Voorhies (1975), Mintz (1971),

Sacks (1976), Seymour (1975), and Van Allen (1972, 1976), to mention only a few examples. See also summary discussion of the effects of modernization by Quinn (1977:184–6).

2 It is perhaps worth noting here that the only detailed descriptions of the women's war have been published by women. Margery Perham (1937:206–20) undertook the task of recording all that was known about the development and the outcome of the riots. Sylvia Leith-Ross (1965:23) drew on this account in her study of Igbo women, several years after the riots, which she conducted in an effort to document the changing role of Igbo women brought on by the British colonial system. More recently, Judith Van Allen (1976) provided an account of the "women's war" in the context of the impact of colonialism on the Igbo women's world.

3 Judith Van Allen (1976:67) says that the Igbo women of this region "came out as second-class citizens" because, although they participated in political and economic affairs, men were better able to afford the costs involved in taking the highest titles because of their control of the land through the patrilineages. See Leith-Ross (1965:105–10) for the description of Southern Igbo female life followed in the text.

4 Leith-Ross (1965:106).

5 Ibid., pp. 105–10. The description of male respect for the right of women to safeguard the fruits of the earth suggests that Igbo female status was based on ascribed, not achieved, rights.

6 Ibid., pp. 87–8.

7 Ibid., pp. 24–6.

8 Ibid., pp. 26–7.

9 Ibid., pp. 28–9.

10 Ibid., p. 30.

11 Ibid., pp. 31–2.

12 Ibid., pp. 34, 38.

13 Ibid., p. 36.

14 Ibid., p. 165.

15 Ibid., p. 34.

16 Ibid., p. 235.

17 A. F. C. Wallace (1969:179).

18 A. F. C. Wallace (1971:374).

19 Ibid., p. 373.

20 Deardorff (1951); see Parker (1912) for the published version of the Great Message.

21 Deardorff (1951:81).

22 A. F. C. Wallace (1971:367).

23 A. F. C. Wallace (1969:261).

24 Jensen (1977:429–30).

25 A. F. C. Wallace (1971:372–3).

26 Deardorff (1951:89, 94, 103).

27 Hoebel (1960:2).

28 It is generally agreed that the language and culture of the Comanche suggest a Northern Shoshonean origin. Information on pre-horse Northern Shosho-

nean culture is, however, lacking. Julian Steward (1938:236) suggests that it is probable that the Northern Shoshone were at one time fundamentally similar to the Western Shoshone (who did not have the horse, nor did they hunt buffalo). Hence, in reconstructing the possible pre-horse Comanche culture, the Western Shoshone are employed as a model.

29 Steward (1938:232).
30 Ibid., pp. 245, 254.
31 Ibid., pp. 242–4.
32 Ibid., pp. 257–8.
33 E. Wallace and Hoebel (1952:35–7).
34 Ibid., pp. 22–4.
35 E. Wallace and Hoebel (1952:212); Hoebel (1940:18–20).
36 For discussion of Comanche political organization, see E. Wallace and Hoebel (1952:210–15). For description of the peace chief, see Hoebel (1940:18–20) and E. Wallace and Hoebel (1952:212).
37 E. Wallace and Hoebel (1952:245).
38 Ibid., pp. 234–41.
39 Ibid., p. 204.
40 Ibid., p. 196.
41 Ibid., pp. 72–3.
42 Hoebel (1960:1–3).
43 Ibid., pp. 7–8.
44 Ibid., pp. 6–11.
45 Powell (1969:Vol. 1, xxiii–5).
46 Hoebel (1960:37–44).
47 Grinnell (1962:Vol. 1; 156).
48 See especially Powell (1969) and Grinnell (1962:Vol. 1, 128).
49 See Limbaugh (1973:8, 15–16).
50 Quoted in Limbaugh (1973:26).
51 Powell (1969:Vol.1, 4).
52 Hoebel (1960:95–6).
53 Grinnell (1918:376), Limbaugh (1973:5).
54 Spencer and Gillen (1968:7).
55 Ibid., pp. 7–11.
56 Ibid., p. 130.
57 Ibid., p. 457.
58 Ibid., pp. 94–5, 107–8.
59 Maybury-Lewis (1965:353–5).
60 Maybury-Lewis (1967:306).
61 Ibid., pp. 31–4.
62 See Hallowell (1955:120, 171–81, 252) for description of Northern Saulteaux attitude toward their environment.
63 Hallowell (1955:299–300).
64 The measure of food stress employed in Table 7.2 is adapted from the code presented by Murdock and Morrow (1970:306–8) entitled Preservation and Storage of Food. This code includes information on the constancy of the food resources used by the society, whether there are techniques of food preserva-

tion, and the prevalence and types of food storage techniques. This is, of course, not the only measure of stress that could be employed. Other measures might yield different results. The relationships presented in Tables 7.1, 7.2, and 6.3 suggest that female political power does not flourish in societies faced with stress either from contact with Europeans, or from an uncertain food supply, or from migration.

8. The bases for male dominance

1 Friedl (1975:7).
2 Divale and Harris (1976:521).
3 These traits form a Guttman scale. Societies in which all traits are absent receive a scale score of 1 and those in which all traits are present receive a scale score of 6. The details of the scale are presented in Appendix F. See Table 8.1 for the order in which the traits appear on the scale.
4 Murphy and Murphy (1974:87).
5 Sūra 4:34. This quote from the Quran was taken from John P. Mason's (1975:649) instructive article on sex and symbol in the treatment of women in a Libyan oasis community.
6 See Appendix F for a detailed discussion of the male dominance measure.
7 Rogers (1975:729). See Quinn (1977:218) for the application of Rogers's concept to a discussion of the relationship between the Mundurucu sexes.
8 Lamphere (1977:613).
9 Ibid., p. 616. Lamphere discusses the work of quite a few anthropologists who argue for the "complementary but equal" position. For a summary of this position and the different ways it has been expressed, see Lamphere (1977:615–20). Lamphere also raises some important issues for future research in this article.
10 Schlegel (1977:261).
11 Ibid., p. 254.
12 Harris (1977a:81).
13 Friedl (1975:135).
14 Ibid., p. 7.
15 Ortner (1974:73–5).
16 Rogers (1978:134).
17 Martin and Voorhies (1975:222).
18 See Martin and Voorhies (1975:222–39).
19 In the total Standard Cross-Cultural Sample of 186 societies, 26 (14%) are classified in the matrilineal descent category, and 38 (21%) follow the matrilocal rule of residence. (See Murdock and Wilson 1972:274.)
20 Murdock (1959:302).
21 Since Martin and Voorhies refer to the same kinds of environmental and social processes that are highly correlated with male dominance and female power, one would expect that matrilineal descent and matrilocal residence would likewise be highly correlated with the same processes. Type of descent

269

and mode of residence, however, are *not* as clearly associated with the ecological and stress factors that this study has found associated with male dominance and female power. Patrilocality and patrilineality are more likely to be found where there is endemic warfare and food stress. Seventy-six percent of the patrilineal societies and 77% of the strictly patrilocal societies engage in chronic warfare as compared with 70% of the matrilineal societies and 66% of the matrilocal–avunculocal societies. Twenty-nine percent of the patrilineal and strictly patrilocal societies face periodic or chronic hunger as compared with 14% of the matrilineal and 16% of the matrilocal–avunculocal societies. These associations between type of descent, mode of residence, warfare, and food stress are not significant, however.

Residence and descent are weakly associated with origin symbolism. Most (64%) of the strictly patrilocal societies have masculine origin symbolism as compared with 36% of the matrilocal–avunculocal societies. When the other types of residence patterns are considered, the results are not so clear cut. Ambilocal–neolocal societies are evenly split between masculine origin symbolism (50%) and couple or feminine origin symbolism. Patrilocal societies with matrilocality as an alternative display masculine origin symbolism in 37% of the cases.

Type of descent displays a similar pattern in relation to origin symbolism. Sixty percent of the patrilineal societies have masculine origin symbolism as compared with 25% of the matrilineal societies. Seventy-five percent of the matrilineal societies have either feminine or couple origin symbolism as compared with 40% of the patrilineal societies. Bilateral societies are split evenly between masculine origin symbolism and couple or feminine origin symbolism.

22 Rogers (1975:747–9).
23 Ibid.
24 Bamberger (1974:263–80).
25 For the Kikuyu tale, see Kenyatta (1953:3–8); for the Bambara tale, see Paques (1954:108–10); for the Jivaro tale, see Stirling (1938:124–9). See Bamberger (1974) for a different interpretation of myths of former female power.
26 Quinn (1977:218).
27 See Epilogue for more discussion of the Hebrews.
28 B. Whiting (1965:126–7); J. W. M. Whiting and B. Whiting (1975:193).

9. Why women?

1 Douglas (1975:234).
2 Ibid., p. 5.
3 Mead (1968:224–5).
4 Turnbull (1961:92).
5 Ibid.
6 Ibid.
7 Turnbull (1961:82; 1965b:263).

8 Turnbull (1961:80–1).
9 Turnbull (1965b:263).
10 Ibid., p. 264.
11 Turnbull (1961:155).
12 Turnbull (1965b:266–7).
13 Reichel-Dolmatoff (1971:50).
14 Ibid., p. 219.
15 Ibid., p. 50.
16 Ibid., p. 97.
17 Ibid., p. 55.
18 Ibid., p. 54.
19 Ibid., p. 219.
20 Ibid., p. 220.
21 Ibid., pp. 220, 225.
22 Ibid., p. 244.
23 Ibid., pp. 218–19, 67–8.
24 Lathrap (1973:94).
25 Lindenbaum (1972:249), Meggitt (1964:210).
26 Lindenbaum (1972:247–8).
27 Meggitt (1964:218).
28 See discussion by Lindenbaum (1972:248).
29 Meggitt (1964:221).
30 Meggitt (1965:107).
31 Berndt (1965:84).
32 Lindenbaum (1972:246).
33 Berndt (1965:81–4).
34 Berndt (1962:48–9).
35 Berndt (1965:83).
36 Lindenbaum (1972:250–1).
37 Ibid., p. 242.
38 Lindenbaum (1979:69, 100–7).
39 Ibid., pp. 117–26.
40 Berndt (1962:54–5).
41 Ibid., p. 72.
42 Ibid.
43 Berndt (1962:67–9).
44 Lindenbaum (1976:57–8).
45 Meggitt (1964:220).
46 Ibid., p. 221.
47 Powell (1969:xviii).
48 Evans-Pritchard (1973:439).
49 Evans-Pritchard (1971:433).
50 Evans-Pritchard (1936:32–3).
51 Ibid., pp. 45–6.
52 Ibid., p. 38.
53 Ibid., pp. 44–5.
54 Ibid., p. 42.

55 Philipps (1926:180).
56 Evans-Pritchard (1971:71–2).
57 Ibid., p. 80.
58 Ibid., pp. 86–8.
59 Ibid., pp. 72–3.
60 Evans-Pritchard (1973:457).
61 Ibid., pp. 451–2.
62 Ibid., p. 463.
63 Evans-Pritchard (1937:261).
64 Ibid., pp. 284–5.
65 Ibid., p. 284.
66 Evans-Pritchard (1934:175).
67 Evans-Pritchard (1957:376).
68 Evans-Pritchard (1971:219, 250).
69 Seligman and Seligman (1932:507, 516).
70 See Evans-Pritchard (1971:251).
71 Richards (1956:34).
72 Richards (1939:20).
73 Ibid., pp. 15–17.
74 Ibid., pp. 24–5.
75 Richards (1956:48–9).
76 Richards (1939:50–1).
77 Ibid., p. 351.
78 Richards (1956:148).
79 Ibid., pp. 148, 157–8.
80 Ibid., pp. 185–6.

Epilogue

1 See Carol P. Christ (1979:273–87).
2 All Biblical quotes are taken from *The New Oxford Annotated Bible* (1973).
3 The phrase "awhoring after foreign gods" is attributed by Patai (1967:278) to the Biblical authors.
4 Kramer (1961:vii–viii).
5 Kramer (1957:71).
6 Patai (1967:187).
7 Kramer (1961:86; 1963:153, 140).
8 Kramer (1961:74–5).
9 Patai (1967:187, 278).
10 Ibid., pp. 32–3.
11 Ibid., p. 61.
12 Ibid., pp. 54, 58.
13 Kenyon (1978:76); see also Patai (1967:60).
14 Meek (1960:116–17).
15 Ibid., p. 117.

16 Patai (1967:271).
17 See Anderson (1975:136–64) on "The Struggle between Faith and Culture"; see Simpson (1952c:441–2).
18 See *The New Oxford Annotated Bible* (1973:xxvii). See also Anderson (1975:207).
19 See discussion of J¹ and J² documents in Simpson (1952c:441–8) and of JEDP documents in Simpson (1952b:194–200).
20 Anderson (1975:194–7).
21 Kenyon (1978:67).
22 Anderson (1975:208).
23 Bewer (1933:60).
24 Ibid., p. 71.
25 Patai (1967:34–43).
26 See Leach on "The Legitimacy of Solomon" in Lane (1970:248–92).
27 See *The New Oxford Annotated Bible* (1973:972) for a comment on the attraction of women to the worship of the "Queen of Heaven."
28 Anderson (1975:146).
29 Ibid., pp. 207, 422–36.
30 See Simpson (1952c:450) for similarities between the Babylonian creation myth and Chapter 1 of Genesis.
31 For a commentary on the meaning of peace in Chapter 1 of Genesis, see Simpson (1952a:487) and Von Rad (1961:59).
32 Patai (1971:13–14).
33 The description of competing sex-role plans among the early Christians in this section uses information presented by Elaine Pagels (1976, 1979) in her analysis of the Jewish and Christian Gnostic texts discovered in 1945 by an Arab peasant in Upper Egypt and believed to be dated the first and second centuries A.D. For the texts themselves see *The Nag Hammadi Library* (1977).
34 Pagels (1979:56).
35 Ibid., pp. 55–6.
36 Pagels (1976:298–9).
37 Ibid., p. 303.
38 Pagels (1979:64).
39 Ibid.
40 Ibid., p. 58.
41 Ibid., p. 65.
42 Ibid., p. 42. According to Pagels (1979:66), "gnostics were not unanimous in affirming the equality of women – nor were the orthodox unanimous in denigrating them." Clement of Alexandria (*ca.* 180), Pagels says, demonstrated "that even orthodox Christians could affirm the feminine in God – and the active participation of women." Most Christians, however, adopted the position of Clement's contemporary, Tertullian, who wrote: "It is not permitted for a woman to speak in the church, nor is it permitted for her to teach, nor to baptize, nor to offer (the eucharist), nor to claim for herself a share in any masculine function – least of all, in priestly office"(ibid., pp. 68–9).
43 Pagels (1976:301–2).
44 Pagels (1979:40–1).

45 Ibid., p. 42.
46 Pagels (1979:xviii–xix). See pages xiii–xvii for an account of the discovery of the texts and their eventual publication in English.
47 Ibid., pp. 98–9.
48 Ibid., p. 101.
49 Ibid., pp. 82–3.
50 From Ntosake Shange's play "For Colored Girls Who Have Considered Suicide When the Rainbow is Enuf." Original cast album, Buddah Records, 1976.

Bibliography

'Ammār, Hāmid. 1954. *Growing up in an Egyptian Village*. London: Routledge & Kegan Paul.

Anderson, Bernhard W. 1975. *Understanding the Old Testament*. 3rd Ed. Englewood Cliffs, N.J.: Prentice-Hall.

Argyle, William J. 1966. *The Fon of Dahomey*. Oxford: Clarendon Press.

Bamberger, Joan. 1974. The myth of matriarchy: why men rule in primitive society. In *Woman, Culture, and Society*, M. Z. Rosaldo and L. Lamphere, eds., pp.263–80. Stanford: Stanford University Press.

Barnouw, Victor. 1963. *Culture and Personality*. Homewood, Ill.: Dorsey Press.

Barry, Herbert, III, Irvin L. Child, and Margaret K. Bacon. 1959. Relation of child training to subsistence economy. *American Anthropologist 61*:51–63.

Barry, Herbert, III, Lili Josephson, Edith Lauer, and Catherine Marshall. 1976. Traits inculcated in childhood: cross-cultural codes 5. *Ethnology 15*:83–114.

Barry, Herbert, III, and Lenora M. Paxson. 1971. Infancy and early childhood: cross-cultural codes 2. *Ethnology 10*:466–508.

Begler, Elsie B. 1978. Sex, status, and authority in egalitarian society. *American Anthropologist 80*:571–88.

Belo, Jane. 1949. *Bali: Rangda and Barong*. Monographs of the American Ethnological Society 16.

Benedict, Ruth. 1934. *Patterns of Culture*. Boston: Houghton Mifflin.

Berndt, Ronald M. 1962. *Excess and Restraint*. Chicago: University of Chicago Press.

1965. The Kamano, Usurufa, Jate and Fore of the Eastern Highlands. In *Gods, Ghosts, and Men in Melanesia*, P. Lawrence and M. J. Meggitt, eds., pp. 78–104. Melbourne: Oxford University Press.

Bewer, Julius A. 1933. *The Literature of the Old Testament*. New York: Columbia University Press.

Boas, Franz. 1898. *The Mythology of the Bella Coola Indians*. Memoirs of the American Museum of Natural History, vol. 2. Publications of the Jesup North Pacific Expedition, vol. 1, 1898–1900.

Bollig, P. Laurentius. 1967. The inhabitants of the Truk islands. Translation. New Haven, Conn.: HRAF Press. (Originally published in 1927, *Anthropos Ethnologische Bibliothek*, Vol. 3, No. 1., Münster in Westphalia: Aschendorffsche Verlags-buchhandlung.)

Boserup, Ester. 1970. *Woman's Role in Economic Development*. New York: St. Martin's Press.

Bibliography

Bossen, Laurel. 1975. Women in modernizing societies. *American Ethnologist* 2:587–601.

Brown, Judith K. 1970. A note on the division of labor by sex. *American Anthropologist* 72:1073–8.

Chagnon, Napoleon A. 1968. *Yanomamö: The Fierce People*. New York: Holt, Rinehart & Winston.

Christ, Carol P. 1979. Why women need the goddess: phenomenological, psychological, and political reflections. In *Womanspirit Rising*, C. P. Christ and J. Plaskow, eds., pp. 273–87. San Francisco: Harper & Row.

Covarrubias, Miguel. 1938. *Island of Bali*. New York: Knopf.

Deardorff, Merle H. 1951. The religion of Handsome Lake: its origin and development. In *Symposium on Local Diversity in Iroquois Culture*, W. Fenton, ed., pp. 77–108. Smithsonian Institution, Bureau of American Ethnology Bulletin 149. Washington, D.C.: Government Printing Office.

De Vos, George, and Lola Romanucci-Ross. 1975. Ethnicity: vessel of meaning and emblem of contrast. In *Ethnic Identity*, G. De Vos and L. Romanucci-Ross, eds., pp. 363–90. Palo Alto, Calif.: Mayfield.

Dinnerstein, Dorothy. 1979. The uses of gender. *New York Times Book Review* (29 July):10–11, 20.

Divale, William Tulio, and Marvin Harris. 1976. Population, warfare, and the male supremacist complex. *American Anthropologist* 78:521–38.

Dobrizhoffer, Martin. 1822. *An Account of the Abipones, an Equestrian People of Paraguay*. London: John Murray.

Douglas, Mary. 1966. *Purity and Danger*. London: Routledge & Kegan Paul.

1970. *Natural Symbols*. New York: Vintage/Random House.

1975. *Implicit Meanings*. London: Routledge & Kegan Paul.

Draper, Patricia. 1975. !Kung women: contrasts in sexual egalitarianism in foraging and sedentary contexts. In *Toward an Anthropology of Women*, R. Reiter, ed., pp. 77–109. New York: Monthly Review Press.

DuBois, Cora. 1945. Analysis of Alorese culture. In *The Psychological Frontiers of Society*, Abram Kardiner, ed., pp. 101–45. New York: Columbia University Press.

Dundes, Alan. 1962. Earth-Diver: creation of the mythopoeic male. *American Anthropologist* 64:1032–51.

Evans, Ivor H. N. 1937. *The Negritos of Malaya*. Cambridge: Cambridge University Press.

Evans-Pritchard, E. E. 1929. Witchcraft (Mangu) among the A-Zande. *Sudan Notes and Records* 12:163–249.

1934. Social character of bride-wealth, with special reference to the Azande. *Man* 34:172–5.

1936. Zande theology. *Sudan Notes and Records* 19:5–46.

1937. *Witchcraft, Oracles and Magic among the Azande*. Oxford: Clarendon Press.

1957. The Zande royal court. *Zaire* 11:361–89, 493–511, 687–713.

1971. *The Azande*. Oxford: Clarendon Press.

1973. The Zande State. In *Peoples and Cultures of Africa*, E. P. Skinner, ed., pp. 437–64. New York: Doubleday/Natural History Press.

Bibliography

Faulkingham, Ralph Harold. 1971. Political support in a Hausa village. Doctoral thesis, Michigan State University.

Firth, Raymond. 1936. *We, the Tikopia*. London: George Allen & Unwin.

Flannery, Regina. 1932. The position of women among the Mescalero Apache. *Primitive Man* 5:26–32.

1935. The position of women among the Eastern Cree. *Primitive Man* 8:81–6.

Fortes, Meyer. 1950. Kinship and marriage among the Ashanti. In *African Systems of Kinship and Marriage,* A. R. Radcliffe-Brown and D. Forde, eds., pp. 252–84. London: Oxford University Press.

Friedl, Ernestine. 1975. *Women and Men: an Anthropologist's View*. New York: Holt, Rinehart & Winston.

Geertz, Clifford. 1973. *The Interpretation of Cultures*. New York: Basic Books.

Geertz, Hildred, and Clifford Geertz. 1975. *Kinship in Bali*. Chicago: University of Chicago Press.

Goldenberg, Naomi R. 1979. *Changing of the Gods*. Boston: Beacon Press.

Gorer, Geoffrey. 1938. *Himalayan Village: an Account of the Lepchas of Sikkim*. London: Michael Joseph.

Grinnell, George B. 1918. Early Cheyenne villages. *American Anthropologist* 20:359–80.

1962. *The Cheyenne Indians*. 2 Vols. New York: Cooper Square.

Hallowell, A. Irving. 1955. *Culture and Experience*. Philadelphia: University of Pennsylvania Press.

Hamamsy, Laila. 1957. The role of women in a changing Navaho society. *American Anthropologist* 59:101–11.

Hammond, Dorothy, and Alta Jablow. 1976. *Women in Cultures of the World*. Menlo Park, Calif.: Cummings.

Harlan, Jack R. 1971. Agricultural origins: centers and noncenters. *Science* 174:465–74.

Harris, Marvin. 1974. *Cows, Pigs, Wars, and Witches*. New York: VintageBooks/Random House.

1977a. *Cannibals and Kings*. New York: Vintage Books/Random House.

1977b. Why men dominate women. *New York Times Magazine* (13 November):46*ff*.

Herskovits, Melville J. 1938. *Dahomey: an Ancient West African Kingdom*. 2 Vols. New York: J. J. Augustin.

Hewitt, John N. B. 1899–1900. *Iroquoian Cosmology*. Part 1. 21st Annual Report of the Bureau of American Ethnology. (Reprinted in 1974 by AMS Press, New York.)

Hoebel, E. Adamson. 1940. *The Political Organization and Law-Ways of the Comanche Indians*. Memoirs of the American Anthropological Association 54.

1960. *The Cheyennes*. New York: Holt, Rinehart & Winston.

Jensen, Joan M. 1977. Native American women and agriculture: a Seneca case study. *Sex Roles* 3:423–42.

Jordan, Winthrop D. 1968. *White over Black: American Attitudes toward the Negro, 1550–1812*. Chapel Hill: University of North Carolina Press.

Junod, Henri A. 1927. The life of a South African tribe. 2 Vols., rev. ed. London: Macmillan.

277

Bibliography

Kenyatta, Jomo. 1953. *Facing Mount Kenya.* London: Secker & Warburg.

Kenyon, Kathleen M. 1978. *The Bible and Recent Archeology.* Atlanta: John Knox Press.

Kramer, Samuel N. 1957. The Sumerians. *Scientific American* (October):71–83.

1961. *Sumerian Mythology.* New York: Harper & Row.

1963. *The Sumerians.* Chicago: University of Chicago Press.

Lamphere, Louise. 1977. Review essay: anthropology. *Signs* 2:612–27.

Landes, Ruth. 1938. *The Ojibwa Woman.* New York: Columbia University Press.

Lane, Michael, ed. 1970. *Introduction to Structuralism,* New York: Basic Books.

Langer, Susanne. 1960. *Philosophy in a New Key.* 4th Ed. Cambridge, Mass.: Harvard University Press.

Larken, F. M. 1926. An account of the Zande. *Sudan Notes and Records* 9:1–55.

1927. An account of the Zande. *Sudan Notes and Records* 10:85–134.

Lathrap, Donald. 1973. The "hunting" economies of the tropical forest zone of South America: an attempt at historical perspective. In *Peoples and Cultures of Native South America,* D. R. Gross, ed., pp. 83–97. Garden City, N.Y.: Doubleday/Natural History Press.

Leacock, Eleanor. 1978. Women's status in egalitarian society: implications for social evolution. *Current Anthropology* 19:247–55.

Leith-Ross, Sylvia. 1965. *African Women.* New York: Praeger.

Levine, Donald N. 1965. *Wax and Gold: Tradition and Innovation in Ethiopian Culture.* Chicago: University of Chicago Press.

Lévi-Strauss, Claude. 1948. *Family and Social Life of the Nambikwara Indians.* Paris: Société des Américanistes.

1966. *The Savage Mind.* Chicago: University of Chicago Press.

Limbaugh, Ronald H., ed. 1973. *Cheyenne and Sioux: the Reminiscences of Four Indians and a White Soldier,* compiled by Thomas B. Marquis. Pacific Center for Western Historical Studies Monograph 3. Stockton, Calif.: University of the Pacific.

Lindenbaum, Shirley. 1972. Sorcerers, ghosts, and polluting women: an analysis of religious belief and population control. *Ethnology* 11:241–53.

1976. A wife is the hand of man. In *Man and Woman in the New Guinea Highlands,* P. Brown and G. Buchbinder, eds., pp. 54–62. American Anthropological Association Special Publication No. 8.

1979. *Kuru Sorcery.* Palo Alto, Calif.: Mayfield.

Lombard, Jacques. 1967. The kingdom of Dahomey. In *West African Kingdoms in the Nineteenth Century,* D. Forde and P. M. Kaberry, eds., pp. 70–92. London: Oxford University Press.

McElroy, Ann. 1975. Canadian Arctic modernization and change in female Inuit role identification. *American Ethnologist* 2:662–86.

McIlwraith, Thomas Forsyth. 1948. *The Bella Coola Indians.* 2 Vols. Toronto: University of Toronto Press.

Martin, M. Kay, and Barbara Voorhies. 1975. *Female of the Species.* New York: Columbia University Press.

Mason, John P. 1975. Sex and symbol in the treatment of women: the wedding rite in a Libyan oasis community. *American Ethnologist* 2:649–61.

Bibliography

Matthiasson, Carolyn, J. ed. 1974. *Many Sisters: Women in Cross-Cultural Perspective*. New York: Free Press.

Maybury-Lewis, David. 1965. Some crucial distinctions in Central Brazilian ethnology. *Anthropos 60*:340–58.

1967. *Akwĕ-Shavante Society*. Oxford: Clarendon Press.

Mead, Margaret. 1963. *Sex and Temperament in Three Primitive Societies*. New York: Morrow. (Originally published in 1935.)

1968. *Male and Female*. New York: Laurel. (Originally published in 1949 by Morrow, New York.)

Meek, T. James. 1960. *Hebrew Origins*. New York: Harper & Brothers.

Meggitt, M. J. 1964. Male–female relationships in the highlands of Australian New Guinea. In *New Guinea: the Central Highlands,* J. B. Watson, ed., pp. 204–24. American Anthropologist Special Publication 66 (4, pt. 2).

1965. The Mae Enga of the Western Highlands. In *Gods, Ghosts, and Men in Melanesia,* P. Lawrence and M. J. Meggitt, eds., pp. 105–31. Melbourne: Oxford University Press.

Meigs, Anna S. 1976. Male pregnancy and the reduction of sexual opposition in a New Guinea highlands society, *Ethnology 15*:393–407.

Mercier, P. 1954. The Fon of Dahomey. In *African Worlds,* Daryll Forde, ed., pp. 210–34. London: Oxford University Press.

Messing, Simon David. 1957. The highland–plateau Amhara of Ethiopia. Doctoral thesis, University of Pennsylvania.

Métraux, Alfred. 1946. Ethnography of the Chaco. In *Handbook of South American Indians,* Julian H. Steward, ed., vol. 1. *BAE Bulletin 143*:197–370. Washington, D.C.: U.S. Government Printing Office.

1951. *Making a Living in the Marbial Valley (Haiti)*. UNESCO Occasional Papers in Education 10.

Mintz, Sidney W. 1971. Men, women, and trade. *Comparative Studies in Society and History 13*:247–69.

Murdock, George P. 1959. *Africa: Its Peoples and Their Culture History*. New York: McGraw-Hill.

Murdock, George P., and Diana O. Morrow. 1970. Subsistence economy and supportive practices: cross-cultural codes 1. *Ethnology 9*:302–30.

Murdock, George P., and Caterina Provost. 1973. Factors in the division of labor by sex: a cross-cultural analysis. *Ethnology 12*:203–25.

Murdock, George P., and Douglas R. White. 1969. Standard cross-cultural sample. *Ethnology 8*:329–69.

Murdock, George P., and Suzanne F. Wilson. 1972. Settlement patterns and community organizations: cross cultural codes 3. *Ethnology 11*:254–95.

Murphy, Robert F. 1957. Intergroup hostility and social cohesion. *American Anthropologist 59*:1018–35.

1958. *Mundurucu Religion*. Berkeley: University of California Press.

Murphy, Yolanda, and Robert F. Murphy. 1974. *Women of the Forest*. New York: Columbia University Press.

The Nag Hammadi Library. 1977. Translated by members of the Coptic Gnostic Library Project of the Institute for Antiquity and Christianity, directed by James M. Robinson. San Francisco: Harper & Row.

Bibliography

Nerlove, Sara B. 1974. Women's workload and infant feeding practices: a relationship with demographic implications. *Ethnology* 13:207–14.

Neumann, Erich. 1955. *The Great Mother: an Analysis of the Archetype.* Bollingen Series 47. Princeton: Princeton University Press.

The New Oxford Annotated Bible. 1973. Herbert G. May and Bruce M. Metzger, eds. Rev. standard version. New York: Oxford University Press.

Okonjo, Kamene. 1976. The dual-sex political system in operation: Igbo women and community politics in midwestern Nigeria. In *Women in Africa,* N. J. Hafkin and E. G. Bay, eds., pp. 45–58. Stanford: Stanford University Press.

Onwuejeogwu, Michael. 1971. The cult of the *Bori* spirits among the Hausa. In *Man in Africa,* M. Douglas and P. Kaberry, eds., pp. 279–305. New York: Doubleday.

Ortner, Sherry B. 1974. Is female to male as nature is to culture? In *Woman, Culture, and Society,* M. Z. Rosaldo and L. Lamphere, eds., pp. 67–88. Stanford: Stanford University Press.

Ottenberg, Phoebe V. 1959. The changing economic position of women among the Afikpo Ibo. In *Continuity and Change in African Cultures,* William R. Bascow and Melville J. Herskovits, eds., pp. 205–23. Chicago: University of Chicago Press.

Pagels, Elaine H. 1976. What became of God the Mother? Conflicting images of god in early Christianity. *Signs* 2:293–303.

1979. *The Gnostic Gospels.* New York: Random House.

Paques, Viviana. 1954. *The Bambara.* Translated by T. Turner. New Haven, Conn.: HRAF Press. (Originally published in 1954, International African Institute, Monographies Ethnologiques Africaines, Paris: Presses Universitaires de France.)

Parker, Arthur C. 1912. *The Code of Handsome Lake.* Albany: New York State Museum Bulletin No .163.

1916. *The Constitution of the Five Nations.* Albany: New York State Museum Bulletin No. 184.

Patai, Raphael. 1967. *The Hebrew Goddess.* New York: KTAV.

1971. *The Tents of Jacob.* Englewood Cliffs, N.J.: Prentice-Hall.

Perham, Margery F. 1937. *Native Administration in Nigeria.* London: Oxford University Press.

Philipps, J. E. Tracy. 1926. Observations on some aspects of religion among the Azande ("Niam-Niam") of equatorial Africa. *Journal of the Royal Anthropological Institute of Great Britain and Ireland* 56:171–89.

Polanyi, Karl. 1966. *Dahomey and the Slave Trade.* Seattle: University of Washington Press.

Powell, Peter J. 1969. *Sweet Medicine: the Continuing Role of the Sacred Arrow, the Sun Dance, and the Sacred Buffalo Hat in Northern Cheyenne History.* 2 Vols. Norman: University of Oklahoma Press.

Quain, Buell H. 1937. The Iroquois. In *Cooperation and Competition among Primitive Peoples,* Margaret Mead, ed. pp. 240–81. New York: McGraw-Hill.

Quinn, Naomi. 1977. Anthropological studies on women's status. *Annual Review of Anthropology* 6:181–225.

Bibliography

Radcliffe-Brown, A. R. 1922. *The Andaman Islanders*. Cambridge: Cambridge University Press.

Rattray, Robert S. 1923. *Ashanti*. Oxford: Clarendon Press.

1927. *Religion and Art in Ashanti*. Oxford: Clarendon Press.

1929. *Ashanti Law and Constitution*. Oxford: Clarendon Press.

Reichel-Dolmatoff, Gerardo. 1971. *Amazonian Cosmos*. Chicago: University of Chicago Press.

Richards, Audrey. 1939. *Land, Labour and Diet in Northern Rhodesia*. London: Oxford University Press.

1956. *Chisungu*. London: Faber & Faber.

Ritchie, William A. 1965. *The Archaeology of New York State*. Garden City, N. Y.: Natural History Press.

Rogers, Susan Carol. 1975. Female forms of power and the myth of male dominance: a model of female/male interaction in peasant society. *American Ethnologist* 2:727–56.

1978. Woman's place: a critical review of anthropological theory. *Comparative Studies in Society and History* 20:123–62.

Rosaldo, Michelle Z., and Louise Lamphere, eds. 1974. *Woman, Culture, and Society*. Stanford: Stanford University Press.

Sacks, Karen. 1976. State bias and women's status. *American Anthropologist* 78:565–69.

Sanday, Peggy R. 1973. Toward a theory of the status of women. *American Anthropologist* 75:1682–700.

1974. Female status in the public domain. In *Women, Culture, and Society*, M. Z. Rosaldo and L. Lamphere, eds., pp. 189–206. Stanford: Stanford University Press.

Schebesta, Paul. 1963a. *The Negritoes of Asia*. Vol. 2, half-vol. 1, *Economy and Sociology*. Translated by Frieda Schütze. New Haven, Conn.: HRAF Press. (Originally published in 1954, Studia Instituti Anthropos, Vol. 12, Wien-Mödling.)

1963b. *The Negritoes of Asia*. Vol. 2, half-vol. 2, *Religion and Mythology*. Translated by Frieda Schütze. New Haven, Conn.: HRAF Press. (Originally published in 1957, Studia Instituti Anthropos, Vol. 13, Wien-Mödling.)

Schlegel, Alice. 1974. Women anthropologists look at women. *Reviews in Anthropology* (November):553–60.

1977. Male:female in Hopi thought and action. In *Sexual Stratification*, A. Schlegel, ed., pp. 245–69. New York: Columbia University Press.

Schoolcraft, Henry R. 1847. *Notes on the Iroquois*. Albany: Erastus H. Pease.

Seligman, Charles G., and Brenda Z. Seligman. 1932. *Pagan Tribes of the Nilotic Sudan*. London: Routledge.

Seymour, Susan. 1975. Some determinants of sex roles in a changing Indian town. *American Ethnologist* 2:757–69.

Simpson, Cuthbert A. 1952a. Exegesis to the Book of Genesis. In *The Interpreter's Bible*, vol. 1, pp. 465–829. New York: Abingdon Press.

1952b. The growth of the Hexateuch. In *The Interpreter's Bible*, vol. 1, pp. 185–200. New York: Abingdon Press.

Bibliography

1952c. Introduction to the Book of Genesis. In *The Interpreter's Bible,* vol. 1, pp. 439–57. New York: Abingdon Press.

Smith, Michael G. 1960. *Government in Zazzau.* London: Oxford University Press.

Spencer, Baldwin, and F. J. Gillen. 1968. *The Native Tribes of Central Australia.* New York: Dover. (Originally published in 1899.)

Spencer, Katherine. 1947. *Reflection of Social Life in the Navaho Origin Myth.* Albuquerque: University of New Mexico Press.

Spindler, Louise S. 1962. *Menomini Women and Culture Change.* Memoirs of the American Anthropological Association 91.

Stephens, William N. 1961. A cross-cultural study of menstrual taboos. *Genetic Psychology Monographs* 64:385–416.

Steward, Julian H. 1938. *Basin–Plateau Aboriginal Sociopolitical Groups.* Smithsonian Institution, Bureau of American Ethnology Bulletin 120. Washington, D.C.: Government Printing Office.

Stirling, Matthew Williams. 1938. *Historical and Ethnographical Material on the Jivaro Indians.* Smithsonian Institution, Bureau of American Ethnology Bulletin 117. Washington, D.C.: Government Printing Office.

Tanner, Nancy. 1974. Matrifocality in Indonesia and Africa and among Black Americans. In *Women, Culture, and Society,* M. Z. Rosaldo and L. Lamphere, eds., pp. 129–56. Stanford: Stanford University Press.

Tocantins, Antonio Manoel Gonzalves. 1959. *Studies on the Mundurucu Tribe.* Translated by Ariane Brunel. New Haven, Conn.: HRAF Press. (Originally published in 1877, Revista Trimensal do Instituto Historico Geographico e Ethnographico do Brasil, vol. 40.)

Turnbull, Colin. 1961. *The Forest People.* New York: Simon & Schuster.

1965a. *The Mbuti Pygmies: an Ethnographic Survey.* Anthropological Papers of the American Museum of Natural History 50:137–282.

1965b. *Wayward Servants: the Two Worlds of the African Pygmies.* Garden City, N. Y.: Natural History Press.

Underhill, Ruth M. 1936. *The Autobiography of a Papago Woman.* Memoirs of the American Anthropological Association 46.

1939. *Social Organization of the Papago Indians.* Columbia University Contributions to Anthropology 30. New York: Columbia University Press.

1946. *Papago Indian Religion.* Columbia University Contributions to Anthropology 33. New York: Columbia University Press.

Van Allen, Judith. 1972. "Sitting on a man": colonialism and the lost political institutions of Igbo women. *Canadian Journal of African Studies* 6:165–81.

1976. 'Aba riots' or Igbo 'Women's War'? Ideology, stratification, and the invisibility of women. In *Women in Africa,* N. J. Hafkin and E. G. Bay, eds., pp. 59–86. Stanford: Stanford University Press.

Von Rad, Gerhard. 1961. *Genesis.* Translated by John H. Marks. Philadelphia: Westminster Press.

Wallace, Anthony F. C. 1958. Dreams and wishes of the soul. *American Anthropologist* 60:234–48.

1969. *The Death and Rebirth of the Seneca.* New York: Vintage/Random House.

Bibliography

1971. Handsome Lake and the decline of the Iroquois matriarchate. In *Kinship and Culture,* F. K. Hsu, ed., pp. 367–76. Chicago: Aldine.

Wallace, Ernest, and E. Adamson Hocbel. 1952. *The Comanches.* Norman: University of Oklahoma Press.

Wallace, Paul, A. W. 1946. *The White Roots of Peace.* Philadelphia: University of Pennsylvania Press.

White, Douglas R., Michael L. Burton, and Lilyan A. Brudner. 1977. Entailment theory and method: a cross-cultural analysis of the sexual division of labor. *Behavior Science Research* 12:1–24.

Whiting, Beatrice. 1965. Sex identity conflict and physical violence: a comparative study. *American Anthropologist* 67 (6, pt. 2):123–40. (Special publication.)

Whiting, John W. M. 1964. Effects of climate on certain cultural practices. In *Explorations in Cultural Anthropology,* W. H. Goodenough, ed., pp. 511–44. New York: McGraw-Hill.

Whiting, John W. M., and Irvin L. Child. 1953. *Child Training and Personality: a Cross-Cultural Study.* New Haven, Conn.: Yale University Press.

Whiting, John W. M., and Beatrice B. Whiting. 1975. Aloofness and intimacy of husbands and wives. *Ethos* 3:183–207.

Wilks, Ivor. 1967. Ashanti government. In *West African Kingdoms in the Nineteenth Century,* D. Forde and P. M. Kaberry, eds., pp. 206–38. London: Oxford University Press.

Witthoft, John. 1961. Eastern woodlands community typology and acculturation. In *Symposium on Cherokee and Iroquois Culture,* W. Fenton and J. Gulick, eds., pp. 67–76. Smithsonian Institution, Washington, D.C. Bureau of American Ethnology Bulletin 180. Government Printing Office.

Woodburn, James. 1968. An introduction to Hadza ecology. In *Man the Hunter,* R. Lee and I. Devore, eds., pp. 49–55. Chicago: Aldine.

Young, Frank W., and Albert A. Bacdayan. 1965. Menstrual taboos and social rigidity. *Ethnology* 4:225–40.

Zelman, Elizabeth Crouch. 1977. Reproduction, ritual and power. *American Ethnologist* 4:714–33.

Index

Index

Brown, Judith K., 77
Brudner, Lilyan A., 77, 78
Burton, Michael L., 77, 78

Canaanite gods and goddesses,
    216–20, 222
    see also deity
Canaanite religion, 10, 70, 218–19,
    221, 224–5
Chagnon, Napolean, 45
Cheyenne, 152, 153, 156, 182,
    199–200
    acquisition of horse, 148, 150
    affection between husband and wife,
        149
    female power, 149
    male dominance, 151–2
    migration history, 148
    pre-horse background, 148, 152
    rape, 151
    sacred symbols of male and female
        power, 148–9, 151
    sexual integration, 157
Chippewa, 74
Christ, Carol P., 215
Christ, life of, 228, 230
Christianity, 35, 140, 216
    see also Christians, orthodox;
        Gnostics
Christians, Gnostic, see Gnostics
Christians, orthodox, 227–30
colonialism, European, 152, 153
    Azande Mbori and, 202
    decline in Iroquoian male role, 141,
        157
    effect on Aranda, 153
    effect on women's world, 8, 130–1,
        133–4, 135, 267 n2
    female farming and, 130
    female trading and, 128
    Igbo female resistance to, 136
    impact on female power, 130, 131,
        156–8, 266–7 n1, 269 n64
    introduction of horse, 135–6, 180
    migration and, 156–7
    movement into marginal areas and,
        152–8
    myths of former female power and,
        180
    response of Shavante, 154–5

Comanche, 122, 152, 153, 156,
    267–8 n28
    acquisition of the horse, 144, 145
    band and political organization,
        145–6
    conception of supernatural power, 147
    evolution of male dominance, 144–8
    female power, 147–8
    male dominance, 152
    male parenting, 63
    pre-horse background, 144–5, 152
    warfare, 146, 148
creation story
    anthropological analyses of, 73–5
    Ashanti, 32, 58, 119
    Azande, 201–2
    Babylonian, 225–6
    Balinese, 17–18, 58
    Bemba, 206
    Biblical story of Adam and Eve,
        220–5
    Chippewa, 74
    classified, 59–60, 239–44
    Dahomean, 71–2
    Desana, 193
    Enga, 195
    Fore, 195
    gender themes in, 57–60
    Genesis, 225–6
    geographical distribution of types of,
        59–60
    Hausa, 36, 58
    inner and outer orientation, 57–60,
        67–8
    Iroquois, 58
    Lepcha, 83–4
    Mbuti, 21, 258 n22
    Mundurucu, 37–9, 58
    Navaho, 70–1, 74
    Papago, 41–2, 58
    reflection of orientation to nature, 57
    reflection of social life, 56, 73–5
    role of sexes in, 16, 33, 73
    Semang, 20–1, 58
    Seneca, 27, 259 n38
    Thonga, 239
    Trukese, 239–40
    Yanomamo, 47–9, 58
    see also creators, types of; gender
        symbolism in creation stories

286

Index

Index

Index

sexual integration, 7, 75, 89–90, 108
  Andamanese, 99
  Balinese, 33, 258 n1
  Cheyenne, 157
  correlates of, 248–9
  cultural configuration of, 84
  female deities and, 84
  in foraging societies, 93
  gender symbolism in origin stories
    and, 84–5
  inner orientation and, 89
  Lepcha cultural configuration and,
    83–4
  Lepcha emphasis on cooperation
    and, 83–4
  Mbuti, 33, 197
  in plant economies, 83
  prevalence of in work activities, 81, 89
  Semang, 21, 33
  in work activities, 83
sexual segregation, 7, 75, 89–90, 108
  Abipon, 122–3
  in animal economies, 81–2, 83
  Ashanti, 28, 33
  Azande, 205
  Bellacoola attitude toward blood and
    female sexuality, 102, 103
  correlates of, 248–9
  dual-sex orientation and, 89
  fear of menstrual blood, 91, 93–4,
    97, 105
  Fore, 198
  gender symbolism in origin stories
    and, 84–5
  Hadza, 93
  Hausa, 35
  Iroquois, 28, 33
  Mundurucu, 37
  outer orientation, 76, 89
  prevalence of in work activities, 80,
    81, 89
  in selected societies, 80–1
  type of orientation, 76–7
sexual symmetry, 170
  Ashanti, 33, 95–6
  conceptual, 5, 44–5, 94–5, 96–7,
    104, 107
  Dahomean, 53
  Hopi, 169–70
  Papago, 44–5

projected onto nature, 78–9
  see also dual-sex orientation
Shavante, 153, 154–5
Shoshone, 145
  Northern, 145, 267–8 n28
  Western, 144, 146, 268 n28
Solomon, 220–1
Spencer, Katherine, 70, 71, 74
Spindler, Louise, 125, 126
Standard Cross-Cultural Sample, 56,
  77, 81t, 232–5, 236, 239, 257 n1,
  266 n22, 269 n19
Stephens, William, 91
Steward, Julian H., 144, 268 n28
subsistence economy, effects of change
  in on gender symbolism, 70–2
Sumerians, 217–18, 221
supernatural power, 6
  conception of creation, see creation
    story
  concept of source of and
    environment, 64–6
  Hausa Bori cult, 36–7
  Papago male and female quest for,
    43–4
  of Papago women, 41
  sex-role plans and, 16
  see also deity

taboos
  Bellacoola avoidance of female
    sexuality, 101, 102
  Desana sex taboos, 192–3
  Enga sexual repression, 194
  general, 93, 94
  regulating sexual intercourse, 7, 46,
    91, 107–9
  see also menstrual blood;
    menstruating women
Tanner, Nancy, xv, 116, 117
tasks, strictly masculine, 77–9
  see also sexual division of labor
Tikopia, 62
Tumbuka, 177–8
Turnbull, Colin, 24, 188, 189, 190, 258
  n22, 263 n8

Van Allen, Judith, 267 n2, 267 n3
Voorhies, Barbara, 130, 131, 176–7,
  178, 179, 269 n21